Acclaim for *Imperial Canada Inc.*

"*Imperial Canada Inc.* is a wake-up call. It details ι Canada's mining industry and demands greater oversight from our governments, not the subservience and active promotion of mining-industry interests that we have now. The authors have created a valuable tool for anyone working for environmental protection, securities exchange regulation, tax reform, and social justice. It is a must-read for Canadians who value our reputation at home and abroad."

– DENNIS HOWLETT, Canadians for Tax Fairness

"Deneault and Sacher set out to answer a key question: Why are the majority of the world's mining companies registered in Canada? The authors make it clear that this question urgently needs to be answered now, at a time when these mining companies are increasingly the bloodied face of Canada in remote and poor regions of the world, accused of grave human-rights and environmental abuses. Deneault and Sacher underpin their study with an examination of the speculative nature of trades in natural resources, the historical role of mining in Canada, and the ongoing close relationship of the industry to government, as reflected in permissive regulatory regimes, corporate subsidies, and lucrative tax arrangements for mining companies."

– MiningWatch Canada

"Through well-documented detail, Alain Deneault and William Sacher show how a permissive domestic policy and regulatory regime and an extreme level of investment speculation combine to allow some Canada-based mining companies to behave deplorably around the world. At a time when the Harper government is rolling back key environmental laws to accelerate resource development in Canada, Deneault's and Sacher's hard-hitting analysis and tone beg a timely question: If Canadians want to export not bad – but exemplary – corporate behaviour to the rest of the world, what standards must we hold our mining companies to here at home?"

– ED WHITTINGHAM, Pembina Institute

"A powerful indictment of Canada's role as a platform for mining firms engaged in highly exploitative and polluting activities in far-flung corners of the global South ... and closer to home. Alain Deneault and William Sacher call for much tighter regulation of the Canadian mining industry and for ethical and responsible investment as an alternative model for the future. The publication of this book represents a strong statement of freedom of expression and strikes a blow to the abusive use of SLAPP (strategic lawsuits against public participation) lawsuits by Canadian corporations."

– PHILIP RESNICK

Imperial Canada Inc.

IMPERIAL CANADA INC.

·Legal Haven of Choice for the World's Mining Industries

Alain Deneault and William Sacher

with
Catherine Browne, Mathieu Denis,
and Patrick Ducharme

Translated by
Fred A. Reed and Robin Philpot

Talonbooks

Talonbooks
P.O. BOX 2076, Vancouver, British Columbia, Canada V6B 3S3
www.talonbooks.com

Typeset in Minion and printed and bound in Canada.
Printed on 100% post-consumer recycled paper.
First printing: 2012
Typeset and cover design by Typesmith
Deneault author photo by Étienne Boilard

The publisher gratefully acknowledges the financial support of the Canada Council
for the Arts; the Government of Canada through the Canada Book Fund and the
National Translation Program for Book Publishing; and the Province of British
Columbia through the British Columbia Arts Council and the Book Publishing
Tax Credit for our publishing activities.

LIBRARY AND ARCHIVES CANADA CATALOGUING IN PUBLICATION

Deneault, Alain, 1970–
    Imperial Canada Inc. : legal haven of choice for the world's mining industries
/ Alain Deneault, William Sacher ; with Catherine Browne, Mathieu Denis and
Patrick Ducharme ; translated by Fred A. Reed and Robin Philpot.

Translated from the French.
Includes bibliographical references.
ISBN 978-0-88922-635-7

    1. Mining corporations—Canada—Foreign ownership. 2. Mining law—Can-
ada. 3. Mineral industries—Canada—Finance. 4. Corporations, Foreign—Canada.
I. Sacher, William II. Browne, Catherine, 1958– III. Denis, Mathieu, 1975– IV.
Ducharme, Patrick V. Reed, Fred A., 1939– VI. Philpot, Robin VII. Title.

KE1790.D4513 2012   343.71'077   C2010-904437-1
KF1819.D4513 2012

Criminality is like a negative of society.

EVA JOLY

INTRODUCTION

Canada: Home to a Dangerous Industry

How did it come to this? Canada, once known as a defender of international peace and noble principles, today has acquired a new reputation as the home of a highly controversial industry. Today, Canada is known around the world as home to oil, gas, and mining companies that choose to register here in order to benefit from our permissive mining regulations and preferential tax structure. Three out of four of the world's mining companies operate out of Canada while often conducting exploration and extraction projects located elsewhere. Ontario alone accommodates more than fourteen hundred of these companies, even though only forty-three mines are in operation in the province. The damage these companies inflict is experienced generally not by Canadians, but by citizens of other countries. As a result, a troubling number of farmers, indigenous people, and other citizens of countries around the world are angry about the actions of Canadian-based mining companies. It is no longer unusual to see the Canadian flag torched or disfigured during public demonstrations in South Asia, Africa, or Latin America.

Canada's controversial role in the world goes far beyond our exportation of uranium and asbestos.[1] Mining corporations, often Canadian, are said to have contributed in one way or another to conflicts that have placed millions of people in jeopardy and have led to deaths, systematic rape, the forced recruitment of child soldiers, and legions of refugees. Multiple sources point out connections between some

Canadian-based corporations and conflicts motivated by "economic development projects" that ultimately are associated with net losses to public treasuries, incidents of corruption (either proven or apparent), and smuggling that destroys people's livelihood. Over the past twenty years, sources around the world have extensively recorded widespread malfeasance by Canadian mining companies, primarily in the South and in Eastern Europe: violent evictions of entire populations, massive unemployment, and homelessness instead of the promised "job creation," long-lasting pollution of large tracts of land, major public-health problems, and tax evasion reaching into the billions. Overall, the record provides convincing evidence that "economic development projects" often leave host countries worse, and not better off, than they were before.

The sources that document these truths form the basis of our argument, specifically, that it is time to speak openly about Canadian government grants and other forms of regulatory and fiscal support that fund Canadian-based mining companies and allow them to develop controversial extractive sites abroad. Perhaps more crucially, it is time to speak openly about the ways in which our legal jurisdiction is used as a base-and-launch facility for questionable projects overseas. Canada stands out as a judicial and financial haven that shelters its mining industry from the political or legal consequences of its extraterritorial activities by providing a lax domestic regulatory structure that it seeks to export through international agencies, diplomatic channels, and "economic development projects."

Although information critical of Canada is abundant overseas, it is hard to find in Canada. The owners or managers of the country's media conglomerates, both private and public (and all of them major financial players), are committed to supporting the mining industry. As a matter of course, Canadian media suppress information about an exploitive process that is described in other countries as abusive or even criminal. Ironically, the citizens of Germany, Belgium, and the United States know more about our grim international reputation than do Canadians. How many of us are aware of the neo-colonial activities of Canadian-based mining companies abroad and the alleged (yet broadly documented) human-rights abuses and environmental tragedies associated with these activities?

Reports of the actions of Canadian-based mining companies in the South and in Eastern Europe come from international sources in Buenos Aires and Kinshasa; Berlin, Brussels, and London; Paris, New York, and Washington; Toronto, Ottawa, and Montreal. All have produced documents that enjoy three levels of credibility: first, they have been produced by authors recognized as credible by a significant number of their peers; second, they have been published by academic journals, public institutions, press agencies, independent organizations, or reputable media institutions; and third, they frequently corroborate one another, or at least arrive at similar conclusions, even though they originate with authors who do not know each other and who work in different disciplines and languages, for different organizations, and for audiences that are located in different cities and continents. This extremely abundant literature is not yet proof in the legal sense, and our purpose here is not to justify these allegations beyond the documents on which they are based. What is most troubling, however, is not their frightening number, but the consistency with which they reach similar conclusions.

Equally troubling are the difficulties that the publication of these documents has brought on the people and organizations that have shared them with us. Almost all have experienced pressure or faced absurd delay tactics or refusals. Their research into the highly problematic action of Canadian mining companies in the South and in Eastern Europe reflects an appalling reality that lies just out of sight, and it is likely that the evidence uncovered is only a fraction of the true extent of the problem.

Of course, the allegations in these reports must be viewed as unconfirmed until they are subject to scrupulous public investigation. Given the seriousness of the allegations, it is clear that under a truly democratic regime, Canadian authorities and the Canadian judicial system would already have launched official inquiries.

To our knowledge, none of the extractive sector corporations mentioned in these damning reports has ever acknowledged the truth of the allegations made against them. The corporate response has been either silence or the usual denials claiming that detailed reports are biased and fancifully imagined. Corporations would have us believe that dozens of critical observers, analysts, thinkers, experts, and witnesses to the activities of the Canadian establishment throughout the world are all aligned in the same conspiracy.

What the sources say about Africa is intolerable. Women living near the Sadiola mine in Mali (partly owned by Toronto-based Iamgold) suffered multiple miscarriages, probably caused by polluted sources of drinking water.[2] Several Canadian-based mining companies (Golden Knight Resources, Prestea Sankofa Gold and Prestea Resources Ltd., and Birim Goldfields) carried out violent expropriations of land in Ghana.[3] Corporations active in Congo-Kinshasa (Lundin, First Quantum Minerals, and Emaxon) signed one-sided deals during wartime with actual or future political authorities of the country, giving them privileged access to promising mining concessions or public assets of high value.[4] DiamondWorks and other companies established themselves in Sierra Leone thanks to a devastating civil war.[5] Heritage Oil profited from instability in Angola.[6] And the list goes on.[7]

But abuses are not restricted to the mining industry. The Canadian International Development Agency supported massive dam projects in West Africa to the benefit of Canadian firms, even though these projects produce large-scale environmental damage without significantly improving the quality of life of people living in the region.[8] Canac, a transportation firm, privatized strategic railway lines in West Africa with the support of Canadian public funds, then closed most train stations to the public.[9] A pharmaceutical company, Millenia Hope, sold drugs in Africa that did not meet the standards of Health Canada or the World Health Organization.[10]

The worst example is surely the presence of Canadian mining firms in the Great Lakes region of Africa in the 1990s, surrounded by belligerents looking for arms and shady business deals. Fought on many fronts, their wars led to millions of deaths, mostly from disease and starvation.[11] Canadian corporations often obtained concessions in the region by negotiating with politicians or warlords who were either preparing for or already engaged in conflict.[12] The United Nations considers it likely that most of the clashes took place for the control of mining deposits.[13]

Mining corporations such as Barrick Gold do not hesitate to use the services of major political and business figures to support their interests at home and abroad. In the 1990s, the firm set up an international advisory board, made up of influential people such as former U.S. president George H. W. Bush, former Canadian prime minister Brian Mulroney, and Canadian businessmen Paul Desmarais Sr. and Peter Munk, to lobby for its interests around the globe.[14] Barrick Gold executives found the advisory board's work highly satisfactory, as shown by the praise lavished on it by CEO Randall Oliphant in a speech to shareholders.[15] That may be because Brian Mulroney has admitted he spent "a fair amount of time in Latin America and China and Africa working with senior management and governments around the world" to represent the corporation's interests.[16] Other former Canadian prime ministers have tackled similar jobs: Joe Clark represented the interests of First Quantum Mining in Africa,[17] while Jean Chrétien represented mining and oil companies in relations with controversial political regimes in Nigeria and the Congo.

A number of international sources raise further troubling questions about the consequences of the presence of Canadian mining companies abroad and the ways in which their presence may have intensified conflicts. In Congo-Kinshasa, for example, a country ravaged by years of warfare, a project known as the Moanda Leasehold involves a ninety-nine-year lease that will formally deprive the Congolese of political and economic sovereignty over resources in the western part of their country.[18] Unless the project is halted, a consortium of investors will gain political authority over the area, where three massive industrial developments are planned. According to the advocates of this neo-colonial project, Canada will participate in the project along with European Union countries, the United States, the World Bank, and the International Monetary Fund (IMF).[19]

Africa is not the only continent having to cope with Canadian neo-colonialism. In Eastern Europe, the pollution caused by mining projects continues to worry local populations. In Latin America, where Canadian mining assets are concentrated,[20] accusations of abuse are as numerous as those on the African continent, and citizens protesting against them are severely repressed by local police forces. One example among far too many, related by the Toronto *Star*, concerns a junior mining firm (Copper Mesa) accused of hiring paramilitaries in 2006 to repress demonstrators opposed to mines in Ecuador that "threaten rainforests and their way of life."[21] In the Montreal *Gazette*, Janet Bagnall reported the assassination in December 2009 of two Salvadorians opposed to Pacific Rim Mining Corp.'s El Dorado project.[22] In El Salvador, the Episcopal Conference in May 2007 denounced the environmental destruction and public-health problems caused by the use of cyanide by gold-mining corporations, many of them Canadian.[23] In Guatemala, Canadian gold giant Goldcorp faces a complaint filed with the Canadian Department of Foreign Affairs and International Trade by communities living near the Marlin gold mine. Their complaint cites depletion of fresh drinking water and pollution, in violation of guidelines set out by the Organisation for Economic Co-operation and Development.[24] In Honduras, the same company's activities are alleged to have led to a massive degradation of the Siria River valley: two studies carried out by academics from Newcastle University describe heavy-metal pollution and acidic-mine drainage, said to be responsible for poisoning people and cattle.[25] In Mexico, Mariano Abarca Roblero, an opponent of an exploration project carried out in Chiapas by a Canadian mining corporation, Blackfire, was killed in November 2009; the suspects are alleged to be actual or former Blackfire employees.[26] Moreover, there are persistent allegations of corruption of local authorities by Blackfire in order to silence the project's many opponents.[27] In Bolivar province, Colombia, small-scale artisanal miners have accused Canadian junior companies of hiring paramilitary forces during the 1990s in order to expropriate the territories where they were mining gold. During this period of nation-wide political violence, more than eight thousand people were displaced after the intervention of "death squads" in the region.[28]

In our previous book, *Noir Canada: Pillage, corruption, et criminalité en Afrique*,[29] we set out to achieve two goals: first, to bridge the public information gap in this country about the practices attributed to Canadian mining companies under our jurisdiction in many countries; and second, to suggest ways of ending the practices that need to be stopped. We called on Canadian authorities to institute an independent commission of inquiry into the practices of the extractive industries based in Canada. Four years later, it is becoming more and more urgent that we shed light on the many cases of abuse and crime allegedly committed by these companies and reported at an international level. The discrepancy between accusations and defence in these cases could hardly be larger. On the one hand, we have a substantial number of alleged misdeeds and dubious, if not criminal, practices attributed to Canadian mining companies by a host of different and reliable sources. On the other, we have the offended denials of the accused firms; denials that they regularly back up with legal actions for libel. An independent commission of inquiry could recommend criminal charges against these corporations if and where appropriate, offer public apologies to the peoples wronged by them, and make strong recommendations as to how to stop such practices and undertake the necessary reparation programs in cooperation with local populations. Because every Canadian government to date has supported the mining industry, this commission cannot take the form of a parliamentary commission consisting only of members of Parliament. This is the reason that, as the authors of *Noir Canada*, we called for an independent commission, at arm's length from governments, which would gather input from parties representing all the interests involved.

While government agencies, private foundations, corporations listed on Canadian stock exchanges, and media groups owned by the country's most powerful financial interests continue to sing the praises of Canada's humanitarian actions around the world, there has been little if any open discussion, scrutiny, or critical analysis of this country's role in the ongoing rapacious practices of the extractive industry, either at home or abroad. Critical information about the mining industry rarely makes the headlines, but fortunately, the authors of this book by no means stand alone. Yves Engler's *The Black Book on Canadian Foreign Policy*[30] and Joan Baxter's *Dust from Our Eyes*[31] have added their voices to Amnesty International, Halifax Initiative, MiningWatch Canada, and *The Dominion* Newspaper Cooperative to alert public opinion and foster critical thinking about Canada's role abroad. Moreover, in 2009, after evaluating Barrick Gold's environmental and social performance in Papua New Guinea, the Norwegian government publicly announced that its sovereign investment fund would divest its shares in Barrick Gold.[32]

Hence the opening line in the introduction to this new book: "How did it come to this?" This book tries to answer that question in two ways. First, we provide a history that shows Canada could not have become what it is – a legal haven for the extractive sector – if it had not allowed the establishment of stock exchanges that orchestrate irresponsible financial speculation on real or imagined resources, leading many small investors to lose their savings in numerous cases of fraud. Since the nineteenth century, Canadian stock exchanges have based the capitalization of shares on financial speculation rather than on the real economy, diverting financial institutions from their original goal of raising capital. Financial speculation is not unique to Canadian stock exchanges: London, Paris, and New York have all had their share of speculative frenzies, leading to appalling social dislocation and global economic decline. The history of Canadian stock exchanges, however, and specifically that of the Toronto Stock Exchange, has been singularly shaped by dubious practices of speculation, primarily on natural resources.

Second, we offer a case study that demonstrates the crucial influence of Canada's origins as a colony of the British Empire. The *British North America Act* of 1867[33] did not liberate Canada from its colonial past. The federal and provincial governments of this country have continued to support practices inherited from their colonial origins. Colonial elites and foreign investors have made immense profits from the ongoing exploitation of natural resources in the "Northwest Territories" (a huge land mass consisting of all of the North American continent that drains into the Hudson Bay), and they have shaped Canada according to their interests, making it a country based on mineral extraction and the exploitation of natural resources. The practices of the extractive industry in Canada from the late-nineteenth century onward, which include exploiting natural resources without any concern other than that of rapid profits, dispossessing first Aboriginal and then any other populations that might have a legitimate interest in and therefore a say on the issues, and continuing to fight for highly accommodating legislation to the benefit of their industry, have driven their economic growth in Canada.

This is not unique to Canada: other colonies and ex-colonies around the world have also channelled their economic activity into one core sector, be it bananas, rubber, or coca. What is specifically Canadian is the fact that practices related to the development of the mining industry, which took shape under colonial conditions in Canada, have been exported abroad. This systemic approach has provided Canada's mining companies with a clear advantage at the highest level of international competition. Now they claim for themselves, wherever they go – in Africa, Asia, Latin America, or elsewhere – the same extralegal status from which they profited so outrageously in their original domestic colonial environment. Our case study unravels the ultra-permissive character of Quebec legislation covering the extractive sector, then discusses the impact of these deficient regulatory measures on democracy and the environment, both at home and abroad.

In this context, it is worth recalling the fact that the Canadian banking sector played a key role in encouraging the development of tax havens in the Caribbean throughout the twentieth century.[34] It would have been logical for Canada, as an advocate of sound legal principles, to oppose such structures. And yet, with the support of the Canadian government, Canadian banks have played a key part in setting up systems to circumvent public taxation or even eliminate it in some Caribbean countries. As a result, the prosperous Canadian extractive industry pays almost no taxes, either in Canada or abroad.[35] Astonishingly, Canada has supported and continues to support a banking industry whose actions are contrary to the financial interest of its own citizens (and usually the interests of the citizens of the Caribbean tax havens as well).

Our country is linked to the tax havens of the Caribbean via Barbados, which as a rule allows companies registered there to access an entire network of offshore jurisdictions providing financial, legal, and fiscal shelters for their profits. There are no unpleasant consequences in Canada for companies that follow this course. The profits they record in jurisdictions of convenience never end up in any bank account opened in Canada, much less as tax revenue in the treasury of Canadian governments. Secrecy is the rule.[36] The fact that these tax havens contradict the fundamental principles of the legal state has never stopped Canada from considering these countries as friends and allies. In fact, Canada formally shares its seat at international institutions such as the World Bank and the IMF with such countries and has even signed a free-trade agreement with Panama.[37]

In Canada, critical thinkers face a political conundrum: their government, which in theory is responsible for looking after the common good and the rule of law, is in cahoots with the extractive industry, which means that it is now part of the problem. As for "civil society," it is led by "experts" who sometimes fail to make clear what position they are defending in woolly discussions about "governance," while citizens see that they have no control over their savings as soon as institutional investors and public fund managers take charge of them.

This book is intended to provide Canadian and international public opinion with tools to help it ask critical questions about Canadian activities in the South and in Eastern Europe, as well as about the role of the Canadian government in relation to these activities. It is hoped that the evidence presented here will encourage Canadians to enter public debate about how the mining industry is regulated in Canada and to form an opinion on this topic independent from the one suggested by official agencies or media that belong to large Canadian financial conglomerates and tend to espouse their interests. Our goal is to deepen understanding of an aspect brought up in *Noir Canada:* the harmful consequences of our ultra-permissive laws regarding the extractive industry, both for countries in the South, and indirectly, for all of us in Canada.

As a state wedded to the interests of mining companies, Canada recently has behaved in ways we may find unrecognizable, doing everything in its power – at the legislative, judicial, economic, financial, and diplomatic levels – to make itself into a legal paradise for the world's extractive industry. Canadian citizens are concerned in this matter. We help fund the extractive industry through their savings, channelled toward the Toronto Stock Exchange by pension funds, insurance companies, and other institutions. We need to talk about the fact that our economy is still shaped by our colonial past. Public debate cannot be stifled forever, and the reality is that we are responsible for how the mining industry is regulated in Canada and how the world extractive industry is regulated here from now on, whether the companies involved were born in our country or have only recently become our guests.

THE ARGUMENT

Canada: Tax Haven for the World's Extractive Sector

Canada promotes stock-market speculation on the mining industry's controversial activities throughout the world – and makes sure the industry is legally protected. The Toronto Stock Exchange, the government of Ontario that supervises its operations, and the government of Canada have spared no effort to transform the capital of Canada's largest province into the extractive industry's world administrative, financial, and legislative nerve centre. Naturally enough, a swarm of professionals concentrated in Toronto – corporate lawyers and academic apologists, geologists and geological instrument manufacturers, bankers, brokers, and financial advisers – hope to sell their services to the industry. This pool of expertise makes it possible for Toronto to promote itself internationally as a city with a "business climate" highly favourable to the international mining industry.

The TMX Group (Toronto Stock Exchange [TSX] and TSX Venture Exchange [TSXV]), and more generally Canada as a jurisdiction, have obvious attractions for the industry. Every year since 2007, the value of transactions on the Toronto Stock Exchange has reached $350 to $450 billion,[1] and between 2007 and 2011, Toronto provided the mining sector with $220 billion in equity financing – more than one-third of the world's total.[2] The TSX in this regard is far ahead of its closest rival, the London Stock Exchange (LSE), which claimed 11.6 percent of the world total in 2011,[3] boosted essentially by the registration in London of Glencore. In 2011, the TSX and TSXV handled 90 percent of the shares issued by mining companies throughout the world.[4]

According to Canadian government sources, the head offices of more than 75 percent of the world's mining exploration or operating firms are located in Canada,[5] and almost 60 percent of them are registered on the TSX,[6] even though their capital is not necessarily Canadian in origin. In fact, the capitalization of many of these entities comes from Australia, Belgium, Sweden, Israel, the United States, or from tax havens such as the Virgin Islands. Strangely enough, many mining exploration firms registered in Toronto do not hold a single mining claim on Canadian soil.

As a financial centre, Toronto provides the world's extractive industry with six substantial advantages. First, the TSX makes it easy for investors to speculate. Second, through generous federal and provincial tax incentives to the extractive sector, Canada specifically encourages investors to put money in mining companies. Third, Canadian lawmakers and political leaders have clearly demonstrated that they have no intention of interfering with Canadian-registered corporations accused of abuse or even crime outside Canadian borders. Fourth, the legal right to "reputation" has a history of taking precedence over the legal right to "freedom of speech," which means that critical voices in Canada are often threatened with costly libel suits. Fifth, rather than remaining neutral, the Canadian government acts as the industry's advocate before Canadian public opinion. Sixth, the Canadian mining industry abroad benefits from the active assistance of Canada's diplomatic services and development agencies.

Any mining concession obtained anywhere in the world, even under the most dubious circumstances, is considered worthy of listing on the Toronto exchange. As the world's mining capital, the Toronto exchange is permissive in the extreme; and the information disclosure rules applying to companies listed on the TSX are ambiguous enough that they encourage greater speculation than do stock exchanges in the United States, for example. Canadian legislation underwrites investment in mining through the awarding of substantial fiscal incentives while it makes civil and criminal legal action against companies very difficult. These "advantages" have made Canada into a key platform for the extractive sector, which, from the Toronto Stock Exchange, controls a global spectrum of exploration and operation activities that generate record profits, often at the cost of serious humanitarian and environmental consequences.

Particularly over the past two decades, Canada has emerged as a judicial and regulatory haven for the world's extractive industry. The country's jurisdiction provides unofficial cover for corporations that may be involved in shameful controversies abroad.

1. UNLIMITED SPECULATION ON WORLD RESOURCES

First in the substantial advantages Canada provides to the world's extractive industry is unlimited speculation on world resources. In attempting to deal with market crises and scandals that have regularly arisen in Canada during the twentieth century, Canadian stock exchanges repeatedly have been faced with a problem equivalent to squaring the circle. How do they persuade companies in search of risk capital to register with them, while at the same time protecting investors against the abusive claims to which they are exposed in the absence of an effective outside authority such as a government regulatory agency? Smooth talkers try to drive up the "value" of shares in the eyes of investors; meanwhile, investors hope to invest in projects of substance. The stock exchange's balancing act is all the more unconvincing in that the actors involved have contradictory interests. Yet only the good faith of these actors can ensure that institutional rules are followed: they are supposed to be "self-regulated." Often mentioned by the various special-interest groups involved in the process, "self-regulation" is in fact the only distinguishing factor between the functioning of the stock exchange and that of a casino.

Resources or Reserves: A Fortunate Ambiguity

The spectacular Bre-X fraud which began on the Calgary Stock Exchange in 1997,[7] as well as several suspect cases on the ultra-permissive Vancouver exchange, showed how pointless were the regulations in effect on Canada's stock exchanges and how feebly they were applied. Until the late 1990s, companies listed on Canadian stock exchanges were given complete freedom to shroud the true nature of their assets in dense fog. In their reports, for example, they were not required to distinguish between "reserves" (precise estimates of quantities of actually exploitable ore in a deposit) and "resources" (gross estimates of the ore of a claim). By publicizing figures that represented "resources" rather than "reserves," they were able to inflate the potential of the deposits on which the share value of their offerings was based, attracting investors to business opportunities that appeared lucrative but were illusory. The "qualified person" responsible for validating information provided by companies listed on the stock exchange was not subject to the slightest degree of supervision by a professional corporation; public regulatory agencies were both indulgent and negligent; and fraudsters enjoyed a high degree of impunity, as the public learned in July 2007 when Bre-X vice-president John Felderhof, accused of insider trading and publishing false news releases, was acquitted by a Superior Court of Justice in Toronto.[8]

In the early 2000s, after the Bre-X scandal, the Toronto Stock Exchange became the central exchange for Canadian-registered mining stocks. (Today, the extractive companies known as the "majors" are listed on the Toronto Stock Exchange, now part of the TMX Group after the merger of the Montreal and Toronto exchanges, while the "juniors" appear primarily on the TSX Venture Index, a capital market made to measure for cash-strapped companies that emerged in 1999 from the ashes of the Calgary and Vancouver stock exchanges.) In response to sharp international criticism, the TSX adopted a more rigorous descriptive and supervisory methodology. New measures were introduced: more stringent standards for disclosure (proposed in July 1998 and in force by February 2001);[9] standards and guidelines for valuation of mineral properties (published in February 2003);[10] and revised and updated mining standards guidelines (effective December 30, 2005).[11] These new standards required Canadian mining companies to make a clear distinction between "resources" and "reserves" and to include this information in documents released to the public. The new guidelines also defined a number of technical obligations concerning the nature of a company's investments, including in what way a "qualified person" might accept, or propose the acceptance of, the information made public by a company.

From then on, rather than being presented in a uniform manner, the ore discovered in a deposit was to be broken down into categories and subcategories, ranging from those with the most detailed criteria to those with the least. One would think that this would make it possible to obtain a clearer understanding of a given company's assets. However, data on the "resources" a deposit may contain, even before a decision has been made to exploit it, are now presented as "inferred," "indicated," or "measured," depending on the quality of the information used to assess their quality. "Reserves" now refer to the ore that may actually be extracted from a mine as indicated by a preliminary feasibility study that outlines the methods and applicability of a production plan. Reserves are in turn broken down into the subcategories of "probable" and "proven" reserves. The difference between the two lies in the affirmative nature of the conclusions of a study. In the case of "probable mineral reserves," it is asserted that exploitation "*can be* justified," whereas in the case of "proven mineral reserves," exploitation "*is* justified."[12]

However, the problem is precisely the continuity between deductions regarding quantity made based on "resources" and the groping preliminary statements made based on "reserves," and this is what has raised concern among international investors. What do statements about reserves really mean? Are they supposed to indicate that we know when, where, and how minerals can be effectively extracted in a profitable manner? But so many factors are involved, and are liable to change, that in fact no judgment is possible. Estimates must continuously be adjusted to take into account real extraction costs, the real mineral content of soils, and above all, the commodity's price fluctuations.

Consequently, the boundary between what are really estimated reserves and what should be viewed strictly as resources constantly shifts. Scott Wright, online analyst for *Zeal Intelligence* and an expert on this issue, admits he has had problems sorting out the wide spectrum of data provided by gold-mining companies. "Maybe this land was surveyed and/or tested in the past, but the market price of gold was so low it was not as economically feasible to extract as it was for the mine next door. But with the rising price of gold, and because the juniors believe gold prices will continue to rise, this deposit is now feasible or will be in the near future ... The price of gold now or in the near future will pay for us to dig a little deeper."[13]

These contingencies not only make it impossible to come up with sound empirical assessments; they also tend to muddle definitions, as what may be categorized as inaccessible resources one day, depending on price speculation or on certain technological costs, the next day may be listed as reserves that "may justify" exploitation. So much uncertainty makes all such notions highly unreliable when it is time to evaluate a project's potential. The estimates provided in the valuation letters of experts and geologists – little better than modern-day letters of exchange – are highly subjective. We find ourselves in the realm of circumstantial "opinions" used to justify the broadest possible interpretation of the word "reserves" as subsumed under the term "resources." These kinds of shifting calculations have enormous potential to generate false or misleading results.

In addition, scientific consulting firms that establish or validate estimates are as completely governed by the profit motive as the mining companies themselves. How, at the risk of losing future contracts, could such consultants ever possibly publish unsatisfactory conclusions? As a result, the consulting firms hired by mining companies may respond first to the requirements of the market, rather than on honest and objective science.

While some investors may be unaware of the confusion between the terms "resources" and "reserves," or may hope to profit from it, others – including some of the canniest – are made uneasy by, and are particularly wary of, the Toronto Stock Exchange, which they see as a market that plays on ambiguity. "Resources are a loose and thorny word in the mining industry. Measured and indicated resources are a commonly stated way of reporting resources among mining companies globally. Different governing bodies assign this different merit though. Canadian regulations not only require but also recognize these terms as a legitimate base for the potential future bankability of ore reserves in their filings, but the Securities and Exchange Commission (SEC) in the United States does not. Because of this you will find that many of the juniors today trade primarily on foreign stock exchanges, where guidelines are less stringent than those of the SEC."[14] In fact, in the United States, regulatory agencies have shown that it is possible to tackle speculation: they prohibit the publication of any data other than reserves. SEC regulations are "intended to reduce the speculation associated with initial in situ, estimated resources, which are invariably greater than the reserves."[15]

In Canada, to these questions of contingency is added a socio-logical factor – the conflict and scientific debate between geologists and mine planners. Geologists are interested in the potential of given soils, while mine planners focus on production costs. Subcontractors argue with each other within each of these groups, and so many questions arise in the process of establishing the data that, in the final analysis, it is a good deal less than dependable. The methodological preferences of either party can lead to asset over-valuation; and the often gaping discrepancies between pre-feasibility studies and the real costs of project implementation are further evidence of the data's unreliability. Virginia Heffernan states the obvious when she writes: "Attaching a price tag to a mine property is never easy."[16]

Thierry Michel's documentary *Katanga Business* (2009) under-lines the weakness of the "scientific" precautions certain financial players claim, either naively or abusively, to be taking. The film focuses on a copper mine being reactivated by a group consisting of Canadian investors, George Forrest (the Belgian potentate of the Congo), and Gécamines, the Congolese state mining corporation carved up by Can-adian and other companies in the mid-1990s in the course of a massive privatization initiative supported by the World Bank. The company that emerged from this process, Katanga Mining, is listed on the Toronto exchange, where it looks for risk capital. "Risk" would appear to be an accurate description: the documentary film closes with the statement that the recent financial crisis has severely affected mining companies in Katanga, with the price of copper dropping by 60 percent and share prices by 80 to 97 percent.[17] Though the film presents multiple points of view – detailed expert assessments from an engineer in good standing, the opinion of an investor (presumably Canadian) who praises what he sees as a "world-class opportunity" for those he represents, and the opinion of George Forrest, who describes copper as a "stable" resource – what is most clear is that valuation has nothing to do with science. It is impossible to ascribe a precise value to a potentially extractable mineral. Stock-market speculation is no less risky than it has ever been. Moreover, the questions raised fall squarely in the public domain, given that pension-fund managers and others whom we hear in the film are actively investing Canadian assets in Katanga.

The Oxymoron: "Self-Regulation"

The new supervisory measures adopted in the early 2000s for Canadian financial markets, such as the standards set out in National Instrument 43-101 *Standards of Disclosure for Mineral Projects* (NI 43-101),[18] have not met with unanimous approval. Though many different mining investors are now more accountable for their activities, some professional groups in the mining sector continue to resist and to challenge the new rules. According to Keith Spence, who co-chaired the committee to develop national standards in Canada, "one of the main challenges of developing valuation standards in the mining business … is the friction between real estate appraisers, who have traditionally dominated the valuation field, and mining professionals, who sometimes resent the use of real estate principles to value mining assets."[19] As a result, years after the Bre-X scandal, some people still express concern about the future impact of these measures, in turn enabling others to advocate a return to greater freedom for the experts who assess deposits. Critics also oppose making experts liable to either civil suit or criminal prosecution based on their recommendations, even though in Canada the risk of legal action against experts is slight. Mining-industry professionals shy away from standardized methodologies, pointing to the deficient nature of the formal procedures currently in force. The proposal to allow experts greater methodological leeway is a way of presenting arbitrariness, which critics pretend to oppose, as the best way to solve the problem of a deficient methodology. The taboo that has lain hidden at the heart of the debate for decades is that of "self-regulation." Mining-industry professionals and investors are unanimous in their hostility to any government involvement in the valuation process, with constant praise for the key concept of "self-discipline"; and the professional corporations to which experts belong are fully independent. But the concentrated presence in one sector of professionals who are invested with so much power obviously increases the risk of insider trading, influence peddling, corruption, incestuous relationships, and simple back-scratching.

The fact that Canadian financial markets are known throughout the world for their permissiveness makes it even more difficult to believe that these regulations and methods, already inherently deficient, could ever be strictly enforced. Despite its democratic pretensions, Canada has acted to concentrate on its territory all the mechanisms for surveillance of its largest financial and industrial players, not to regulate them in accordance with the rule of law, but to provide them, in the manner of a tax haven, with a political, financial, and legal environment that is as unconstricting and as apathetic as possible. This was one of the main arguments put forward in *Noir Canada*.[20] The TSX, Queen's Park, and Ottawa, by failing strictly to supervise investors and Canadian-registered companies, have actively contributed to creating for them a space in which everything is possible. The consequences of this generosity are felt even at the international level.

William J. McNally and Brian F. Smith, economists at Ontario's Wilfrid Laurier University, have shown how badly the Toronto Stock Exchange, and the Ontario Securities Commission (OSC) that supposedly supervises it, apply existing regulations that govern release of information in cases of insider trading. Unlike what is common practice in the United States, many cases are never even investigated. One in eight transactions are said to involve TSX companies buying up their own shares. The OSC budget does not allow consistent monitoring, and incredible as it may seem, the data available to it on a daily basis are less precise and less complete than the monthly data published by the TSX itself. The lack of monitoring is extraordinary, and the weakness of Toronto regulations has raised the hackles even of seasoned investors such as Claude Lamoureux, who denounced their laxness when he was president of Teachers, the powerful pension fund for Ontario public school teachers.[21] For people in the know, insider trading in Toronto is child's play; meanwhile, the general public, lacking information, is in constant danger of losing its shirt. In the rare instances when the guilty are arrested, the sanctions imposed are sometimes less than the profit made on the illegal trade. "Almost half of the purchasing firms fail to report their trades to the OSC."[22]

In the United States, following a number of major corporate scandals, including cases such as Enron and WorldCom, in 2002 Washington enacted a bill known as the *Sarbanes-Oxley Act* on "public company accounting reform and investor protection." Section 404 of *Sarbanes-Oxley* requires corporations to exercise internal control over financial reporting in compliance with a control framework established by a normalization agency.[23] The adoption of these stricter rules in the United States led Canada to enact what have proven to be only superficial changes to its model of a self-regulating financial sector. In Canada, the permissive approach to which the government had reiterated its commitment in 1994 based on the Dey report[24] still prevails. Canada's utopian idea is that the market will induce brokers and share-issuing companies to behave themselves in order to make their shares credible. "Market and social pressures are supposed to lead companies to adopt governance standards that will contribute to maximizing value," explains Université de Montréal law professor Stéphane Rousseau.[25] Yet Canada has refused to adopt regulations inspired by Section 404 of the

American law, a section that is described as "controversial because of the costs it entails."[26] Thus the proposed Canadian regulation on internal control over financial reporting, which dealt with the same issues, did not include a similar constraint.[27] Introduced in February 2004 in all jurisdictions except British Columbia, the proposed regulation was withdrawn in March 2006 when Canadian Securities Administrators determined not to proceed with proposed changes.[28] Instead, a complementary regulation on corporate governance guidelines establishes a distinction between mandatory disclosures and other voluntary, completely optional disclosures. These optional disclosures are in fact a catalogue of good intentions; for example, the members of a company's board of administrators ought to be "independent" and should satisfy itself "as to the integrity of the chief executive officer (the CEO) and other executive officers and that the CEO and other executive officers create a culture of integrity throughout the organization."[29]

Well-versed in the art of using euphemisms, Rousseau refers to the intention "to regulate governance in a level-headed manner."[30] Under Canadian law, the only restriction is that the corporation is required to ask an audit committee, consisting of three independent administrators, to examine the links between internal and external auditors and to oversee the work of the external auditors. This committee also participates in the process of disclosing information based on the company's financial statements. In other words, in the absence of a normative framework, the credibility of the financial world rests once again on the degree to which it trusts itself, since only the social agents belonging to the brotherhood of finance are given the right to assess the real independence of actors whose behaviour is dictated by the logic of the marketplace. As ever, the legal basis of the Canadian economy is dictated by the interests of powerful shareholders, rather than those of employees, partners, or communities affected by the economy's operation. "In Canadian law, the theory of shareholders' primacy has imposed itself, both in case-law and as a doctrine, as the dominant conception of society's interest."[31] Finance makes law. The late Raymond Favreau, who served as attorney and scientific adviser for ATTAC-Québec (an association to promote taxation of international financial transactions), pointed out that Canadian judicial authorities have shown surprising complacency with respect to economic crimes. Recent examples are those of Paul Eustace, manager of Portus Alternative Management, or of the Norshield Financial Group.[32] Favreau extensively researched the loopholes that make the Toronto exchange's oversight methods look like a sieve. "In the case of significant economic crimes committed in Canada, if the company involved is listed on a U.S. exchange, the U.S. authorities will often take action," notes Favreau, who spent decades charting these and similar failings.[33]

Canadian leniency toward financial crime is an open secret. "Want to be a corporate criminal? Move to Canada" read a headline in the August 9, 2009, edition of the Globe and Mail. In Canada, court sentences for so-called white-collar crime bear far fewer consequences than in the United States. The judicial system moves slowly, and bail conditions are generous. (In the same edition of the Globe and Mail – a conservative newspaper – columnist Lawrence Martin wrote that the Ontario justice system had given a "shining green light" to "patronage as usual" and "dirty politics as usual" by acquitting former Ottawa mayor Larry O'Brien of influence peddling.)

Existing financial regulations and procedures look good on paper. But who actually complies with them, and how can we believe that there is compliance when we know that legal provisions have no real force? According to Africa specialists Jean-Pascal Daloz and Patrick Chabal, a responsible democratic state is defined less by its formal laws and regulations than by the way in which these measures are enforced. Weak states, by contrast, are characterized by the ingenuity with which they play with their legal restrictions, elude sanctions, flirt with the sublegal, take advantage of loopholes, and operate in darkness.[34] "What is at issue is not the inadequacy of rules and regulations, but the fact that they are systematically disregarded; from this point of view old and new regulations share the same fate. In other words, rules and regulations are designed as obstacles to be avoided, points of reference around which procedures are invented to develop new relations."[35]

In this context, experts in civic morality, tasteful academics, and other duly authorized representatives of "civil society," despite their good faith, are trapped in a fruitless attempt to control the extractive industry strictly through the adoption of new formal regulations. Their proposals, always "concrete," are rarely anything more than a decorative flourish on a policy framework that is designed to be ineffectual. Proposals developed as part of "roundtables"[36] – or whatever other structure of "good governance" happens to have been established at any given moment – are the product of multiple and sometimes dubious compromises between "social partners"; these proposals are developed by people who never ask whether the government, if it ever were to adopt new regulations, would know how to enforce them or would have any real intention of doing so. "While, intuitively, corporate governance is being enhanced as an instrument to maximize enterprise wealth, it has a long measure to go toward providing consistent and measurable practice."[37] The only true imperative is still the enrichment of private actors.

In any event, it is understood that certain interests will be protected. Disclosure of information on the conditions in which corporations earn profits is a question that should be of concern to any democratically minded person. However, the only considerations that must be disclosed are those based on the interests of corporations or their shareholders. A careful reading of existing regulations shows that nobody is paying serious attention to circumstances such as human-rights violations or environmental, political, social, and fiscal abuses, of which many companies listed on Canadian stock exchanges stand accused around the world. According to continuous disclosure guidelines, which define the obligation to disclose information on securities in Canada,[38] managers must keep markets closely informed of the "uncertainties" of their activities with regard to market "performance" criteria; but in the area of "risks" an organization can tolerate with regard to the ecosystem, or the life or political organization of populations, these factors must be reported only if the data is likely to have a "market impact," or to influence a "reasonable investor" in his or her decision to purchase a stock.

Since the prevailing economic anthropology assumes that our model investor is interested only in gain, a large amount of information on the damage inflicted by extraction projects is suppressed, because it is considered irrelevant to the extreme self-interest of the imagined investor. In fact, in Toronto, the definition of financial information that must be disclosed is strictly based on the narrow concept of "material information," which "is that which either results or could be expected to result in a change in the market price or value of the company's stock."[39] The sole determining factors are the criteria adopted by the stereotyped "reasonable" (read: grasping) investor and "market impact." Those who read between the lines will also understand that the "environmental liabilities" that corporations are required to disclose[40] appear in the eyes of "reasonable" investors more as a handicap than as an objective piece of information. New environmental reporting guidelines,[41] introduced in October 2010, continue to provide not a single restrictive measure in social or environmental terms.[42] Only "risks" on environmental matters must be disclosed with respect to the determining factor, which is the materiality factor that might have an impact on the issuer's "performance," meaning its financial performance related to environmental issues mainly with respect to financial issues.[43] As for the euphemistic jargon that the business world defines as "corporate social responsibility," Canada actually "obliges" companies to boast of their feats in this area. "If your company has implemented social or environmental policies that are fundamental to your operations ... describe them and the steps your company has taken to implement them."[44] The same holds true for the Global Reporting Initiative, a set of voluntary guidelines for reporting on economic, environmental, and social performance. Canada is thus unable to do more than urge or invite mining companies to maximize the marketing impact of their alleged "social" or "green" investments. Mining companies respond to the invitation in the storytelling mode, relating their social concerns in cloying business-speak, singing the praises of voluntary commitments and programs that may or may not have any real impact in countries where, in any case, the companies are paying almost no taxes.[45] "These texts consist of several smaller narratives: here, children are given scholarships; there, a Tanzanian student is supported at a leading Canadian university; somewhere else, we build a primary school. No figures are produced but there are repeated references to individual beneficiaries of the company's generosity, demonstrating how corporate charity has changed their lives. We also find vaguely worded declarations of principle distantly related to the company's actual practices," writes Gaétan Breton, professor of accounting at the Université du Québec à Montréal, in an article on the community commitments of Barrick Gold.[46]

According to the European Parliament, voluntary measures in the Canadian manner, with their "restrictions" of convenience, are altogether insufficient. In November 2007, it rejected a recommendation by the Brussels-based European Commission to the effect "that voluntary reporting guidelines would be sufficient" in the mining and energy industries – a system that would have mirrored Canadian practices.[47]

Although some members of "civil society" may find it sufficient to insist that investors show some sensitivity to environmental and social

these countries. In the 1990s, children in the Great Lakes region of Africa were handed Kalashnikovs to guard or seize deposits of coltan needed to produce millions of video-game consoles given as gifts to children in the West.

Around the World: Mining Laws Based on Canada's Example

All over the world, Canada can claim responsibility for the appearance of a new generation of mining codes. These codes provide corporations and shareholders with the same generous provisions as the Quebec and Ontario mining codes: negligible taxes, full socialization of costs, disregard for customary and native rights, contempt for environmental issues, absence of regulations governing corporate behaviour, and the list goes on. Particularly in countries with a developed mining sector, whenever new, neo-liberal rules of "good governance" were imposed on the population, at the same time a legal, financial, political, and human resources framework was established to suit the needs of the extractive industry. Canada has been active in drafting a number of these mining investment policies in countries in the South, including Colombia, Botswana, Zimbabwe, Guinea, and Zambia. Mining-industry companies, 75 percent of which are registered in Canada according to official sources,[72] were also invited to participate in drafting these policies, while the World Bank consulted eighty firms to have a clearer view of the Eldorado that these indebted states would soon become. An explosion of Canadian mining investment has taken place in recent years: it reached a high of $12.5 billion in 2011.[73]

The new mining codes that Canada has exported throughout the world – partly through the Canadian government's influence on agencies such as the IMF and the World Bank – all share one troubling characteristic: in contrast to earlier formal and informal codes in many of these countries, the new rules do not explicitly recognize the right of Aboriginal peoples to exploit the resources of their traditional lands, where they often carried out artisanal small-scale mining linked to local capital. Instead, public authorities are set up to "solve" the thorny issue of the ancestral presence of indigenous peoples on these lands, by subordinating it to the interests of Western corporations.

According to Amnesty International, Canada exerted intense diplomatic pressure to convince countries of the South to join it in opposing the 2007 UN Declaration on the Rights of Indigenous Peoples.[74] It is perhaps not surprising, then, that Canada should show no concern when a country draws up a mining code without any consultation with its indigenous peoples. This is what happened in Colombia in 2001, even though the redefinition of "indigenous territory" was a violation of Colombian law. The new Colombian code modified the redistribution of benefits from the extractive sector so that they no longer need to be paid to local (Aboriginal) communities.

Canada intervened directly in the Colombian restructuring process. As early as 1996, $11.3 million were given to "improve" the institutional operations of the Colombian ministry of mines and energy and the ministry of the environment. A portion of the funds came from the Alberta-based Canadian Energy Research Institute. [75] CIDA also approved financing in the amount of $241,861 in technical assistance to the Colombian government's Plan Pacifico.[76] Nearly one-third of this amount was paid out to Ottawa-based Radarsat International Inc., which in conjunction with the Canadian Space Agency markets a satellite technology for analyzing soil and subsoil relief.[77]

Ironically, according to international financial institutions, tax revenues – to be reinvested in "development" – are supposed to be the chief advantage of the "reforms" imposed on mining countries in the South. But the new mining codes that have proliferated there during the past century provide very substantial tax advantages for mining investors. Even to calculate royalties and tax payments to be included in contracts, countries of the South are forced blindly to trust the production forecasts of mining professionals, yet they generally have no prior experience of the financial speculation characteristic of the extractive industry and are unable to estimate future earnings. In any case, whatever amount is owed to the state, it is clear that substantial sums contrive to evade tax authorities, given the absence of even the most elementary governmental supervision of the mining companies' operations.

In Ghana, for example, where Canadian firms hold half of all mining concessions, the latest version of the mining code is completely unfavourable to the government in practically every area where it might have expected to garner tax revenues: equipment to be used in mining installations is tax exempt; expatriates pay no fees when they transfer funds abroad; in order to buy equipment, investors are allowed to deposit 25 percent of their income, or more, in a foreign currency account. As a result, in Ghana the mining sector does not seem to account for more than 2 percent of the country's GDP.[78]

In Tanzania, a report entitled *A Golden Opportunity?* underlines the shortfall faced by the government as a result of new tax laws for the mining industry enacted in the late 1990s. The authors state that "the combined loss to Tanzania of a low royalty rate, unpaid corporation tax, and tax evasion is at least US$400m over the past seven years" and that "the concentration of gold mining in the hands of large multinational companies at the expense of artisanal small-scale miners has put 400,000 people out of work."[79]

In the Democratic Republic of Congo, the mining code stipulates that only 4 percent of a mine's "operating capital" (their costs, not the value of the materials they extract) shall be returned to the government in the form of royalties, which is less than half the rate of neighbouring countries where royalties are already low.[80]

With the minimal regulations embodied in the mining codes, mining countries in the South are unable to collect the tax revenues that would enable them to support economic development projects or foster the growth of their own industrial sector. Meanwhile, Canada or other organizations involved in funding "development" are underwriting Canada's own powerful extractive industry. Not only do Canadian pension funds invest in Canadian mining companies, but agencies such as Export Development Canada and the Canadian International Development Agency, as well as a variety of one-off initiatives designed to "help" the African continent, also tend, in fact, to support the industry's expansionist aims.

In addition to the investment guarantees that we mentioned earlier, Export Development Canada provides the extractive industry with insurance, and political risk is one of the threats against which companies are protected. As one analyst explained in 2009: "EDC has been making substantial efforts to broaden and market its presence in the mining sector, and its Political Risk Insurance product is part of that strategy. The EDC coverage protects against a variety of threats ranging from political violence, currency conversion or transfer restrictions and foreign government non-payment or repossession threat."[81]

Export Development Canada has financed and insured politically high-risk projects in countries such as Madagascar, DRC, Tanzania, Eritrea, Congo-Brazzaville, and Mauritania. The case of Madagascar is one example of a controversial project. In 2009, Canadian interests, including natural-resource company Sherritt and engineering heavyweight SNC-Lavalin, held a 45 percent interest in the Ambatovy open-pit mine in the Toamasina region. Export Development Canada's contribution was worth $400 million in the form of insurance against the political risks engendered by the project: mining companies had insured themselves against the consequences of the fact that the population of Madagascar was angry.[82]

transport during its military operation."[94] The military trial that found them not guilty remains controversial.

In 1998, Kabila arbitrarily reviewed the mining concessions he had granted. For example, the 82,000-square kilometre exploration concession which former president Joseph Mobutu had given Barrick Gold in 1996 – a contract countersigned by Kabila soon after he overthrew the government and became president[95] – was suddenly reduced to 55,000 square kilometres.[96]

Kabila's dissatisfied political allies, Rwanda and Uganda, were frustrated by his inconsistency and there were attempts to overthrow him, allegedly with the help of commercial partners; the allegations often mention the Canadian junior American Mine Fields Inc. (AMFI), now known as Adastra, which was later acquired by First Quantum Minerals.[97] The war resumed, and among its beneficiaries were private corporations able to profit from a world of chaos.

The 2010 UN High Commissioner for Human Rights report notes: "During the second war, foreign companies rarely controlled the source of the minerals or other goods they were purchasing, and sometimes paid the armed groups directly ... In a number of cases, foreign or multinational companies were directly involved in negotiations with perpetrators of serious human-rights abuses, paying armed groups or providing them with facilities or logistics in order to exploit natural resources."[98] As early as 2002, however, a report by the UN Panel of Experts on the Illegal Exploitation of Natural Resources and Other Forms of Wealth of the Democratic Republic of Congo included a list of companies in violation of OECD codes of behaviour.[99] The report invited certain jurisdictions, Canada being implicitly among them, to investigate the activities of multinational corporations and mineral exploration firms in the African Great Lakes war zone between 1996 and 2003. The number of dead as a direct or indirect consequence of this war is estimated at five million people.[100]

is funded by the World Bank, once again to the detriment of people in the South.[90]

3. PROVIDING FIRMS WITH LEGAL COVER

Third in the substantial advantages Canada provides to the world's extractive industry is legal protection for mining firms. Canada can be relied upon to provide, unofficially, full political and legal cover to companies registered in its jurisdiction even when these companies are facing well-established and documented allegations of abuse. Many documents, including those produced by two United Nations agencies, the UN High Commissioner for Human Rights and the UN Committee on the Elimination of Racial Discrimination (CERD),[91] deal with the exceptionally serious impact of the extractive industry in the countries of the South.

A report from the United Nations High Commissioner for Human Rights on the violation of basic human rights in the Congo between 1993 and 2003 implicates transnational mining companies in these violations.[92] During this decade, the simmering conflict between the rebel forces of the Alliance of Democratic Forces for the Liberation of the Congo, backed by Uganda and Rwanda, and the regime of long-time dictator Joseph Mobutu flared into open hostility. Yet rebel leader Laurent-Désiré Kabila was able to rely on support from the mining companies to build up his war chest. "During the AFDL's advance on Kinshasa in 1996, before it had even formed a government, Kabila was allocating mining concessions to private companies. Many of these transactions were conducted illegally."[93]

Employees of Anvil Mining are among the Canadian individuals and corporations mentioned in the report. "An Australian-Canadian mining company was accused of supplying the army with logistics and

Finance Corporation gave Canada $3 million to be administered by CIDA-INC;[86] the purpose of the funding was to underwrite eventual investors in the mining sector, particularly in pre-feasibility and feasibility studies, training, technology transfer, and consulting services.[87]

Corporate investments also received support from the Canadian government in 2011 when then minister of international cooperation Bev Oda, pretending to believe that the development of the Canadian mining industry leads to poverty reduction and improved standards of living for people living near mining sites, used "development aid" funds to create a program supporting the mining industry. The stated goal was "to reduce poverty in Colombia, Peru, Bolivia, Ghana, and Burkina Faso" by funding the activities of civic organizations such as World Vision, Plan Canada, and the World University Service of Canada.[88] The "partners" with whom these organizations were said to be "working" – Barrick Gold, Iamgold, and Rio Tinto Alcan – were hardly lacking in financial resources. Further, the minister made her announcement, not to desperately poor populations, but at the Devonshire Initiative CEO Summit. Some of Canada's most scrupulous actors in the field of international cooperation, such as the general Coordinator of the Andean Indigenous Organizations (CAIO), Miguel Palacin Quispe, were highly critical of this alliance; Quispe wrote that Canadian mining corporations of this kind "are the source of many conflicts because of the dispossession of lands, destruction of water sources, and the ignoring of international rights."[89]

Who benefits from this kind of international "development aid"? In Madagascar, according to local residents, Rio Tinto's titanic iron-ore mine is causing both ecosystem disruption and major social and economic problems. Further, the ore extracted in Madagascar is then processed in Sorel, Quebec. The process of extracting the ore, which benefits the company and a small number of people working in Quebec,

Since 2001, Export Development Canada's decisions with regard to projects have been related to environmental policies. However, the Canadian Network on Corporate Accountability notes the persistence of many blind spots: "EDC still lacks sufficient levels of transparency to ensure accountability. The corporation does not disclose its due diligence process for proposed projects, or reveal the specific standards that a project is deemed to have met. Besides, EDC does not require companies to consult with communities that would be affected by proposed investments."[83]

Now that the private sector is immune – thanks to Canadian taxpayers – to the political responses of populations confronted on a daily basis with corrupt dictatorships, who will still genuinely care about the fate of these people?

Thanks to another unexpected source of financing, the extractive industry was able to count on $100 million from the Canada Investment Fund for Africa (CIFA),[84] set up with public funds by Jean Chrétien after the creation by Western countries of the New Partnership for Africa's Development (NEPAD). CIFA's capital was allotted to projects in DRC, Nigeria, Rwanda, Senegal, South Africa, and Tunisia. Exploration company Banro Corporation, for example, received millions of dollars in public funds in support of their projects in Eastern Congo, in the heart of the war-torn African Great Lakes region.

CIDA supports the extractive industry in other, even more unexpected ways. It operates the Industrial Cooperation Program (CIDA-INC), whose stated goal is to provide financial and technical assistance to Canadian industrial start-ups in developing countries or countries in transition to a market economy.[85] The program is described as the developing world's single-largest source of credit available to private sector companies; the yearly value of agreements signed under its auspices is estimated at US$12 billion, with oil, gas, and extractive industries holding first rank. In 2004, the World Bank's International

All over the world, countless documents from reliable sources show how often indigenous peoples, such as peasant farmers and artisanal small-scale miners, oppose the presence of Canadian mining companies on their lands, whether for exploration or exploitation. Wherever Canadian mining firms are to be found, the same extremely serious allegations are heard: allegations of massive pollution and ecosystem destruction, brutal eviction at the hands of paramilitary forces, corruption, tax evasion, and even the murder of people opposed to mining activity. Hundreds of these denunciations have been aimed at Canadian mining firms, particularly in Latin America and Africa, but also in East Asia and in some industrialized countries.[122] The multiplicity of these denunciations lends support to the idea that Canada today is the keystone of a predatory international mining resource system.

Canadian authorities continue to turn a deaf ear; they decline to investigate transnational corporations as long as the allegations made against them "have not been corroborated."[123] And they never will be, for the government never investigates them. The vocal denials of the companies take precedence over all other testimonials.

Canada presents itself as a legal haven for the world's transnational mining companies. Registered primarily in Canada, they are subject to virtually no supervision of their potential wrongdoing beyond Canada's borders. Canada provides them with legal, political, and moral cover, while their subsidiaries, enjoying bank secrecy in the Caribbean, rake in the profits acquired by looting Africa and other continents. This means it is almost impossible to get a judgment in Canada, in either civil or criminal courts, against Canadians or Canadian entities that may have committed abuses or crimes abroad.[124]

The possibility of domestic legal action against abuses that may have been committed abroad is not as utopian a proposition as it might seem. Precedents have been established in Germany and Belgium.[125] In the United States, though it is far from adequate and was weakened by legal decisions in 2009, the *Alien Tort Claims Act* (ATCA)[126] allows federal district courts to hear human-rights lawsuits even where the plaintiffs are foreigners and the facts alleged have taken place outside American borders. It is under this law that the Sudanese Presbyterian Church filed suit in the United States against Talisman Energy of Calgary (registered on the TSX), which was accused of complicity in the violation, by the Sudanese regime, of the fundamental rights of civilians living next to the company's concession. Talisman requested that the American court drop the case, to no avail. New York Southern District Court judge Denise Cote did not declare American courts incompetent to hear the case, ruling that there exists no possibility for human-rights litigation under Canadian jurisdiction.[127] Yet the Canadian government brought its full weight to bear in an attempt to influence American justice: "The Canadian government sent a 'Statement of Interest' to Cote claiming the lawsuit would have a 'chilling effect' on trade by Canadian companies in the Sudan."[128] The American court then chided the Canadian authorities, pointing to a "lack of understanding about the nature of the claims."[129]

The *Sudan Peace Act*,[130] a program of sanctions adopted by Washington in 2002 against the Sudanese government to restrict its public investments, also pointed an accusing finger directly at companies such as Talisman. Though it does not apply to the Canadian firm, a representative of Talisman Energy recognized that the *Sudan Peace Act* focused a great deal of attention on the company.[131]

While we may rejoice at these measures, they may have unintended negative consequences. Court decisions brought down under the *Alien Tort Claims Act*, for example, tend to assign a private character to international debates that are political in nature. But in Canada, there is no need even to discuss such a contingency, since no comparable measure exists in Canadian law. In the area of universal criminal jurisdiction, the *Crimes against Humanity and War Crimes Act*,[132] adopted by Ottawa in 2000, opens the door to judging, on the basis of a restrictive list, crimes committed abroad by Canadians. Over and above matters of legal procedure (obstruction of international justice), the law lays down sanctions in such extreme contexts as genocide, crimes against humanity, and war crimes, in relation to murder, extermination, enslavement, deportation, imprisonment and torture, sexual violence, and persecution. However, it allows no recourse for the victims of major economic crimes, of which Canadian bodies corporate or physical may be either the perpetrators or accomplices.

These judicial procedures are, moreover, extremely difficult to enforce. Only the attorney general (the federal minister of justice) can consent to the prosecution of such offences. However, this system contravenes the principle of the separation of powers between the judiciary and executive branch of government. Canadian political authorities have proven reluctant to authorize lawsuits that might cast an unfavourable light on themselves, given their substantial support for Canadian companies abroad. The Canadian International Development Agency backs controversial Canadian mining companies around the world;[133] Export Development Canada has used taxpayers' money to set up an opaque insurance fund that directly benefits these firms,[134] while the Canada Investment Fund for Africa finances highly controversial projects on that continent.[135]

Under both liberal and conservative governments, there is nothing ambiguous about Canada's official policy with regard to its overseas industries: it is up to the host country to enforce the rules to be applied within its jurisdiction, even if the poverty in which the country is maintained by the international economic system makes it unable to fulfill these functions. Canada has also been doing everything in its power to lessen the scope of the tools that might enable it to seek out irregularities in the way business is transacted by Canadian companies abroad. "With subtle strokes of the pen, it appears that the Conservative government has been systematically changing the language employed by the foreign service, and as a result, bringing subtle but sweeping changes to the traditional Canadian foreign policy," writes Michelle Collins in *Embassy*.[136] For example, in the world of Canadian international politics, "child soldiers" do not exist; instead, they are vaguely described as "children in armed conflicts." Moreover, the adjective "humanitarian" finds itself deleted from the concept of "international humanitarian law."[137]

However, the relevance of this transfer of responsibility to the host country is refuted by elementary analyses. In 2005, the UN Sub-Commission on the Promotion and Protection of Human Rights reported that crimes committed by private companies in the world result most of the time from complicity, support, partnership, and direct or indirect assistance in the violation of human rights, especially on the part of the host country.[138]

But Canada does more than ignore these analyses. On the ground in the host countries, not only does Canadian diplomacy put pressure on local authorities, but the mining lobby also throws its full weight into the balance to influence the decisions of political authorities. The former Argentine minister of the environment, Romina Picolotti, admits to having been forced to resign in 2008, following insistent representations by the mining lobby. According to her, as summed up in the Toronto *Star*: "Barrick, the world's biggest gold producer, was so successful in convincing the Argentine government to block legislation affecting one of its operations that the cancellation became known as 'the Barrick veto'."[139]

Filing a complaint is a battle in itself. The case of Cambior, a Quebec-based mining company, shows the de facto immunity enjoyed in Quebec by locally registered mineral firms in relation to abuses committed abroad. In 1995, the collapse of a tailings pond at the Omai mine in Guyana brought about a disaster of unprecedented proportions, contaminating the country's water system with cyanide and causing grievous harm to the public health of nearby communities as well as the long-term destruction of flora and fauna. A group of 23,000 Guyanese then filed suit against the company in Quebec Superior Court. On August 14, 1998, the court, while declaring itself competent to hear the case, concluded that the Guyanese judicial system had greater competence. In its ruling, the Quebec court raised the lack of a real connection between the victims and Quebec.[140] A Guyanese court later declared a mistrial and compelled the citizens' group to pay the company's court costs.

In another emblematic case, an association of Congolese law students in Canada, the Association des juristes et étudiants congolais en droit du Canada (AJEC-Canada), unsuccessfully demanded that Canada launch criminal proceedings against Montreal-based Anvil Mining. Charges related to a massacre perpetrated by the armed forces of Congo at Kilwa in 2004, in which seventy-three were killed close to the company's mining site, and in which the company may have been complicit. The RCMP told AJEC-Canada to ask the federal minister of justice to provide authorization for it to carry out an investigation in Congo-Kinshasa; at the same time, the RCMP warned that it did not have the resources to carry out this investigation. AJEC-Canada's few exchanges with the federal government or its agencies were by telephone, leaving no paper trail, not even an acknowledgment of receipt.[141]

On November 8, 2010, Anvil Mining was finally brought to court by a group of DRC citizens, working with the Canadian Association against Impunity, for its alleged role in the Kilwa massacre. However, it seems there will always be a Canadian court ready to turn a blind eye to allegations of atrocities committed elsewhere by Canadian mining companies. On January 25, 2012, the Quebec Court of Appeal overturned the judgment of the Superior Court that allowed the case to be tried in its jurisdiction.[142] The court told the parties to return to the DRC, because it offered a more appropriate forum for decision despite the fact that it was a military court that had heard the case there earlier,[143] confirming how difficult it is for populations who say they have been harmed by the industry to be heard by the legal system in Canada.[144]

Hudbay Minerals, a Canadian corporation, has also been sued in Canada for $12 million by Angelica Choc, the wife of Guatemalan activist Adolfo Ich Chamàn, over the death of her husband in September 2009 in Guatemala, where the mining company operates a nickel mine.[145] In another case tried by the Ontario Superior Court, three community leaders from Intag valley in Ecuador sued Copper Mesa (formerly Ascendant Copper), as well as the Toronto Stock Exchange, for $1 billion. The three Ecuadorians alleged, on the basis of video evidence, that the company employed the services of a paramilitary organization to expel them violently from their lands. They also claimed to have received death threats. An indicator that the market is quicker to react than the courts, the Toronto exchange in an exchange bulletin issued on January 19, 2010, confirmed that it had removed Copper Mesa from TSX listings. The official reason given: "For failure to meet continued listing requirements of TSX …"[146] Nevertheless, in this case Canadian courts once again confirmed Canada's status as a legal haven. In March 2011, the Court of Appeal of Ontario confirmed a previous decision of the Superior Court and rejected the Ecuadorians' demand because it presented "no reasonable cause of action."[147]

In cases such as these, the international dimension adds a layer of complexity to citizens' initiatives, both in terms of costs and of competence to hear cases. The chances of success are slender. Palestinian citizens attempted to sue two Montreal-based companies, Green Park and Green Mount, in relation to their activities in Jewish settlements in Palestine, but the case was dismissed in the fall of 2009.[148] According to an Oxford University study, Canada has a narrow concept of the territorial limits of judicial competence, allowing private companies to take advantage of the doctrine of *forum non conveniens* to argue that the Canadian jurisdiction is not qualified to judge cases beyond Canada's borders, no matter what the involvement of Canadian actors.

Oxford Pro Bono Publico's critique of Canadian jurisdiction is telling: "The state of Canadian law with respect to corporate social responsibility, and extraterritorial corporate social responsibility in particular, is generally recognised to be insufficient. Few options are available to non-nationals seeking to pursue Canadian corporations in Canada for wrongs committed abroad, excepting general principles of private international law. The instances of extraterritorial criminal responsibility are narrowly provided for, and are clouded with doubt as to whether they apply to corporate activity. As a result, Canadian corporations have been forced to defend their actions before American courts in actions having no connection with the United States."[149]

As long as mining companies enjoy near-perfect impunity in Canada, it seems likely that world capital will continue to flow into Canadian financial centres, where it will generate windfall profits at the cost of devastating consequences for local populations.

4. USING THE LAW TO SILENCE CRITICS

Fourth in the substantial advantages Canada provides to the world's extractive industry is legal action against critics. In the South, the mining industry finds invaluable allies among ruling elites in its attempts to subject its critics to prosecution. In the wake of Washington's "war on terror," and bowing to American pressure, many governments have adopted laws penalizing legitimate defenders of human rights and ecosystem integrity. Accusations include terrorism, eco-terrorism, sedition, and sabotage, and political leaders are arbitrarily detained. In Canada, where freedom of expression is subordinated to particularly restrictive libel laws and the mining sector looms all-powerful, cases of the legal system being used against critics are legion. In other words, companies can explore and exploit the world's resources with total impunity as to the conditions in which these activities are carried out, yet it can be extremely dangerous to call attention to the mining industry and its practices or even to discuss the international consequences of its methods.

In recent years, in Ontario, eight indigenous Canadian leaders were sentenced to six months in jail (these sentences were later reduced and the leaders were released after sixty-eight days of detention) for having peacefully demonstrated against platinum and uranium mining projects on their territory. On March 17, 2008, the Ontario Superior Court stated that "the desire of Aboriginal communities to protect their land, cultural heritage and way of life does not supersede a court order granting a [mining] corporation the right to proceed with economic development activities on its land."[150] The First Nations involved had good reason to believe that the authorizations issued by the Ontario ministry of mines to Platinex, an exploration company, and to Frontenac Ventures Corporation, which had already begun operations on their lands, did not comply with Supreme Court judgments regarding their rights.[151] The communities opposed to the mining projects on their lands "have proposed a joint panel to investigate what led to these conflicts and recommend new approaches to mineral exploration on First Nations' lands, but have received no reply from Ontario premier Dalton McGuinty."[152]

Nothing seems to be able to stop the mining industry from imposing its peculiar concept of "justice" in these matters. Corporate legal action against a government minister may be undertaken if necessary, as in Romania, where the Canadian mining firm Gabriel Resources filed suit against the former minister of the environment, Attila Korodi, and against the secretary of state, Silviu Stoica, seeking €100,000 in damages.[153] The two, by virtue of their public responsibilities, had

organization Ecojustice (formerly the Sierra Legal Defence Fund) provides pro bono legal support for environmental activists helping ensure equitable access to the legal system.[166] Canada's poor reputation for freedom of expression reached a new low in 2008 when the American Political Science Association openly stated they would not hold their 2009 convention in Canada because they were afraid they might be sued by interest groups, or even the Canadian government, if they dared to express divergent ideas.[167]

In 2007, a professor of law at McGill University, Roderick Macdonald, tabled a report to the Quebec justice department on the issue of SLAPPs (strategic lawsuits against public participation). According to this report, punitive or abusive lawsuits against citizens or political figures raise serious issues of "unequal access to justice, 'political manipulation' of judicial power, weakening of democratic participation, de facto limitation of freedom of expression, and potential tension arising from simultaneously permitting physical and moral persons to seek recourse from the courts, and recognizing the rights of citizens to make their views known."[168] In 2009, Quebec's National Assembly adopted one of Canada's first anti-SLAPP laws.[169]

SLAPPs undermine the last political prerogatives left to citizens of modest means because of the way democratic processes have evolved. After all, what today is still genuinely common to all? The two key faculties of will and thought remain as the ultimate, inalienable rights of the person who has no particular prerogatives in public life. SLAPPs are expressly designed to attack the potential to think freely and to engage in an act of free will. These lawsuits undermine citizens' ability to act by intimidating and inhibiting them to the point of self-censorship. Acts of free will, beyond the standardized limits set out by the regime, suddenly appear presumptuous. To think freely becomes an unnatural effort in which natural language must give way before the coded language of the judicial system. However, even the spectre of arraignments has not yet managed to stop all intellectuals and social activists in the world from speaking publicly on these issues.

5. A MADE-IN-CANADA PROPAGANDA OFFENSIVE

Fifth in the substantial advantages Canada provides to the world's extractive industry is intervention in the education system to engender support for mining. Ensuring the legitimacy of market relations in the eyes of Canadians was one of the public policy objectives outlined by Industry Canada in the early 1990s: "Policy-makers must not lose sight of the central role for government in creating a foundation for market interactions that is perceived as legitimate."[170] Using the most seductive possible terms, the federal government joined forces with the provinces, mining-industry marketing departments, and the mining lobby in working to make the Canadian public believe in the legitimacy of the extractive industry.

Over the past fifteen years, the mining industry has actively worked to make Toronto into a "world-class city" where the marketing and packaging of knowledge, science, and culture, all of which are heavily subsidized, are completely aligned with its industrial objectives. The methods used would probably be described by many as "propaganda" if they were employed by distant foreign governments. In the event, hardly a street corner in Toronto avoided the onslaught. Health-care institutions have been given the names of their corporate patrons: the McEwen Centre for Regenerative Medicine, named for gold-mining magnate Rob McEwen (Goldcorp, US Gold Corp.), or the Peter Munk Cardiac Centre, named for the founder of Barrick Gold. Companies such as the Swiss Xstrata have sponsored the Royal Canadian Opera Company's Ensemble Music School, while the Royal Ontario Museum (ROM) has become a vessel for "charitable" operations bearing industry labels.

These contributions have had an impact on the content of the museum's exhibitions. In the fall of 2008, when South African mining giant De Beers was inaugurating operations at Snap Lake in Canada's Far North,[171] the ROM opened an exhibition on "The Nature of Diamonds."[172] The founder of the South African firm, Cecil Rhodes, was presented as a philanthropic visionary whose fortune benefited the students of Oxford University (not exactly the students most in need of financial help). The exhibition avoided all unpleasant topics, including the brutality of British colonialism in Southern Africa and the fact that the fortunes amassed by De Beers or another South African sponsor of the exhibition, Anglo American, were primarily based on their monopoly position under apartheid.[173]

To the point, though, the chief beneficiaries of the Canadian mining industry's "philanthropy" have been Canadian educational institutions. "Today, there is not a university in Toronto that has not accepted mining-industry charity, named a building or a program after a mining executive, or awarded a mining-industry executive an honorary degree."[174] Mining-industry sponsors began showing their "generosity" toward institutions of higher learning at a time when environmentalists, native activists, labour unions, and grassroots organizations, in Canada and around the world, were challenging the industry's views. The industry responded with an aggressive public-relations campaign aimed at the entire education system, from primary school to university.

The Mining Matters educational program was established in 1994 by the industry's chief lobby group, the Prospectors and Developers Association of Canada. A veritable program of indoctrination, it subjected Ontario's young people to the uplifting message of the industry before they could be expected to have developed critical faculties. The program was applied with particular zeal to the students of Ontario's First Nations schools, located where significant diamond deposits had just been discovered.

The mining industry was successful in convincing the Ontario ministry of education to integrate 70 percent of its recommendations into its science curriculum, providing disturbing evidence of what the regime would like students to learn. Curriculum guidelines currently state: "Because rocks and minerals are such an integral part of our lives, it may be hard for students in Grade 4 to see the issues clearly … Therefore, it is critical that they be given opportunities to look at the issues from the standpoint of all stakeholders [including mining companies] … In communities where mining or related manufacturing processes provide the livelihood for parents of many students, teachers must be sensitive to the feelings of all students when discussing the costs and benefits of using everyday objects and products made from rocks and minerals."[175] In other words, the Ontario government "is warning teachers against being too critical of the mining sector in their classrooms, or taking too strong an environmentalist framework, and is demanding that they highlight the perspectives of mining companies as well as the benefits of mining products for a consumerist society."[176]

The Mining Matters program produced a teaching kit adapted to the fourth-, seventh-, eleventh-, and twelfth-grade curricula. In it, the mining industry is systematically depicted as a model of virtue while political questions are reduced to near opacity, as social unrest, trade-union opposition, environmental disasters, and public policy issues are addressed strictly as exercises in problem solving.

This "educational" program provides for "debates," the premises of which are biased from the start. As a role-playing exercise, pupils are called on to cast themselves as mining investors, government officials, or members of an affected community. According to the assumptions embodied in the script, the mine operator has the highest respect for governmental standards, draws up an excellent reclamation plan, and is devoted, body and soul, to the populations involved. In fact, the company's primary concern is to provide local populations with training

programs and jobs. The government's job is to help the company carry out its projects. In the Mining Matters program, unwilling communities are represented as caricatured minorities who set up a "Life without a Mine Is Just Fine" committee to confront the "Concerned Citizens for Progress" set up by the right-thinking majority. Since the script asserts that the company's development plan is perfect in every respect, the child has no way of understanding why local communities or governments might need to consider both the advantages and the drawbacks of any given project. Once the "debate" is over, the class is invited to enact the moment where the project takes concrete form: a "participation process" is set up to approve the establishment of the mine, despite the inequality between the various parties involved in the process.

Meanwhile, younger pupils take part in a contest to describe Canada's underground wealth in the form of a poem, essay, or poster. The winner receives a prize worth between $50 and $150. In recent years, the "pedagogical" process has expanded to include Barrick Gold shares among the prizes.[177]

The idea is to instruct young people in acquiescence; to trap them in a circuit of discourse closed to the outside world, in which they are entirely removed from the social issues surrounding this controversial industry. Collusion among the industry, professional associations, politicians, departments of education, and the academics who help design the programs is so developed that parents or teachers opposed to such methods would have a problem finding an authority to whom they could appeal.

At the University of Toronto, Pierre Lassonde has financed a program and an institute that bear his name and that are specifically designed for the mining industry. Courses are taught by mining-industry executives, the curriculum is designed along the lines recommended by industry experts, and the program is managed by administrators drawn from the industry. According to a study done by Stuart Tannock,

a student at the Lassonde Institute of Mining can complete his degree without having taken a single course that seriously addresses the environmental, social, cultural, political, or legal issues raised by the presence of mining companies anywhere in the world.[178] Such questions are restricted to the marginal field of "critical non-technical aspects of rock engineering projects."[179]

Lassonde himself, in the course of his career, has been associated with projects that have been bitterly criticized in Peru, Mexico, and Romania.[180] Indeed, he was involved in the Rosia Montana adventure. He had previously spent some time on a soapbox denouncing environmentalists in a completely unscientific manner, saying they are "like two-year-old kids. All they can say is, 'no', "and claiming that the populations of countries in the South where the industry encounters resistance "generally [do] not understand what mining is all about."[181]

In a similar vein, Peter Munk, to whom the University of Toronto owes the Munk Centre for International Relations, has expressed his surprise at the fact that God "for some unique and obscure reason" has chosen to distribute gold not in the heart of Paris or Manhattan, but in the subsoil of backward peoples of the South living in "the middle of the Tanzanian jungle" or "on top of the Andes mountains."[182]

Before pressure from the student body forced the university administration to rewrite the contract, the University of Toronto had formally agreed that the Munk Centre for International Relations would cooperate with the Barrick Gold international advisory board (which at one time included Brian Mulroney, George Bush Sr., Peter Munk, and Paul Desmarais Sr.),[183] failing which the company reserved the right to withdraw its financial support for the centre. The agreement between the university and Lassonde is similar: the donor may demand restitution of his investment (with interest) if the program is subordinated to "other engineering causes than mining."[184]

At McGill University, a poster inviting the public to a conference entitled Public-Private Partnerships for Sustainable Development: Toward a Framework for Resource Extraction Industries can only be described as a work of propaganda worthy of the Stalinist era. The poster shows a desert in which three indigenous people, their backs turned to the camera, appear to be walking toward a distant mining site; dominating the horizon next to the mining installations are the gigantic silhouettes of two, undoubtedly Western, technicians.[185] This scholarly event was "made possible in part" by "generous funding" from CIDA and three corporations: Rio Tinto Alcan, SNC-Lavalin, and Teck Resources.

These are the institutions that educate the next generation of people who, in Toronto, will be viewed as qualified to evaluate the relevance of mining projects, as well as work as geologists, engineers, financiers, academics, and legal experts trained to expedite the business of the mining industry. The presence of special-interest groups within Canada's educational system and research faculties has never been publicly debated. The Mining Matters "educational" program has made it clear that in Canada, all that matters is mining. Stuart Tannock, to whom we owe this information and analysis, notes that this form of "education" is "industry-driven."[186] In a 2005 Lassonde Institute newsletter, for example, a student returning from the Bulyanhulu mining site in Tanzania praised "the weather, people, culture, and peaceful environment" he had observed; this is a site described by twenty-nine civil society organizations from all over Africa as one of the "most controversial and contested [extractive industry] projects in Africa."[187]

Another student who visited the same area came away with very different observations – possibly a sign that he had been shaped by a different educational approach. Dennis Tessier, a master's student at the University of Western Ontario and the University of Dar es Salaam in the Institute of Development Studies, reports interviews conducted

in 2004 that many Tanzanian inhabitants had painful memories of the eviction that had taken place during the summer of 1996 on land conceded to a Vancouver company, Sutton Resources. Tessier repeats allegations that several thousand small-scale local miners were driven away by bulldozers; as many as fifty of them may have been buried alive during this operation.[188] The Council on Ethics of the Norwegian government pension fund in its 2008 report,[189] and the UN special representative of human-rights defenders in a 2002 report,[190] also referred to the case. We are still waiting for the establishment of an independent commission of inquiry to investigate.

6. A DIPLOMACY OF CONVENIENCE

Sixth in the substantial advantages Canada provides to the world's extractive industry is diplomatic support overseas. In addition to offering spectacular advantages to the mining sector within its own borders, Canada ardently supports its transnational mining companies abroad. The Canadian Network on Corporate Accountability found that Canada has developed a political structure and a diplomatic network that enable it to provide the mining industry with financial support, insure its risky projects, support the autocratic political regimes under which the industry operates, intervene whenever it faces legal action at home and abroad, bring pressure to bear on countries of the South to adopt the mining codes that suit it, defend international trade regulations that neutralize the authorities of countries impoverished by this system, and support trade missions whose objective is to ensure the appropriation of natural resources by transnational companies registered in Canada.[191]

Canadian diplomatic support for mining companies that could at best be described as "controversial" is today widely recognized. The book *Noir Canada* describes some of the more conspicuous examples. Acres International has continued to receive the support of the Canadian

International Development Agency and the World Bank,[192] even after its representative was sentenced on corruption charges by a Lesotho court.[193] The Canadian government has brought pressure to bear on the Tanzanian authorities to override the decisions of Tanzanian courts and to consider that the presence of artisanal small-scale miners on the concession acquired by Sutton Resources at Bulyanhulu was illegal.[194] At Manantali, Mali, CIDA financed the construction of a dam that flooded valuable agricultural land,[195] in addition to underwriting the privatization of the Bamako-Dakar railway, totally destabilizing the regional economy.[196] Moreover, several former prime ministers have successfully privatized privileged government information acquired during their term of office by working in countries of the South for Canadian mining companies whose activities have been sharply criticized: Brian Mulroney, as a member of the Barrick Gold international advisory board and a director of the company;[197] Joe Clark for First Quantum Minerals;[198] and Jean Chrétien with a wide range of controversial firms in the oil, mining, and pharmaceutical industries active in Africa, Latin America, and elsewhere (not to mention the advantages he enjoys through his privileged connections by marriage with the Desmarais family).[199] This privatized use of privileged state information is not confined to the federal level in Canada: by 2006, former Newfoundland premier and federal minister Brian Tobin was acting as executive chair, president, and CEO of Consolidated Thompson Iron Mines, acquired in 2011 by Cliffs Natural Resources Inc.[200]

Canadian diplomats and former officials are clearly involved in supporting the mining industry in the South, whatever the cost. Their often-obvious conflicts of interest can become embarrassing. Joe Clark, associated with First Quantum Minerals, was mandated in 2006 by the Carter Center to observe the electoral process in Congo that resulted in the election of Joseph Kabila, son of rebel leader Laurent-Désiré Kabila, as president.[201] In late 2009, sources revealed that the

Canadian ambassador to Congo-Kinshasa, backed by Hillary Clinton, had brought pressure to bear on the Congolese government not to abrogate its partnership contract with Vancouver-based First Quantum Minerals, a "partnership" that had been negotiated illegally, according to the conclusions of the Congolese commission set up to scrutinize the mineral contracts awarded during wartime.[202] Canada engaged in an even more active attempt to defend the corporation during the Toronto G20 Summit in June 2010.[203]

In July 2009, Jean Chrétien was appointed senior international adviser to Ivanhoe Energy,[204] a company established by controversial mining tycoon Robert Friedland. Friedland had previously founded AMFI, a Canadian company well known for its questionable activities in the Congo during the Great Lakes conflicts of the 1990s,[205] as well as Galactic Resources, which has been accused of considerable environmental damage in Summitville, Colorado.[206]

Accidents of history sometimes provide information that enables us to make educated guesses about current international events. What can be learned, for example, from the kidnapping of Canadian diplomats Robert Fowler and Louis Guay in Niger in December 2008? Officially, the two men had been mandated by the UN to "solve all the humanitarian problems in the region" (no less), as well as the "conflict resulting from the Tuareg rebellion."[207] But suddenly, they vanished. It was later revealed that they had recently visited a site belonging to Semafo, a Canadian company operating in Niger, without the UN's knowledge.[208] However the visit is analyzed, troubling conclusions are inevitable. Either Fowler and Guay were in fact carrying out their UN mission, and had entered into secret discussions with the mining company with a view to resolving the conflict between the Tuaregs and the extractive companies, which would make the Canadian company an unofficial political actor in the region (and not just a business); or the two diplomats were not acting on behalf of the UN and were using their mission as a smokescreen, for covert or personal reasons. In either case, something is radically at odds with ordinary standards of official behaviour in these incidents. From an outside perspective, Louis Guay would seem to be at the same time a diplomat who put aside his responsibilities to go to work in the mining industry (at Placer Dome), and a mining businessman who made a lateral move into diplomacy.[209] As for Robert Fowler, on returning to Canada, he quickly wrote a book entitled *A Season in Hell: My 130 Days in the Sahara with Al Qaeda*[210] that firmly located his misadventure in the realm of human interest, with no mention of his business relations. These relations became much more difficult to disregard in 2012 when he joined the new "corporate social responsibility advisory board" of the formidable gold-mining company, Barrick Gold.[211]

Canadian diplomatic influence and its leverage over local authorities have given Canadian corporations a significant edge abroad. Benjamin Little, senior vice-president, corporate affairs, of Toronto-based Iamgold, has candidly confirmed that Canada's mining companies are the first to benefit from Canadian diplomacy: "We can access, as needed, prompt Canadian diplomatic support for management issues in countries like Ecuador, Peru, and Colombia."[212]

Canada tells the world that it needs to provide zealous diplomatic assistance to the mining industry because it is important to protect the savings of Canadians, invested on the Toronto Stock Exchange via the investment, educational, and retirement funds to which citizens have entrusted their money. But perhaps the diplomatic corps is also attempting, through this spin-doctoring of its international role, to avoid having to confront the socio-economic, cultural, and ecological consequences of its policies in the South. The look on the face of Canadian diplomat Jenna MacKay-Alie in Chile, as shown in Martin Frigon's documentary *Mirage of El Dorado*, is genuine astonishment. This representative of Canada is suddenly faced with the fierce indignation of people opposed to Barrick Gold's Pascua-Lama extraction project, which threatens a large mountain glacier and its related ecosystem. The diplomat titters uneasily, tries to stick to her text, and tells the angry citizens to take it up with their government – it is *their* government's job to deal with the dislocation caused by the Canadian presence. All of a sudden, this fine rhetoric obviously sounds hollow, even to the person whose job it is to present it with brio. Instead, it insults our intelligence. Surrounded by her bodyguards, the diplomat heads for the elevator: the meeting is over, it's "not our problem."[213]

Canadian diplomats explicitly invoke the welfare of Canadian citizens to account for their repeated intercession on behalf of the mining industry. The first secretary of the Canadian embassy in Guatemala, commenting on an extraction project in that country by mining company Glamis Gold that had encountered vocal protest among the local population, told Radio-Canada: "We're not just defending the company ... We're not just talking about one Canadian corporation; we're talking about the thousands of Canadians who have invested in the Toronto exchange, which provided the financing, the capital that Glamis Gold needed to operate here in Guatemala. It's our job to see that they don't lose their investment."[214]

Within international bodies, Canada does not hesitate to identify with the mining lobby. Working through the World Bank and the IMF, it has promoted permissive mining policies designed to favour its extractive industry in the South. In 2009, it used its veto at the Paris Club to block, on a technicality, a debt-relief initiative drawn up for a country whose political decisions did not suit the Canadian mining companies already established there.[215]

From a strictly formal standpoint, Canadian indifference to the consequences of resource exploitation in the South is well established. It is clearly expressed in the preparatory texts to a free-trade agreement between Canada and Peru. A 2005 "initial Environmental Assessment

(EA) of the Canada-Peru Foreign Investment Protection and Promotion Agreement (FIPA)" sets out to measure the environmental impacts of Canada-Peru trade agreements; it deals only with the "environmental impacts in Canada." Even more explicitly: "it is outside the scope of this study to analyze the potential environmental effects of the Canada-Peru FIPA on Peru." Environmental damage, such as "air emissions, water contamination and sedimentation, soil contamination, and habitat destruction" caused by its mining industry in Peru, continue to leave Canada completely cold.[216]

There are many problematic aspects to Canada's presence in Peru. Before the adoption of a new Peruvian *Mining Code* in 1995, Canadian resource extraction investment in Peru was virtually non-existent. Today, 40 percent of all mining investment in that country is Canadian.[217] Investors include majors such as Teck Cominco and Barrick Gold as well as some seventy juniors. Several Canadian mining companies also operate in Peru through subsidiaries registered in tax havens.[218] In the wake of this massive influx, conflict quickly broke out between the *càmpesinos*, 55 percent of whose lands are threatened by concessions, and the mining companies.[219] At Tambogrande, a Canadian firm, Manhattan Minerals, encountered particularly fierce resistance. The company intended to extract copper, zinc, and gold from an open-pit operation that would have destroyed part of the town and led to the eviction of 8,000 to 25,000 people.[220] The project included diverting the Piura River and threatened to pollute the water reserves vital to a primarily agricultural region. Faced with massive protests, the government withdrew its concession in 2005, forcing the company to abandon the project. The land itself had a rich history: in two generations, the local peasants had transformed a desert into productive cropland.

Despite all the evidence, the document in which the Canadian Department of Foreign Affairs and International Trade explains the Canada-Peru FIPA rejects the "hypothesis" that Canadian companies

take advantage of weak environmental legislation in countries of the South to exploit their natural resources at bargain-basement prices. According to the document, which gives priority to a rather selective philosophical skepticism over common sense, the "pollution havens" hypothesis suffers from a "lack of conclusive evidence."[221] In other words, Canada is telling the world that it will consider cases of environmental destruction by its companies only when their "systematic" nature can be "proven." Thus, any exception to the rule is sufficient to justify Canada's complete passivity, while "proof" is constituted by the ordeal inflicted on the bodies of people exposed to these experiments.

Even worse, if one day the "systematic" destructive nature of the operations were to be proved, Canada has found another rhetorical device that will allow it to remain unperturbed: it will then be necessary to demonstrate that the shameless exploitation of the countries of the South is "definitive" (in other words, it cannot be put right).

In other words, only when mining operations create lasting and definitive prejudice to the populations of the South will Canada begin to sit up and take notice. Such are the pirouettes of self-justification by which the Canadian political authorities have transformed laissez-faire into a global neo-liberal system.

Canada's staunchest allies on the international scene are often officials of foreign governments that have signed advantageous contracts with mining companies. Thanks to the colossal investments of Canadian companies in the South, Canada can count on docile political partners. An indication of this kind of acquiescent compliance in the face of Canadian foreign policy was provided by Ecuadorian president Rafael Correa who, in a shocking display of ignorance or opportunism, in 2009 described the behaviour of the Canadian mining industry as "exemplary."[222] Another example is Jaona Ravaloson, former ambassador of Madagascar to the UN, who today styles himself an "international financial consultant," and who has requested that Canada interfere in

his country's affairs. In the pages of Montreal daily *Le Devoir* on April 22, 2009, he invited Canada "to contribute to the establishment of a new order" in Madagascar by ensuring "direct investment flows."[223] Canada accounts for more than one-half of foreign investment in Madagascar. In geopolitical terms, this principle amounts to legitimizing direct Canadian interference in the internal affairs of any state as soon as Canadian-based companies exploit its resources.

Canadian officials are assiduous promoters of an industry that is loathed around the world. Former minister of foreign affairs and international trade Pierre Pettigrew, speaking at the 2009 Africa Forum held in Montreal, could find nothing but praise for "our reputation," which he described as "well founded" without a hint of irony colouring his fulsome enthusiasm.[224]

Conclusion: Ottawa Confirms Canada's Status as a Legal Haven

In 2006, the Canadian government was under pressure to draft and pass legislation that would oblige the extractive industry to comply with minimally restrictive standards in its overseas operations. The Paul Martin government chose instead to punt, setting up a series of "National Roundtables on Corporate Social Responsibility and the Extractive Industry in Developing Countries." Using the consensus-seeking model of "good governance," representatives of the mining industry, civil society organizations, trade unions, universities, and current or former employees of the extractive sector held hearings and deliberated in a number of Canadian cities. During the tour, which lasted several months, briefs were submitted and discussed and protesters organized demonstrations to express their point of view. But in the end, the recommendations formulated in the March 2007 report were minimal.[225] It was suggested that the government

appoint an ombudsman and that Canadian financial assistance to the industry be made conditional on the acceptance of voluntary safety and human-rights principles. The report also provided for the possibility of launching criminal proceedings, in Canada, against Canadian companies alleged to have violated these principles. However, this last proposal was later publicly undermined even by the authors of the report representing "civil society," although they had been unanimous in signing it.[226]

Two years later, on March 26, 2009, the Canadian government delivered a stinging rejection of the report's proposed measures, even though they were little more than decorative. In an official public statement entitled *Building the Canadian Advantage*, the government confirmed Canada's status as a judicial haven for the extractive industry. The document imposes no human-rights obligations on mining companies registered in Canada or listed on Canadian exchanges: "Obligations under international human-rights conventions apply to states and do not directly create obligations for companies."[227] With regard to "the relations between the extractive industry and security providers," the document states that Canada "has applied to join the Voluntary Principles on Security and Human Rights" developed by a partnership of governments, corporations, and NGOs in 2000; these guidelines are intended "to help corporate actors anticipate and mitigate most risks related to the deployment of public and private security." The Canadian government is apparently unaware that prominent Canadian firms were financed or founded by arms dealers or experts in mercenary activities (Adnan Khashoggi for Barrick Gold,[228] for example, or Tony Buckingham for Heritage Oil).[229] Though it cannot be presumed that either is more likely to have committed human-rights offences because of their previous employment and expertise – only an exhaustive investigation could tell us if this were the case – the very fact of economic partnerships with powers involved in hostilities places

them in potential violation of the principles set forth in *Building the Canadian Advantage.*

The Canadian policy announcement also established Canada's first corporate social responsibility counsellor to fulfill a function characterized entirely by its limits. The job description might just as well have been inspired by a directive produced in a Caribbean offshore tax haven: "The Counsellor will not review the activities of a Canadian company on his or her own initiative, make binding recommendations or policy or legislative recommendations, create new performance standards, or formally mediate between parties."[230] Besides, the "Counsellor" will only undertake reviews with the consent of the involved parties. The possibility of criminal proceedings against Canadian companies active abroad is clearly not on Ottawa's agenda.

The person appointed to fill the new position, Marketa Evans, presumably enjoys the support of the inner circles of the Canadian mining industry: "Evans was the founding director of the University of Toronto's Munk Centre – named for and funded by Peter Munk, founder [with Khashoggi's financing] of Canada's Barrick Gold."[231]

At the same time, then federal international trade minister Stockwell Day confirmed Canada's status as a judicial haven for Canada's extractive industry, stating that Canadian legislation would not affect Canadian mining activity overseas in any way: "the companies do not need it."[232]

Canada's reluctance to assume legal responsibility for corporations registered within its jurisdiction impressed few at home[233] or abroad.[234] Though the consequences of Canada's generosity to the extractive industry are international, Canadian authorities still maintain a total blackout on serious allegations of environmental destruction, looting, smuggling, tax evasion, violent evictions, and economic abuse levelled against companies under their "supervision." Canada seems more intent on facilitating speculation on assets acquired abroad in frequently questionable circumstances, and on maintaining judicial loopholes that allow the extractive industry to continue to commit abuses while amassing profits beyond Canada's borders.

In international "development" organizations, diplomatic forums, and free-trade agreements, Canada has also asserted its intention of promoting an ultra-permissive model for Canadian companies operating abroad. It has mandated the Canadian International Development Agency to defend the "Canadian advantage" internationally by strengthening the "capacities"[235] of countries in the South to restructure their institutions and legislative and regulatory frameworks; this will enable countries to adopt mining codes that provide Canadian companies with exorbitant advantages. The mining codes of Canadian provinces will continue to be imposed as models throughout the world.

Anemic Draft Legislation

Although they form an ineffective minority and act with exaggerated timidity, some opposition members of Parliament, supported by intellectuals and activists, are willing to act on these issues. This attests to the fact that we live in an age when, contrary to what Max Weber noticed in his own time, people have begun openly to question the effectiveness and even the legitimacy of the stock exchange as an institution.

In 2009, at the same time as the Canadian government made public its official position on the international extractive sector, the Liberal opposition introduced an extraordinarily timid piece of legislation, Bill C-300, the *Corporate Accountability of Mining, Oil and Gas Corporations in Developing Countries Act*.[236] On paper, the proposal looks encouraging: ethical criteria are established to determine whether agencies such as CIDA, Export Development Canada, or the Canada Pension Plan should support Canadian mining companies, and the role of an ombudsman dealing with foreign populations, to be attached to Canada's Department of Foreign Affairs, is defined. However, the wording of the bill maintains the ineffective principle of voluntary performance guidelines to be observed by Canadian companies, gives political authorities absolute discretionary power, and deprives the Canadian people, or citizens' groups who feel they have suffered a prejudice abroad, of any recourse. Despite its extremely cautious wording, the draft legislation gave its author John McKay an existential ordeal at the hands of the mining lobby, which is clearly prepared to intimidate anyone who dares to raise the issue of its methods abroad. "I have to be extremely careful because the mining companies have made it very plain to me that: 'We will sue your ass off, in fact, if you make any allegation of our companies and cause reputational damage'"[237]

Even though McKay's bill was probably innocuous from the point of view of the industry's interests, it was defeated on October 27, 2010, in the House of Commons by a vote of 140 to 134, having been vigorously rejected by a Conservative minority government supported by a number of opposition MPs. In a fatal but unsurprising move, thirteen Liberal members of Parliament, including then Liberal leader Michael Ignatieff himself, did not show up to vote that day.[238] This graceless action was denounced even by the Montreal daily *La Presse*, normally very conciliatory, which spoke of "shame."[239]

What happened to Bill C-300 in Parliament confirms the shortcomings of the pseudo-regulatory mechanism known as good governance, adopted in recent years by those authorized to speak in the name of "civil society" in formal exchanges with industry and public authorities. In fact, these forums are structured to exclude civic actors who do not accept rules for discussion in which "consensus" with mining-industry representatives is a mandatory prerequisite; as a consequence, they lead to negotiations with the central government that are based on the most minimal demands. Given the contradictory interests of the players and the disparities in the power they wield, this process of "negotiation" makes it extremely difficult to arrive at a thorough diagnosis of the problems to be dealt with, even though these problems are extensively documented.

Worthwhile results cannot be expected from the "good governance" approach. It is guaranteed to fail, and this failure can perhaps be illuminated by Edward Said's musings on the contemporary figure of the "expert": "To be an expert you have to be certified by the proper authorities; they instruct you in speaking the right language, citing the right authorities, holding down the right territory. This is especially true when sensitive and/or profitable areas of knowledge are at stake."[240] The late Columbia University professor was explaining why he never agreed to act as a paid consultant or expert. Politics may require the contribution of experts, but cannot belong to them alone.

During the same parliamentary session, another much more promising mining bill emerged, which partisan politics have since consigned to oblivion. Bill C-438, the *Extraterritorial Activities of Canadian Businesses and Entities Act*, introduced by then Bloc Québécois MP Johanne Deschamps, provided for the establishment of a permanent "Canadian Extraterritorial Activities Review Commission" independent of government. The bill's merit was that it vigorously insisted not on the commission's capacity to receive complaints originating in other countries, but on its ability to carry out investigations on its own initiative. In other words, it would be in a position publicly to call on the Department of Foreign Affairs to take action against companies that had committed offences, and not merely to deprive them of public funding (as provided by Bill C-300). The commission could "by order, cause to be seized, frozen or sequestrated … any property located in Canada and owned by a Canadian." It would also publish an annual report detailing cases studied and

THE HISTORY

Stock Market Speculation: Historical Wellspring of the Canadian Economy, or How Toronto Became the Place Where the Mining Sector Goes for Capital

Those were the good years. Despite all the tremors that sent prices up and down, the stock exchange seemed to be an institution you could bank on – endorsed by serious thinkers such as Max Weber In a pamphlet entitled *Stock and Commodity Exchanges*, written in 1894, he illustrates the fundamental theoretical benefits of the institution, rebuking those whose "boundless superficiality" and "ignorance"[1] cause them to doubt its legitimacy, its efficacy, or its relevance. Weber's categorical positions have long typified the defenders of this particular financial instrument. And when argument fails them, they move to intimidation.

Canada is still at it today. The panegyric that masquerades as the history of the Toronto Stock Exchange, written by those who have interests to protect, expresses this spirit. Whether in the exchange's supremely self-aggrandizing descriptions, in the lyrical outbursts of the financial elite, or in the Canadian government's rhetorical flourishes, the dithyramb knows no respite. James West, who tracks speculative trends in the gold market for the Gold World website, solemnly assures us that "the TSX Venture Exchange is the greatest stock market on earth, in terms of appreciation and performance ... Long live the TSX Venture Exchange, the most transparent, profitable and individual investor-oriented stock market in the world!"[2] Why hide such a dazzling light beneath a bushel? *Superbrands Canada* magazine, an overview of successful branding and promotional strategies throughout the North American markets, presented the Toronto Stock Exchange in its premiere 2004 edition as "a national icon in Canada, respected as a symbol of quality, integrity, and financial leadership in the capital markets."[3]

The "rationalization thesis," grounded in an analysis of the dominance of the West in modern times as theorized by Weber, is considered so self-evidently clear that none can question it. According to Weber, the stock exchange can be summed up as follows: though it has the same objectives as a traditional market, its activities take place on a much greater scale. Its increased complexity requires a division of labour between those who work in its productive apparatus and those who finance and manage its economic development projects. The stock exchange places the seal of impersonality on the financial and professional relationships between members of civil society. Shareholders possess a portion of a given corporate enterprise, but do not know the other shareholders personally, and even less the employees who work in it. They have virtually no access to the company's books (annual reports excepted). Various quantities of shares change hands between people of different social categories, who also do not know each other. In principle, the stock exchange organizes capitalism or the institution of shareholding, but not individual capitalists or shareholders. The role of the stock exchange is to keep capital in circulation; otherwise, it might remain in the same hands, stagnating unproductively.

What motivates industrialists to finance their projects through the specific mechanism of the stock exchange? Weber answers the question by citing the example of the mining industry. The stock exchange is the best source of funding when projected developments are on such a large scale that more modest sources, such as cooperatives, lack the organizational capacity to carry them out. At this point, because everything is on a much bigger scale, projects need financial professionals who are able to deal with all investment-related issues. "Historically ... the 'company' that jointly owned a mine itself also took charge of excavating the mineral ore through collective work ... Later, as ... the systematic working of a mine came to require significant additional 'resources' for that end, the property-owning group gradually separated off from the working group [today: hired wage-workers]."[4] Theoretically, according to the great sociologist, this would be the typical sequence of events when a business "goes public."

How do these investment professionals identify themselves, culturally? A glance at Weber's classic, *The Protestant Ethic and the Spirit of Capitalism*, suggests that their interest in high finance is motivated by greater moral virtues. The wealth accumulated and concentrated in the hands of these professionals proves their rigorous observation of the prevailing moral rules of Protestant culture. "[Money] is thought of so purely as an end in itself, that from the point of view of the happiness of, or utility to, the single individual, it appears entirely transcendental and absolutely irrational."[5] From this point of view, an accumulation of money indicates that an explicitly utilitarian Protestant ethic has been successfully applied.

In fact, of course, history demonstrates that the stock exchange regularly falls prey to powerful "irrational" impulses driven by a handful of financial players. Nothing can be done to correct this irrationality; it has been present from the beginning. If the intention in establishing the stock exchange was to create a rational instrument of economic development, then that intention has always been perverted.

In the mid-nineteenth century, economist Pierre-Joseph Proudhon already viewed the stock market as a commercial mechanism devoid of ethics. For Proudhon, the purpose of the stock market was not to provide society with a useful service by organizing operations that implied an element of risk for which compensation was to be provided; rather, risk had become distinct from any useful operation. Proudhon uses the word "*agio*" (agiotage, stockjobbing) to describe the movement toward speculation. *Agio* "belongs to the same category as wagers and gambles, not to say swindling and theft: it is illicit and immoral. Speculation, from this point of view, is nothing more than the art – always associated, however, with luck – of getting rich without work, without trade, and without genius."[6] This view of speculation is precisely the one embodied in the stock exchange at a time when Canada was beginning to play a role in the modern world. In Proudhon's terms, while an "incomplete legality" might define as lawful the spectacular fortunes suddenly manifesting themselves on the stock market, these fortunes were nonetheless "perfectly illegitimate in terms of conscience," since they were usually the product of "corruption, violence, or fraud."[7]

The stock-exchange behaviour known as financial speculation consists, in fact, of irrational conduct motivated by greed. We can always *attempt* to differentiate between such conduct and that of rational investors acting in the real economy; but there is no historical evidence of a clear-cut distinction between them. The speculation to which European stock exchanges were more and more obviously exposed from the nineteenth century on was more than just an incidental side effect of stock market activity. Speculation was rampant as shady operators quickly grasped that they could deliberately play the market for short-term gain. An investor could purchase a share only to resell it immediately for a modest profit or wait a while to make a killing. Good money could be made by infinitely repeating this operation. However, shares traded on the market refer only to themselves; there is no inherent relation between share prices and

It was also an era of hysterical swings, such as the upsurge of railway share prices when Queen Victoria took a train (just as today, share prices sometimes suddenly increase on a Monday when a star golfer wins a tournament on Sunday).[13] The real economy cannot possibly keep up with what the fantasy of the stock exchange expects of it. "The claim that the mines could produce more gold than Europe required was taken seriously."[14] Eventually, of course, the mining boom of the 1820s in London was revealed as irrational, leading to a spectacular collapse in mid-decade for which the weakest would pay the steepest price.

No sooner had this speculative bubble burst than the railway bubble began to take shape. The new railway schemes involved colonial economies and the newly consolidated American market, as well as the domestic British and German markets. Conflict of interest was rampant; a blatant example was George Hudson, the British "Railway King," who sat on the board of railway companies and was also a member of Parliament. Once again, things seemed to be upside down: investors did not speculate on the anticipated value of revenues generated by railway operations; instead, railway lines were planned to make share prices rise and to justify, retroactively, their over-valuation. The frenzy was such that fifty new railway companies had been registered and sixteen new track-laying projects had emerged by January 1845; some of these conflicted with each other to the point of absurdity.[15] Companies vied with each other in announcing new railway projects, seeking to checkmate competitors and increase the value of certain shares.

As capital was channelled toward speculation, the real economy suffered. "Money was diverted from the normal channels of business to pay for land, iron, timber, and, above all, labour."[16] Capital flowed toward railway shares that existed only to mobilize capital; the shares were backed by companies doomed to bankruptcy. The only people to benefit were financial swindlers who bought or sold at the right moment, making a personal fortune in the process. Laissez-faire economics gave the authors of such institutional appropriations a free hand.

Canada, as a colony, was the product of this economic culture, which it would later appropriate and reinforce as an independent nation. "The colonial movement was in the nature of a speculation. Columbus himself was a speculator, and North America the greatest speculative prize of all. The first American colonies were established as joint-stock ventures."[17]

Starting from this initial speculative impulse, the history of Canada unfolded with the development of economic institutions such as the Toronto Stock Exchange and a variety of colonial state structures. Stock market evaluations were not based on Canadian production. The opposite was true: like Latin American mines and British railways, Canadian production sites were developed to give substance to market evaluations. Here again, it was not that speculators gambled immoderately on industrial projects that were already under way or completed; rather, industrial projects were launched in order to support absurd increases in stock prices. Stock prices provided the impetus for the development of the real economy, and not vice versa.

Fraudulent Dealings in Toronto

Historian Christopher Armstrong is one of the few critical thinkers to have studied the institutions connected with the Toronto stock market and their essentially speculative nature. The history of these institutions does not confirm the principles laid down by Max Weber: Armstrong's research shows a wide gap between the theory and the actuality of the stock market's workings. In the "boiler rooms" (exchanges that artificially drove up share prices and totally dislocated the real economy) he describes, the greed of some and the naivety of others opened up a game that cannot be reduced to any form of strictly economic rationality.

In the late nineteenth century, Canada was notable for the small size of its population and for its colonial-style economy built on abundant natural resources. To finance commercial operations, banks accredited in the British manner generally provided short-term support for players in the commercial, mortgage, and agricultural sectors, while insurers took on long-term industrial projects. Most of these transactions took place on the Montreal and Toronto exchanges; the former hosted companies active in established areas such as railway transportation, while the latter attracted riskier segments, particularly the mining industry. "But Canadian exchanges picked up only the odds and ends of the market. The big money was spent – or came from – elsewhere."[18] Neither Montreal nor Toronto could compete with the New York financial colossus or with the City (London's financial district). In fact, Canadian investors were more and more likely to invest their money directly in the United States. In the world of stock market trading, New York and London set the tempo.

Toronto, however, was becoming the administrative centre of the extractive industries. "By the turn of the century, worthless stocks in fly-by-night undertakings were being peddled by smooth-talking con men who, it was said, did not scruple to offer a simpleton shares even in the blue sky above."[19] And as such, Toronto was also becoming the locus of financial intrigues that were making the stock market itself less and less justifiable in economic terms. The Toronto exchanges encouraged speculation so relentlessly that they could no longer be taken for anything but casinos. Armstrong's history of Canada's stock exchanges reads like an encyclopedia of clever forms of fraud worked on powerless authorities – authorities who end up looking like the Keystone Cops rather than elected public representatives responsible for the democratic oversight of the common wealth.

In the spirit of the times, the Toronto exchanges displayed an implacable indifference to any consideration other than shareholders' interests. As a consequence, interested parties established a weak regulatory system that was tailor-made for them. The fact that exploration or economic development projects might create huge numbers of victims among Aboriginal or settler communities was a matter of supreme indifference. Nor would environmental, cultural, social, or political concerns ever cause any breach in the wall erected by money. Behind this wall, in Toronto, mining issues could be reduced to a matter of profits, regardless of whether the profits in question were real, potential, estimated, or imagined. Daily life at the stock exchange continued as though the institution's activities were of concern only to shareholders and never to citizens in general, even though society must live with the consequences of the market's wild swings – and pick up the pieces.

The Toronto exchanges were defined by their willingness to set up ways of getting rich that bore no relation to the institution's official pretensions. Clearly the intention was not to finance projects, but to trade in shares of risk, and whatever economic rationalism had ever existed was forgotten in the heat of the gambler's passion.

Until they merged in 1934, the two Toronto exchanges were characterized by weak regulation that encouraged an extreme level of financial and mining speculation. The regulatory structure did little or nothing to stop fraud and repeated crises of confidence. In fact, both exchanges witnessed one scandal after another. Time and again, the same scenario was played out: no sooner was one case of trickery revealed and new regulations drawn up to prevent a recurrence, than the next fraud and the next crisis came along. New regulations, always announced with aplomb by stock-exchange administrators who swore they would discipline themselves this time around, were part of an ongoing game that is apparently still being played in Toronto to this day.

As an intrinsically speculative exercise, the mining industry has always been perfectly suited to these speculative games. Canada's exchanges came into being at the same time gold was being discovered on Canadian soil. The Toronto Stock and Mining Exchange was established seven years after the Toronto Stock Exchange, in 1868, after gold had been found in the Madoc region of Ontario. Both were fragile institutions that rested primarily on trust. "Companies were under no obligation to release news or financial data, so in that period … information and rumours were exchanged on the floor and then disseminated onto the 'street,' rather than vice versa."[20] Furthermore, subpar shares were traded alongside the exchange – shares that the TSE described as "unlisted mining securities," and that it promoted in 1897 to attract brokers who wanted to deal directly with speculators. Organizations offering shares for sale on this basis had no obligation to comply with the most elementary rules of the stock exchange, to disclose standard information, or to pay any fees.

For brokers in the mining sector, the stock exchange was strictly a tool for speculation. A number of them eventually set up their own organization, the Toronto Mining Exchange, which in 1899 became the Standard Stock and Mining Exchange (SSME). This confirmed Toronto as the heart of the North American mining sector, and also made it the continental capital of stock market fraud. The SSME throve on orchestrated hysteria following the discovery of gold and silver in Northern Ontario: self-styled mining-claims specialists raked in fortunes while defrauding some 400,000 investors of a total of $100 million over three decades.[21] The competition between the two exchanges led to a race toward the bottom in terms of regulation and oversight, as each sought to attract brokers looking for ever more flexible and permissive structures. Many brokers were active in both institutions.

To stay competitive, the TSE opened its doors to mining companies with unsavoury reputations. Share prices rose and fell in arbitrary fashion, touching off resounding collapses that were easily identified as arising from insider trading, as illustrated in the case of the War Eagle mine.[22]

Many of the swindling techniques identified by Armstrong throughout the history of the Toronto Stock Exchange are still in use today. The "wash trade," for example, is a recurrent feature in cases of fraud. Swindlers relying on this technique use stock-exchange channels to churn out false data. By using entities and subsidiaries under their control to sell themselves shares they already own, they build up an artificial interest in a given stock. Brokers become aware that it is being sold (albeit through dummy transactions), and advise their customers to buy it. The number of transactions increases even more until the price begins to rise on its own, with no further need to stoke the fires. The idea is to sell one's shares at a high price before the public realizes what has happened.

"Bucketing" is a ruse by which a broker pretends to carry out a buy order for a client without doing so on the spot. He holds on to the instruction while the price drops and buys the share later, at lower cost; then he bills the client the price listed at the time he was supposed to carry out the transaction, and pockets the difference.

Another well-known ploy, known as fly-by-night, is equally elusive. It consists in negotiating the value of a share on the basis of information obtained outside the official framework of the exchange. These forms of insider trading are endemic. Despite all their claims to the contrary, stock exchanges have never held a monopoly on transactions. Alongside formal structures, there is always the possibility that informal agreements will influence the behaviour of stock prices. These "street" or "gutter" markets undercut any kind of self-regulation.

Armstrong's work shows that the administrators of Toronto's exchanges have been unable to keep financial flows sufficiently under control to guarantee investors that market results always provide an accurate picture of financial realities. The sharpies of the financial world have simply made their methods more sophisticated, or in some cases, have continued to rely on the time-honoured methods developed by their predecessors.

Promoter vs. Speculator: A Fuzzy Distinction

Weak stock market regulation began as the result of a compromise, which has since been constantly renegotiated, between the owners of corporations listed on the exchange, known as promoters, and brokers, seen essentially as speculators. The promoters, who rely on the market to raise the capital they need for their enterprise, argue for a serious business framework; since, according to them, the capitalization of their industrial assets is based on projects that are part of the real economy.

The brokers have an entirely different view. As speculators, they seek a rapid yield on their assets based on marginal gains that multiply whenever a share changes hands. Share trading for speculative purposes has more to do with a buyer's belief that he will later be able to sell his shares at a profit than with real economic values as the basis of share prices. The money that speculators invest is often borrowed, since they hope that the price of the shares in which they invest will be more than sufficient to cover the interest they pay on their loan.

Traditional capitalists view these methods as an unsavoury form of gambling and will sometimes describe it as "illegal" in the business press. They are afraid that the inflation of share values caused by speculation will concentrate capital in the hands of commercial paper vendors, to their detriment as managers of the real economy. But the more they try to emphasize the genuine meaning of investments in real industrial projects, the more the power of speculators, and their investments in the financial sphere, increase – to such a degree that the speculators ultimately shape the entire system according to their interests.

A critical examination of stock-exchange speculation as a historical phenomenon leads us to deconstruct the classical opposition between the real and speculative economies that was dominant in the nineteenth century. According to this classical opposition, practices related to the real economy were to be found on the Montreal exchange, where shares in heavy industry, and particularly railways, were traded, while more speculative activity, essentially related to mining and natural resources, was represented on the Toronto exchange. In fact, however, not only were railways themselves built precisely in order to provide some consistent basis for their dangerously soaring share prices, but their construction found its ultimate justification in giving access to the country's natural resources. In other words, the real economy developed because people were speculating on the value of the land and subsoil on which railway lines would be built. Real and speculative economies were – and are – aspects of a single process.

The opposition between promoters and speculators can also be deconstructed. While starchy railway promoters presented themselves as serious businessmen contributing to the country's economic growth, they were no strangers to fraudulent and speculative practices. Beginning in the 1850s, railway incorporation charters were granted in profusion to such luminaries as Allan MacNab, Francis Hincks, Joseph-Édouard Cauchon, and John Ross, successively ministers and premiers in cabinets that frequently changed colour, but whose members never deviated in their propensity for "shady dealings" and dedication to the "well-being of their children," as the Right Honourable MacNab would later delicately put it. Gustavus Myers, an American reformist, attempted a century ago to chart the squalid speculative manoeuvring and insider trading that marked their fortunes or misfortunes, and that they carried out either collectively, or to each other's detriment. The First World War put a stop to Myers's initiative after a first volume, but his portrait of the founding fathers of the Canadian parliamentary system was despicable. They sold railway company shares to a group of investors of which they were secret members – a group that then resold them at an inflated price before the first share offering. Right-of-ways passed through their land, which they sold at a profit. They bought public land at a low price, then sold it at a much higher price as soon as the coming of the railway line was announced. They bought railway company shares at low prices the day before major government financial assistance was announced, and they took bribes during the railway charter attribution process. If flagrant wheeling and dealing forced the director of a company, who happened to be premier of the United Canadas, to resign, he could always sell his insider's knowledge to a competitor. So it was that Allan MacNab "always contrived to make a fortune, or a ruin, of every railway project he found interesting," wrote George Brown, publisher of the Toronto *Globe* (and who was premier of the United Canadas for a little more than forty-eight hours in 1858).[23]

"Railways are my politics!" said MacNab one evening, and Hincks, Cauchon, or Ross could have said the same thing. These landowners treated public property as a lever to promote their speculative enterprises. Under their guidance, the Legislative Assembly of United Canada adopted, in 1849, a motion that proclaimed the young state's active support for the railway industry: this was God's gift to domestic and foreign speculators alike. While some $60 million in foreign capital had been invested in Canada over the preceding two decades, almost twice that amount ($100 million) was invested, primarily in the railway sector, in the 1850s alone.[24] But what the investors really coveted was not so much the opportunity of building railways as the millions of acres of public land that were being made over to railway companies at bargain basement prices, often in highly obscure circumstances.[25] Land was the true focus of the frenetic stock market activity in which the majority of the members of the Legislative Assembly were actively participating. Francis Hincks proved to be particularly gifted at turning a personal profit from the game of sale and resale that drove railway company share prices long before the companies had even hired their first employee. Hincks, who headed United Canada's major railway projects (including the Grand Trunk), had great credibility when, in his other role of inspector general of public accounts (equivalent to today's finance minister), he gave potential investors prospectuses in which the close ties between railway companies and politicians were presented as a guarantee of future dividends; for the Grand Trunk, the figure was 11.5 percent.[26]

To describe the history of railways in Canada as one of visionary nation-builders is profoundly inaccurate. The vision that predominated was that of the short-term profit sought by investors on the London, and later the Montreal, stock exchanges where the railway companies were listed. The railways suffered, and their users paid the price. Lines were too short, and companies built too many of them, having designed them primarily in order to be able to make impressive-sounding announcements. The result was not a network that would create a national infrastructure: entire regions remained unconnected; meanwhile, lines were built to link the lands held by private investors. The materials used in construction were of inferior quality, so that trains running when it rained or snowed, or on hilly terrain, often derailed. Stations sprang up as though at random, dictated by speculation on lands along the right-of-way. Historians who emphasize the huge amounts of capital brought into play to construct the Canadian railway system often forget to mention how volatile that capital proved to be, and how the inflated share prices of a railway company listed on the London or Montreal stock exchanges would often collapse as soon as work actually began, leading to bankruptcy in many cases. The capital invested seemingly had one sole aim: to be resold at a profit – whether or not the railways were suitable for industrial or commercial infrastructure purposes, or whether they were even built at all.[27]

In the final analysis, the population of Canada's provinces, cities, and towns ended up footing the bill for the country's railway network, for which they paid more than 50 percent of the total cost; this is the most commonly accepted figure since Myers's study. A significant portion of the private capital invested never ended up in the actual network and was withdrawn as share prices fell. Canadians paid a high price for a system that socialized only costs while making (and losing) fortunes for speculators during the golden age of the Montreal Stock Exchange. When railways were nationalized in the early 1920s, Canadian National inherited a multitude of spur lines, many of which were unfinished, and a $550 million debt.[28]

Throughout this era, Montreal maintained its position as Canada's leading stock exchange. Toronto began to threaten its hegemony in the 1920s, but during the stock-exchange boom, the annual number of transactions on the Montreal exchange grew from three million (1924) to twenty million (1928);[29] a listing in Montreal cost $27,000 in 1921,[30] and close to $225,000 on the eve of the crash.[31] The reason for Toronto's emergence as Canada's major exchange had nothing to do with different practices observed in each city, but with the fact that mining better lends itself to stock-market speculation, and was to become its principal object during the twentieth century. As it turned out, most of the country's mining firms were listed on the Toronto exchanges – Montreal could only boast a mere handful.

Mining is particularly well adapted to the culture of speculation because from a geological viewpoint, evaluation of deposits is itself a speculative exercise. What is the geological potential of any given subsoil? In what way is the price of its wealth most likely to evolve on world markets? What psychological impact will the announcement of one mining discovery or another have on speculators? These questions, and others like them, make it impossible to separate speculation on mineral resources, which are assessed on the stock exchange for purposes of exploitation, from purely financial speculation on the predicted value of shares traded on the markets.

For this reason, by the early twentieth century the mining industry was asserting its presence on the Toronto exchange, as discoveries (real or rumoured) of gold and silver in Northern Ontario were announced. Newspapers played a key role in amplifying stories of mineral discoveries. One of the rackets most esteemed by Toronto mining speculators consisted of driving up a share price by publishing full-page ads on ore deposits that were described as promising but actually did not exist. When these ads appeared, the city's daily newspapers, which at the time all boasted a reporter assigned to the mining beat, took up the good news. Leading personalities lent their name to the promotional prospectus, and engineers confirmed the high ore concentrations to be found at the new site, which had been carefully scattered with a few extracts of ore mined elsewhere. An aggressive sales campaign orchestrated in the boiler rooms would finally get the share price moving up; the company had incurred very few expenses to achieve this result, and its real assets consisted of precisely nothing. Canada was already a "haven" allowing more laissez-faire than the United States. While victims were often Americans, in the early 1930s salesmen in boiler rooms "manned banks of phones to deliver high-pressure pitches to prospective customers all across North America,"[32] escaping the so-called blue-sky laws passed in the United States requiring sellers to register new offerings so officials could vet their quality and protect investors.[33]

Memories of the Klondike gold rush of the previous decade were still fresh, and cities quickly developed around mining sites. Although Northern Ontario developed rapidly, the speculative bubble greatly exceeded real industrial development. In 1901, one million shares traded daily on the TSE,[34] but share prices proved to be as volatile as the speculators were fickle. Northern Star's share price plummeted from 32 cents to 3 cents (after what was represented as a blind reaction of the market); but the company needed only to announce the discovery of a vein of silver for wild enthusiasm to sweep through the market again, and the share price soared overnight to 17 cents.[35] Keeping track of financial developments also became increasingly difficult. Shares that posted a 50 percent profit one day could collapse to 5 percent the following day. Speculation on mining shares so enlivened the country's economic life at the turn of the twentieth century that a specialized exchange, the Standard Stock and Mining Exchange, as mentioned previously, was set up in Toronto, establishing the city as the mining centre of North America, and by extension, the capital of the most unrestrained speculative and fraudulent practices in the industry. Speculators of every description, promoters of suspect sites, bogus brokers, and greedy investors all fixed their sights on the mining industry. "Prior to the First World War very few companies except mining ventures, which were speculative by their very nature, actually raised funds by floating shares directly onto the market."[36] At the speculators' feet yawned a chasm into which poured the capital of all those who hoped to get out of the market before the inevitable collapse. For that was the ultimate goal of their speculation. It became indispensable to forecast which way the wind of the financial institutions was likely to blow, preferably by relying on informers inside the mining corporations. Insider trading became an integral part of successful professional practice.

Toronto emerged as the place where stock market speculators gradually brought their peculiar culture to prevail. Insiders made considerable profits in this new context. As a result, small investors progressively ceased to trust in the exchange, viewing it as a huge casino where share prices were arbitrarily set, if not manipulated. Gambling pervaded other aspects of social life. John Maynard Keynes had observed the phenomenon in the United States, and in 1936 wrote:

> Even outside the field of finance, Americans are apt to be unduly interested in discovering what average opinion believes average opinion to be; and this national weakness finds its nemesis

in the stock market. It is rare, one is told, for an American to invest, as many Englishmen still do, "for income"; and he will not readily purchase an investment except in the hope of capital appreciation. It is only another way of saying that, when he purchases an investment, the American is attaching his hopes, not so much to its prospective yield, as to a favourable change in the conventional basis of valuation, i.e., that he is, in the above sense, a speculator.[37]

Canada Becomes an American Colony

Sir Wilfrid Laurier's prediction that the twentieth century would "belong to Canada" turns out to have been true, to the extent that it can be extricated from its euphemistic form. What the phrase undoubtedly means is that Canada "belonged to the twentieth century." The British, and later the Americans, were to make abundant use of Canada. Those were the years when it was said that the United States could invade Canada just as easily as a thief could pick up a pebble from the ground for the sole pleasure of slipping it into his pocket. At the turn of the nineteenth and twentieth centuries, one-third of the assets of Canadian corporations consisted of American capital. Ever greater numbers of bankers, investors, and promoters arrived from Boston, Cleveland, New York, or Philadelphia to open mines, build hydro dams, lay the foundations for industrial projects, plan railways, and establish factories. The environmental consequences of this "economic development" were already difficult to hide, and settlers thinly spread across the vast territory proved unable either to protect or to advance their interests. "Harnessing the 'new staples' to a continental market perpetuated Canada's role as a resource hinterland, and the linkages forged by American corporate investment were, if anything, much tighter than the older economic ties with Britain."[38]

in addition to costly and lengthy procedures, there was also a risk of reprisals and countersuits.

The Comedy of Self-Regulation

The creation of the Ontario Securities Commission (OSC) in 1931 seemed to herald an era of stricter supervision, although in fact it did little to stop questionable trading practices. To make it easier to supervise economic activity, the Ontario government was able to force the merger of the Standard Stock and Mining Exchange and the Toronto Stock Exchange in 1934, following a new upsurge of speculative frenzy over a gold discovery on the Standard. The OSC acquired more sophisticated investigational tools, and was given the right to audit brokers' accounts unannounced. Criminal law was brought into play. In 1935, the OSC arrested leading members of the TSE for falsifying prices: "Quoting prices that were a few points below the market for sales and above for purchases allowed the difference to be channelled directly into the pockets of the traders."[48] One hardly knew whether to worry about the level of fraud or rejoice that it was brought to light.

Only in moments of shock did the government feel it had the authority to intervene. (During the period just before the creation of the OSC, a series of major frauds had been uncovered by the press, particularly by the American journalist Frederick Paul, writing in *Saturday Night*, and by Floyd Chalmers in the *Financial Post*.) However, periods when prices collapse are not the best time for market reform. Government intervention is far more necessary when the market enters into one of its phases of acute indiscipline, when the economy overheats, when share prices soar sky-high, when players get carried away and speculation consummates the divorce between finance and the economy.

Government policy has been, then as now, to expect that speculators obsessed with profit should regulate themselves.

Marketing techniques and communication technologies also helped amplify the phenomenon of stock market speculation. Always prepared to tell tall tales in order to seduce small shareholders, market touts could now peddle their moribund financial products – mining stocks in particular – in the comfort of investors' homes. "Mining companies were employing their listings as selling tools in tip sheets and high-pressure telephone campaigns. Members who held low-price options on treasury shares were urging clients to buy the stock without disclosing their interest, which constituted misrepresentation."[49] No sooner had home sales been declared illegal in 1934 than brokers began to hound potential investors by mail, telegraph, and telephone. Faced with these new ploys, public authorities continued to lag behind in their regulatory efforts.

For the first time, public opinion began to criticize the concept of self-regulation and call for the *Criminal Code* to be applied to the stock market – a demand that is still heard today.

Far from being concerned with limiting abuse, the main financial players sought to disguise as normal behaviour the risk involved in the casino-like stock exchange. The exchange was equated with a gamble – but a "classy" gamble, not to be compared with vulgar activities like horse racing. Balmer Neilly, secretary of McIntyre Porcupine Mines, put it rather bluntly in his March 1939 address to the Ontario Prospectors and Developers Association: "With the best intentions in the world we have got the prospectors all tied up in red tape. With our legislation we have lost track of the fundamental aim – making mines … Fear is congealing prospecting." He went on to say: "Let the government recognize prospecting for what it is: an outright gamble. Let us have no strings on the prize, an adventure without any restrictions … Surely it is infinitely better that a man should gamble on a prospect than a race horse or an Irish Sweepstake. On those, if you lose, you lose. When money is gambled on prospects, if you lose the money stays in Canada and more is known about the mining country."[50]

The extractive industry was also able to distract a section of the public by draping itself in the Canadian flag, making its development one of the themes of Canadian mythology. Resource exploitation was presented to Canadians as a guarantee of wealth; against this nationalistic backdrop, "junior" mining companies were presented as discoverers upon whom national prosperity depended. Insignificant discoveries, shouted from the rooftops, obscured the controversial nature of a stock-market system specifically devised to favour prospectors, promoters, and speculators.

The higher stock market profits soared, the more difficult it became for the OSC to crack down on irregularities, even though rising prices were often an indicator of these irregularities.

As time went on, the industry's backers lost whatever inhibitions remained. This was especially true of brokers and mining exploration companies, which depended entirely on liquidity obtained from the market. Mining exploration companies called for nothing less than the abolition of almost all regulations, which would have made Canada into a true mining company's paradise. The "search for new mines to replace old ones is suffering from the most serious decline in experience because of the rules and regulations of the Ontario Securities Commission," stated the Ontario Prospectors and Developers Association menacingly in 1939, while fraud and scandal continued to rock the industry.[51]

At the first sign of falling prices, mining-industry players would chalk up their failures to excess regulation. The Ontario government finally buckled under pressure: on April 1, 1939, the OSC loosened its regulations to the benefit of Ontario-registered exploration firms. This made little difference to the industry's public position in favour of ever less supervision. As for mining companies' methods, they remained exactly the same; only the scale would change. The atomic age ushered in by the Second World War touched off a keen interest in uranium and other strategic metals among Canadian prospectors. Trading in mining shares drove the Toronto exchange to heights that have never since been equalled. On April 3, 1956, no fewer than 12,682,000 shares changed hands on the TSE. Military-related secrecy had lent speculation something approaching legitimacy. "Until the end of 1956, for security reasons the U.S. government banned the release of figures for ore reserves and production levels by uranium producers. In the absence of reliable information, investors could only guess at the commercial viability of such companies. In fact, when the ban was lifted, only state-owned Eldorado Mining was actually producing ore in Canada, so that the other prospects were rank speculations. This situation, of course, was tailor-made for fraudsters."[52]

Tendentious advertising, misrepresentation, and high-pressure selling were still the rule, despite the fine rhetoric of self-regulation. A share bought for 5 cents could rapidly be traded at 90 cents by using aggressive sales techniques. Prospectuses held out the promise of non-existent geological discoveries. Shares that did not yet exist were traded by telephone. Ever more creative accounting found ways around formal obstacles.

New abuses followed new remedies, despite the founding in 1947 of the Broker Dealers Association of Ontario (BDA), set up to "guarantee" once again that brokers' behaviour would be cleaned up … on condition that government was not involved in regulation. The financial world regulated itself, viewing supervision strictly in terms of the mutual interests of its players, never of the people who experienced the impact of the market without participating in it.

Mining and oil share trading on the Toronto exchange concentrated on a limited number of assets that were constantly being revalued.

In 1954, 850 million shares were traded on the TSE, compared with 520 million in New York – but the value of shares traded in Toronto totalled only $1 billion, as compared with the US$14.2 billion that underwrote New York securities.[53]

In the early 1950s, the TSE claimed it had discovered a way to cool the enthusiasm of mining-industry speculators. "The exchange board did finally move to require underwriting and option agreements for listed stocks to include 'escalator' clauses, so that insiders could not continue to take down very low priced stock even after market prices had moved sharply upward, benefiting themselves at the expense of a company treasury."[54] Effective though they may have been, such measures remained both partial and marginal.

The scandals continued to fly thick and fast. "Red hot markets for Canadian resource stocks made it all the easier for promoters to manipulate prices."[55] Shell companies multiplied, boosting the price of shares by buying and selling them to each other. For no visible reason, in 1955, Midcon Oil and Gas shares rose from 42 cents to more than $2 in less than a month. Shortly thereafter, the share price plummeted again to a little more than 80 cents.

Two years later the TSE, in the throes of another scandal, reached new levels of opacity. The share price of Aconic Mining Corporation fell suddenly from $11 to $1. A TSE investigation pointed to a conflict of interest involving an administrator of the company who was also a member of the exchange's listing committee. But when the time came to reveal the degenerate details of the affair, such as actual sums of money and the names of people involved, the facts were kept secret and the financial press learned nothing.

By the late 1950s, the American regulatory agency – the Securities Exchange Commission (SEC) – was warning investors against the aggressive marketing of unlisted shares by Canadian brokers, threatening to disqualify the latter on the American market.[56] In 1959, even

Merrill Lynch's Toronto manager stated at a press conference that neither the Toronto Stock Exchange nor the OSC were trying hard enough
to discipline their stock promoters.[57] Moreover, unlike their Canadian
colleagues, American academics joined the fray in the 1960s, radically
questioning the self-regulation principle.[58] OSC director O. E. Lennox's
reply was essentially to say that the aim of his regulatory agency was to
promote mining investment in Ontario, and that buying shares issued
by junior mining companies was always a gamble. He denounced the
United States for wanting to oversee financial markets in a "dictatorial"
manner,[59] wording that announced what Canada was to become: a
regulatory paradise for the mining industry. This is the doctrine that
Toronto's financial actors are still preaching today.

In the meantime, financial networks were becoming more international, and as the number of shares traded increased due to overseas
transactions, scandals tarnished Toronto's international reputation. In
1961, a few timid steps were taken: the TSE limited the more extrava-
gant kinds of marketing used for certain shares. Rules governing listed
companies were also tightened. Under pressure from the Ontario government of Red Tory John Robarts, the TSE attempted to guarantee the
neutrality of its managers: in 1960, for the first time, the organization
appointed a president who did not belong to one of the member firms,
and the new appointee, Howard Graham, undertook to monitor the
nature and scope of transactions on a day-to-day basis.

These restrictions put a damper on mining speculation, but
could not stop the white-collar crooks of the financial world from
devising ever more sophisticated methods. Misrepresentation was the
preferred investor bait, while promoters and brokers worked hand
in glove to pump up share values artificially. Rampant speculation
remained the rule. Despite the superficial measures it had adopted,
the Toronto exchange continued to conceal dubious practices that
produced false data and benefited speculators: "The most glaring

abuses arose from permitting speculative mining and oil companies to continue the primary distribution of their stock through the exchange at the same time as secondary trading in previously issued shares continued."[60] The extractive industry remained at the heart of these controversies.

During the 1960s, TSE president Howard Graham made a number of threatening noises, establishing standards and directives to tighten supervision and disclosure procedures for firms listed on the exchange. This did not stop Toronto from reaffirming its guiding principle: "to facilitate purchase and sale of shares between investors," a principle that ultimately favoured speculation. The new directives carried little weight against the power of the mining industry, which accounted for 40 percent of all TSE industrial listings. Moreover, in 1962, 76 percent of all mining transactions in Canada took place in Toronto. In a 1962 TSE document, the principle of financing companies in need of funds for large-scale projects was relegated to the section on the history of the exchange, as if it were no longer relevant.

The TSE also proved ultra-permissive in its policy on the information that companies were required to disclose. To obtain a listing, a mining firm had only to claim a well-located property that could be expected to contain a certain amount of surface ore. A start-up fee of $50,000 sufficed to ensure the "seriousness" of the mining operation. Worse yet, it was common knowledge that even these minimal rules were broken: "Promoters were aware that the TSE often did not adhere to its published standards. For example, mining companies sometimes got listings even if they had only half the required amount of cash in the treasury, and it was suggested that $30,000 was a sufficient sum to finance exploratory work to discover whether a property had realistic prospects or not."[61]

Believing in the sincerity of the TSE's assurances of self-regulation became increasingly difficult: "*The Financial Post* complained that the rules were not nearly so hard to evade as the exchange pretended. Members were only required to report their short positions biweekly, and the TSE published nothing but aggregate figures for each stock, making attacks harder to detect."[62]

The notorious Windfall Oils and Mines scandal of 1964 confirmed these suspicions and destroyed the credibility of Canada's regulatory system. The tale itself reads like a grotesque caricature. During a golf game involving TSE shareholders and speculators, word leaked out that George MacMillan, a well-known prospector who with his wife, Viola, headed a prospecting firm called Texas Gulf Sulphur Company, had discovered traces of copper, zinc, and silver near Timmins, in Northern Ontario. As evidence of the claim, the market relied on eight ore samples that had been sitting in MacMillan's car for a month. Little did it matter that no analysis results had been published, and that exploratory drilling had not begun: the stock took off. Tens of thousands of shares were issued. Prices doubled. Not the slightest additional information was provided to the TSE. Exchange president Howard Graham, alerted to the void on which the latest rumours were based, kept silent to avoid panic. In the absence of any conclusive assay results, rumour and demand continued to drive share prices upward. A few weeks later, however, the TSE was unable to satisfy OSC representatives. Viola MacMillan asserted that the mine's expected yield could sustain the speculative boom; on her word alone, share prices kept soaring. Then in late July, after a month of drilling, the brutal truth was revealed: the alleged deposits were pure wind. Calm returned to the market; the share price fell suddenly from $4.75 to 80 cents. The Canadian Mining Hall of Fame today presents the MacMillans as exemplary figures in the industry's history. Which is what they are, from a certain point of view.

White-Collar Crime

The historical balance sheet is hardly reassuring. Between 1907 and 1953, of 6,679 public mining firms listed in Toronto, only 348 ever produced a significant amount of ore. And a mere 54 ever paid dividends. Of the $850 million invested in Canada between 1953 and 1960, $510 million went to promotion and sales, while only $150 million were invested in exploration. Thirty percent of all transactions involved brokers' private accounts.[63]

These were the findings of the Porter Royal Commission on Banking and Finance established in 1964 by the Canadian government. The commission criticized the exchange for not obliging firms to provide investors with the strategic data that would guide their choices. In Toronto, no information whatsoever about company assets was required.

The Porter Commission concluded that the TSE was always one subway train behind the fraudsters; that the spirit of the law was systematically ignored; and that deficient supervision was powerless against the cycle of fraud.

Leaked information and insider trading were secretly encouraged, while prospecting continued to boost share prices even before drilling had begun. Moreover, the Ontario and Canadian governments were unable to offset the impact of acquisitions and mergers on the market.

The self-presentation of the stock exchange as a huge casino was an accomplished fact; government measures were an object of derision.

In their study of white-collar crime, John Hagan and Patricia Parker turn their attention to Ontario to explain how investors, as part of the social class that holds power, have been able to construct administrative and symbolic structures that provide them with virtual impunity. They apply the theories of criminologist Edwin H. Sutherland on financial crime. Sutherland maintains that the power elite wield the necessary tools to shelter themselves, structurally and symbolically, from irregularities that can be described as crimes. "Organizations, especially formal business organizations, make resources available for the perpetration of grander crimes than is otherwise the case, and … organizations also frequently provide effective covers for the commission of these crimes."[64] As an economic colony of the United States, Canada has encouraged and promoted exploitation of its resources to attract foreign capital. Basing themselves on the work of Wallace Clement and attorney Lawrence Krizanowski, Hagan and Parker write: "The result was an unequal alliance in which the United States became the 'extractive power', dominating much of Canada's industry and its resource market. Through most of this century, therefore, Canada has been much more concerned with stimulating than restricting capital investment, much of which was foreign, but some of which was domestic. Predictably, the regulation of securities was of low priority during this period, and the manipulation of securities was common."[65]

In addition, the social structures in which the major financial players operate allow them to use their employees as a buffer on issues of responsibility.[66]

Criminologists have noted that the extreme complexity of modern-day financial vehicles makes it difficult even for a judge to grasp their full scope. Companies duplicate themselves, change their names, and carry out transactions with their subsidiaries, which in turn are spread over several distinct legislative jurisdictions, some of which are tax havens. They are thus free to carry out financial crimes far more difficult to plan, and far more ambitious in scale, than a simple downtown hold-up. Given Canada's dependent relationship with foreign capital, "these markets were given as free a rein as possible." In the wake of Watergate in the United States, for the umpteenth time Ontario promised to tighten its regulatory system; however, as the president of the OSC proclaimed in the early 1980s: "our role is not solely investor protection, but it is to create an environment which leads to an efficient market place."[67]

Twice Upon a Time in the West

The crisis of confidence that shook Toronto in the aftermath of the 1964 Windfall Scandal – sky-rocketing prices based on eight ore samples in a car – worked to the advantage of regional stock exchanges such as Vancouver and Calgary. Exploration firms (juniors), promoters, and brokers migrated to British Columbia, bringing the illicit methods responsible for their fortunes along with them. But fraudulent activity was already under way before they arrived. Canada's financial "Far West" had long been identified with Vancouver and Calgary.

The laxness of the Vancouver exchange was illustrated in the 1970s by the Irving Kott affair. Kott's company, listed on the VSE, touted a technology developed by two McGill University researchers that promised to recover gold residues from the sludge left over after extraction. The almost alchemical promise to transform industrial wastes into gold was perfectly in tune with the dreams presented to dazzled speculators by Canadian stock markets. (Kott was also a master of the "wash trade" technique: his company sold and re-purchased its own shares via offshore companies based in London, Luxembourg, Montevideo, or elsewhere; as the shares moved from one account to another, their price continued to rise until they became objectively attractive.)[68]

In their investigation of the Vancouver exchange, David Cruise and Alison Griffiths recall that in 1974, the Coordinated Law Enforcement Unit estimated that between 20 and 30 percent of all trades on the VSE had been the result of manipulation, and that between twenty-five and fifty people involved with the exchange had a criminal record.[69]

The VSE even managed to overtake Toronto in the bad reputation sweepstakes. Said *Forbes* magazine on April 27, 1981: "If you have a faint heart or slow wits, steer clear of the Vancouver exchange. It's that simple."[70] Eight years later, the same publication described Vancouver "Scam Capital of the World."[71] Absolutely anything could be listed, and was: even a non-existent airport in a region where no airplane ever flew. Sects such as Scientology used it to raise funds.[72]

The *Financial Post* described the speculative frenzy of brokers who paraded their wealth in Vancouver as "'a monstrous betrayal of the confidence of the Canadian people' and 'a cynical exploitation of public confidence.'"[73] Or as the prominent Vancouver businessman Altaf Nazerali put it: "a sucker gets out of bed every morning; it's up to us to find him and turn him into a customer."[74]

On the national level, in 1997 Canadians were reminded of the reality principle when another huge fraud case rocketed into the head-lines: the Bre-X scandal. The scam practised by this company, first listed in Calgary before being registered in Toronto, plunged some fifty thousand savers into severe economic distress while forcing institu-tional investors to cover colossal losses. The crudeness of the gambit behind the fraud, which involved sprinkling gold on ore samples from the Busang mine in Indonesia to drive up the firm's share price, quickly became an international scandal. A mere "junior" had even succeeded in fooling the world's largest gold-mining major.[75] "Barrick spent years and many millions of dollars and used its very substantial connections, a former American president, a former Canadian prime minister, a businessman married to a member of the royal family of Jordan and others to influence events and the Indonesian government to get a share of Busang."[76] Following the Bre-X bankruptcy, other Ontario-based exploration firms suddenly expressed doubts about the information they themselves had provided regarding their own assets. The value of most mining shares dropped with the fall of Bre-X.

The affair revealed once again the structural inadequacies of all Canadian stock exchanges: Vancouver, Calgary, and of course, Toronto.

In each case, the terminology used to designate the nature of the ore deposits of a mine stood exposed as lax in the extreme, and professional structures to supervise and regulate the accurate and reliable disclosure of that information were shown to be non-existent.

In another area involving shares also traded on the TSX, the bankruptcy of Canadian electronic giant Nortel demonstrated, in 2001, that it was legally possible in Canada to conceal years of operating deficits through creative accounting that showed only income.[77]

In the end, the TSX regained its position as Canada's sole mining-investment stock exchange, tightened yet again its self-regulatory standards, and created a venture-capital market fully adapted to the exploration companies: TSX Venture. Today, the controversial questions that keep arising from the international actions of Canadian mining companies must be dealt with in Toronto, and these questions have an ethical dimension. How much longer will we tolerate speculation on mining concessions acquired or exploited in a context of war, violent evictions, massive pollution, political collusion, tax evasion, and smuggling? In Max Weber's time, people generally accepted the relevance and legitimacy of the stock exchange as an institution; today the fact that intellectuals, activists, and some opposition members of Parliament are ready to act on these issues tells us that this is no longer so.

Today, the approximate ratio of speculative transactions to those that take place in the real economy is a dizzying fifty to one. For French economist François Morin, a former member of the governing body of the Banque de France, the time has come to wrest control of the stock market from those who seized it long ago from within. "Can we possibly imagine an international community that is united enough to finance actions other than those strictly related to the financial sphere? Actions dealing with our planet's environmental issues, with the challenge of sustainable development, or with world poverty, for example."[78]

As a key tool of the financialization of the national and global economies in the twentieth century, and particularly over the past thirty years, the stock exchange has made this impossible. It is now clear that the principles on which its creation was supposed to have been based, as described by Max Weber, are utterly foreign to it. Jean-Luc Gréau, a former high official of two associations of French corporate executives (Conseil national du patronat français and Mouvement des entreprises de France), today scathingly denounces the "financial obsession" that characterizes share trading and is gnawing away at capitalism.[79] Not only does today's investor screen out from his awareness the environmental, social, psychological, and cultural impacts of his activity in history; he even eliminates the actual enterprise of which he is a shareholder. A shareholder, but in no way a stakeholder, today's institutional investor provides no long-term stewardship of his firm; he is prepared to let it disappear as long as he can manoeuvre to increase his own assets. The process of investing, in his eyes, refers to nothing more than owning shares, which are in turn reduced to nothing more than an objectified business opportunity in the financial and not the economic sphere.

In the late twentieth and early twenty-first centuries, at a time of insistent pressure created by a strong world demand for minerals, the dramatic impact of mining speculation on the environment and on human beings is easily observed. Unsurprisingly, the TSX as the heart of world mining finance, and more generally Canada as a privileged jurisdiction, are playing a key role in this process.

Examples continue to abound. In 2012, suspicions regarding Sino-Forest, a forestry company that appeared to have exaggerated its activities and carried out fictitious business transactions, prompted the OSC to produce a report on foreign corporations listed on the Toronto Stock Exchange whose share value represented $37 billion in April 2011.[80] The OSC gave the public the benefit of its usual parrot-like statements on the self-regulation of financial ogres, despite the fact that these ogres are well known to be completely obsessed with money. "In our view, the level of rigour and independent-mindedness applied by boards, auditors and underwriters in doing their important jobs – management oversight, audit, due diligence on offerings – should have been more thorough," stated the agency.[81] The regulatory agency promised to continue its work of "oversight," a commitment that will doubtless leave the industry terrified.

In another example from March 2012, a \$4 billion class-action suit was launched against Kinross, a Canadian mining company, on behalf of shareholders claiming that the company had been guilty of misrepresentation as to the quality and quantity of gold ore contained in a Mauritanian mine.[82]

"What we are observing is more than a game of purely statistical representation. In practical terms, we find ourselves at the heart of what drives the market and its players ... We are moving toward a total financialization of the world economy at a steadily accelerating pace; ... this process, and the values it enshrines, carries with it great risks for our planet, and for our humanity."[83] Investment has now been reduced to the sole purpose of profit-taking. Moreover, its numerical representations, as praised by the stock exchange, carry within them something that is indisputably threatening.

A CASE STUDY

Quebec Colonial Ltd.

In an article published in the Montreal daily *La Presse* on National Patriots' Day in 2009, Quebec premier Jean Charest attempted to appropriate the legacy of the Patriotes of 1837,[1] claiming these uncompromising nineteenth-century thinkers as the originators of the "democracy, justice, and freedom" that he sees as characteristic of today's Quebec. The insurgents of yesteryear would probably be surprised by Charest's odd comparison between the current status of Quebec and the democratic vision that inspired them: a vision of people taking power and making their own decisions regarding the nation's political, economic, social, and cultural affairs.

According to conventional wisdom, Quebeckers (and Canadians) enjoy the benefits of a state in which they democratically supervise their public affairs through structures ensuring that elected representatives consult the population. It is asserted that in this manner, the state apparatus works for the common good of the majority of Quebec's citizens.

These claims are not supported by analysis when it comes to the exploitation of the province's immense natural resources, particularly its mineral wealth. In Quebec as elsewhere, it seems that the "economic development" promised by mining companies often destroys the habitat and lifestyle of indigenous people and produces pollution over extensive areas, threatening the health of present and future generations. In this chapter, we take a closer look at the Quebec mining sector.

Our thesis is that the Quebec mining sector stands totally outside the logic and effective mechanisms of democratic oversight, and that it contributes nothing to the common good despite the billions of dollars in revenues that the mining sector generates for private companies every year.[2] The interests of the Quebec people and those of the mining industry are about as compatible as those of citizens and narcotics producers in what are known as narco-states, areas that have been taken over and are controlled and corrupted by drug cartels and where law enforcement is effectively non-existent. By analogy, we believe that Quebec might well be called a mineral state; in other words, a state entirely dedicated to the interests of its extractive industry.

A mineral state is characterized by eight features. First, it is a territory with a strong geological potential for extractible mineral resources. Second, its public institutions, whether formal or informal, are structured in such a way as to transfer public mineral wealth and the profits it generates to a minority of private owners or corporations. Third, the state uses civil law or military force, or both, to guarantee unlimited access to resources for private players involved in the exploitation of its mineral deposits. Fourth, it provides a network of infrastructures making it easy to convey human and material resources to mining sites and to send minerals on their way to export markets. Fifth, through formal and informal channels, it makes it easy for companies to send profits back to their country of origin without having to deal with overly finicky tax audits. Sixth, it ensures that standards for working conditions or environmental protection are kept to a minimum. Seventh, it provides the extractive sector with cheap access to its energy and hydroelectric potential. Eighth, through a carefully balanced interplay of forces, it gives the mining industry enormous influence over government officials and actions. Foreign and national entrepreneurs are invited to invest heavily in mining, which is presented in a highly favourable manner as one of the pillars of the country's economy.

A Case Study

As a jurisdiction, Quebec has won high praise from the international mining sector. It has often ranked first in world lists established by corporate investment analysts and been cited as an example of a state offering "best practices" to the extractive industry. We have chosen to focus on Quebec because, in our opinion, this particular jurisdiction provides the best example of a state appropriated by the mining industry. However, it is worth mentioning that other Canadian jurisdictions such as British Columbia, Alberta, Newfoundland, Saskatchewan, and particularly Ontario also provide mining operators with some of the best business environments in the world, helping to make Canada the most attractive country for the international mining industry. It follows that not only Quebec, but almost every Canadian province and even Canada as a whole, can be described as a mineral state, given that the federal government offers unfailing support to the mining industries registered in this country.[3]

As a major shareholder of the Bretton Woods institutions, Canada has often emphasized the fact that it plays a significant role in the governance of the World Bank and the IMF.[4] It is perhaps no accident, then, that these institutions have induced the world's poorer countries to adopt mining codes that bear an eerie resemblance to the Canadian model. The Democratic Republic of Congo is a case in point. Beginning in 2000, the World Bank and the IMF worked to reshape the country's legal and institutional framework, with particular emphasis on mining; the new *Mining Code* adopted in 2002 ensured the least possible leeway for government intervention.[5]

A Land for the Taking

In Quebec, hydroelectricity, the boreal forest, and of course deposits of gold, copper, zinc, uranium, nickel, platinum, palladium, iron, and diamonds all represent a world-class potential for exploitation. Quebec's industrial tradition has in fact been built on its mineral wealth. The demand for raw materials is rising, chiefly because the economies of China and India are rapidly expanding.[6] As a result, mining is more than ever a lucrative branch of activity.

In 2009, the Quebec Mining Association (QMA) declared that the Quebec mining industry was enjoying "the most significant period of expansion of the past twenty years."[7] Today, the Charest government's "Plan Nord" continues the enterprise of colonization and looting of natural resources that has been under way for the past five centuries on the American continent.[8]

Thanks to its immense geological potential, Quebec has been the site of intensive industrial mining activity since the establishment of the great asbestos mines at the end of the nineteenth century. In the twentieth century, demand generated by the industrialization of Europe and the United States, and above all by the Second World War, led to the creation of veritable mining empires in the province. Noranda, for example, a copper company established in the 1920s, was one of Canada's mining giants throughout the rest of the twentieth century.[9] (Noranda merged with Falconbridge and then was acquired by a Swiss corporation, Xstrata, in November 2006.)[10] In the years after the Second World War, the Western world under reconstruction and on its way to hyper-industrialization devoured increasing amounts of raw materials. Unprecedented prosperity was the consequence for Quebec mining companies, particularly in the Abitibi region where huge deposits were identified and explored. This was the Duplessis era when it was said that minerals went for a penny a ton[11] – a practice that did have its critics, however, even at the time. On August 8, 1956, in the pages of *Le Devoir*, editorialist Gérard Filion indignantly denounced the "big corporations that benefit from tax holidays … exploiting the province's natural resources for ridiculous royalties."[12] Until the early 1960s, Quebec's French-speaking citizens had almost no control over

A Case Study

the province's economy. They were massively exploited in the mines where they laboured under conditions not far removed from slavery – conditions that were challenged by workers during famous strikes at Asbestos in 1949 and Murdochville in 1957.[13] Foreign corporations were the sole beneficiaries of the province's mineral wealth. "The industry, of which over 60% was under American control, shipped massive amounts of Quebec ore to the United States where foreign factories made it into finished products."[14] In this way, Quebec was deprived of the substantial economic benefits associated with value-added secondary and tertiary industries.

The Quiet Revolution of the 1960s stood out as a period of government interventionism under premier Jean Lesage, whose victorious campaign slogan was "*Maîtres chez nous*" (Masters in our own house).[15] During this period, the Quebec government created the Société générale de financement (SGF), an investment fund focused on supporting Quebec companies; Sidbec, which attempted to develop a Quebec-based steel industry; and SOQUEM, which supported mining. The government used Hydro-Québec to nationalize the hydroelectric sector and created the Caisse de dépôt et placement du Québec to manage public pension funds.[16] In Quebec's universities, geology departments were established and French-speaking engineers were trained.[17]

Despite these measures, the mining industry continued to elude any kind of government control. Moreover, despite the emergence of a horde of new junior exploration firms set up by French-speaking engineers, even today the key positions in the industry are still held by English Canadians and foreign investors. In fact, the situation has changed little in Quebec since the first great mineral rush of the 1920s. Today, among the largest extractive mining companies, we find Agnico-Eagle Ltd., Iamgold, Breakwater Resources, Richmont Mines Inc., Wesdome Gold Mines, First Metals Inc., Alexis Minerals, Century Mining Corporation, Campbell Resources Inc., Aurizon, and Xstrata.

With the exception of the Swiss giant Xstrata, all are registered on the Toronto Stock Exchange, along with almost all other mineral exploration firms active in Quebec (and the world).

Quebec: A "Mining Paradise"

Neo-liberal thought, which idealizes society as a meritocracy, loves classifications: the top universities, the biggest fortunes, the largest corporations, the "most developed" nations – categories in which countries under foreign domination generally lag far behind, which makes perfect sense, since the classification criteria are drawn up by dominant nations. But in one area, Quebec stands at the top of the podium: it is considered "the most favourable jurisdiction for mining."[18] Every year, it ranks among the top ten jurisdictions, and has often come first, in the rankings established by the Fraser Institute for the international mining sector. These rankings are based on an extensive poll of hundreds of mining companies and leading industry players.[19] The institute bases its calculations on close scrutiny of profit maximization indicators that measure: "the effects on exploration of government policies including uncertainty concerning the administration, interpretation, and enforcement of existing regulations; environmental regulations; regulatory duplication and inconsistencies; taxation; uncertainty concerning native land claims and protected areas; infrastructure; socioeconomic agreements; political stability; labor issues; geological database; and security."[20]

Environmental concerns, working conditions, and issues relating to the just distribution of the profits earned from mineral extraction are seen as negative or irrelevant considerations. All of which would be cause for alarm in any society concerned with the environment and with its own economic sovereignty.

A Case Study

A Visionary Fiscal Policy

Mining generates huge revenues. Six of the seventeen mining majors operating in Quebec appear in the Toronto *Globe and Mail*'s ranking of Canada's Top 1000 revenue-producing companies.[21] Since maximizing profits is the overriding aim of any business entity, mining companies do their best to ensure minimal taxation of their cash flows in whatever jurisdiction they operate. In the South's dictatorships or dictatorships-disguised-as-democracies, tax evasion causes enormous losses and is often facilitated by the corruption of the tax system's key players. In Quebec, mining companies are theoretically subject to three types of taxes: income tax, capital tax, and an industry-specific tax known as royalties. The latter is intended to provide compensation to the public for the fact that companies are extracting the non-renewable resources of the state. The reality, however, is that an entire set of mechanisms located within the state structure make tax avoidance as fully legal as in any offshore tax haven. From giant mine operators to junior firms and small-time stock-market speculators, all of the mining industry's players are able to enrich themselves by exploiting Quebec's immense geological potential, while producing a minimum amount of economic spinoffs for the community. In fact, the mining industry regularly praises the "competitive fiscal environment" of the province and its "visionary policy of investment stimulation."[22]

A report issued by Quebec auditor general Renaud Lachance in April 2009 denounced the permissive nature of the tax system to which the mining industry is "subject." His findings embody a devastating verdict on the actions of Quebec's ministry of natural resources and wildlife (ministère des ressources naturelles et de la faune, or MRNF).[23] The MRNF describes its mission as follows: "to ensure the development and optimal use of land, energy, forestry, and mineral resources in Quebec from a sustainable development perspective, for the benefit of the entire population."[24] According to the auditor general's report, however, the "benefit" accruing to "the entire population" is minimal. "Mining companies benefit from several measures and allocations that allow them to lessen their profits, or even reduce them to zero,"[25] which would explain the fact that "for the 2002–2008 period, 14 companies paid no mining tax even though they had combined gross annual production values of $4.2 billion. As for the other companies, they paid, for the same period, $259 million, namely 1.5 percent of the gross annual production value."[26]

In Quebec, as in Ontario and other Canadian provinces, mining royalties are profit-based. A more accurate way of measuring minerals actually extracted would be to calculate the value of the resources produced. When royalties are based on profits, companies can reduce them by reducing the profits they declare. This is easy to do under Quebec law, which offers many helpful credits and allowances: credit on duties refundable for losses, depreciation allowance, allowance for exploration, mineral deposit evaluation, and mine development, additional exploration allowance, processing allowance, additional depreciation allowance, additional allowance for a northern mine.[27] Mining firms in Quebec and Ontario are also allowed to deduct, from the profits they make at any particular mine, the expenses incurred in other mining operations. These measures allow companies to declare little or no profits even when they are doing substantial amounts of business.

A research report by Laura Handal of IRIS, Quebec's Institut de recherche et d'informations socio-économiques,[28] confirms the obvious disparity between the lavish support provided by the Canadian and Quebec governments to the mining industry and the sparse benefits that accrue to the public from this sector of the economy. Handal's report also indicates that no information is available regarding most government measures. In other words, companies' annual profits, which determine their royalties, can easily be manipulated through multiple tax breaks, many of which are not made public.

Handal notes that the practice of basing royalties on profits rather than production value has been strongly criticized for its deficiencies and the potential abuses it favours, even by the World Bank[29] – an institution that can hardly be suspected of excessive hostility toward the extractive sector.

With profit-based royalties, the amount of royalties paid does not bear any relationship to the value of the minerals actually extracted. If a firm's profits are zero, no tax is paid, no matter how much the minerals taken from the ground are worth.

In 2010, even Quebec finance minister Raymond Bachand complained in his budget document that "many mining operators are in a position to reduce their mining duties payable to zero for many years in a row. This situation is of even more concern since some metals have reached record prices in recent years."[30] The Quebec government therefore announced that royalties payable on corporate profits in the mining sector would be increased to 16 percent by 2012.[31] Though the ineffectiveness of this measure is laughable (if a company's royalty payments currently amount to zero, then an increase to 16 percent or even 100 percent would still be zero), the mining industry nonetheless opposed it. On April 23, 2010, Fraser Institute analysts published an opinion piece in *Le Devoir* in which they asserted that mining companies did not object to paying taxes, but that the proposed change to the province's tax regime was unacceptable because the companies had already done the financial planning for mining projects premised on the then 12 percent tax level.[32] How can we accept this logic? Given the lifespan of mining projects, this would result in postponing any tax increase for fifteen to twenty years. In the context of these ineffectual debates, the government's position is simply cynical.

The Quebec government's March 2012 budget made slight changes to the rules applying to tax credits for expenses. For companies that do not develop mineral resources, the tax credit rate for expenses will be reduced by 10 percent. However, they can regain 10 percentage points if they give the Quebec government an option to acquire an equity stake in the development.[33] Overall, we may expect the effect of these changes to be negligible, but they serve the purpose of providing the government with ammunition to answer its critics.

In any case, cosmetic changes to Quebec's budget and tax regimes will not alleviate the Quebec auditor's concern over the opaque way in which the MRNF handles information about the mining sector, since the ministry no longer systematically analyzes statistics or publishes information on the industry.[34]

In his concern to see genuine democratic accountability applied to this sector and enable the MRNF to accomplish its mission (to "take into account the principal costs and benefits associated with public intervention in the mining sector"),[35] auditor general Renaud Lachance challenged the MRNF to bring its "mineral strategy" out of mothballs for a public airing. The government had promised that before the end of 2007, it would adopt a "strategy" that would define a framework for future mineral exploration and operation. However, another eighteen months elapsed before the government finally published its report *Preparing the Future of Quebec's Mineral Sector: Quebec Mineral Strategy* in June 2009.[36] Meanwhile, the MRNF had organized a program of public hearings in the fall of 2007, inviting interested persons and organizations to express their views on its website, and then launching an "individual consultation of more than 50 organizations."[37]

Speaking of strategy, there is another "strategy" that is often adopted by government officials when the interests of multinationals are called into question: playing for time. One way of doing this is to set up mechanisms for consultation and negotiation under the heading of "good governance."[38] Since the parties that are consulted have no decision-making powers, there is no guarantee that opinions expressed during the consultations will be taken into account. The government, however, will find many opportunities to cite the consultations as evidence of a democratic process.

For this reason, there was some cause for pessimism concerning the outcome of the MRNF's "consultation," even before the ministry made it clear that the aim of its "mineral strategy" would be "to generate further wealth and jobs in a sector that is crucial to many Quebec regions."[39] This uplifting rhetoric actually translates as the continued colonization of Northern Quebec and destruction of the boreal forest.[40] The "strategy" described in the document that was the ultimate outcome of the consultation, *Preparing the Future of Quebec's Mineral Sector: Quebec Mineral Strategy*,[41] looks more like a public relations campaign than a policy to regulate mining activities. The document's copyright page indicates that it is the product of "collaboration" with two powerful lobbies, the Quebec Mining Association and the Quebec Mineral Exploration Association. Thus it comes as no surprise to find that it deals with the advantages of privately led exploitation of mineral resources, and the programs the government intends to implement to support it. The "Strategy" is full of buzzwords and phrases such as "sustainable development" and "community participation" and the feeble rhetoric to which they always seem to give rise. On the vexatious issue of fiscal demands that might be imposed on the industry, the "Mineral Strategy" does not set any targets. At most, it recognizes that "the mining royalties regime must also be examined to ensure that Quebec receives its fair share from the mining of its non-renewable natural resources."[42]

The "Strategy" episode had at least one merit: it made it impossible for the Quebec government to go on disguising the fact that the province faces a tax-related revenue shortfall in the mining sector – a shortfall directly and increasingly associated with the province's inability to balance its budget. A detailed, independent, cost-benefit analysis of mining activity in the public interest, as called for by the auditor general, might well lead to devastating results for the current government. Under today's laws, regulations, and taxation policies, it is hard to see what advantages, if any, mining operations present for Quebec, especially as the wealth created by mine operators seems to flow irresistibly toward other countries.

An argument regularly put forward by the mining sector when praising itself is that it creates jobs. However, the number of jobs involved is rather small; many of the jobs are temporary; and many depend on the price of raw materials, which tends to fluctuate. Nor should it be forgotten that mining is one of the most dangerous industrial sectors in Canada in terms of occupational risks.[43] In the best of circumstances, a mine is likely to remain active for fifteen years, at the end of which the workers – perhaps afflicted with silicosis, berylliosis, or some other illness – are forced to relocate with their families, leaving ghost towns behind them.[44]

The problems with royalties identified by the auditor general are not the only examples of the Quebec government's generosity toward the mining industry. A complex series of interrelated tax incentives to the extractive sector also explains the silver medal awarded to Quebec by the Fraser Institute for its taxation regime. According to the auditor general's report, between 2003 and 2008, the cost of tax abatements granted by the government was more than one-and-a-half times greater than the royalties collected (and as much as seven times greater in 2004).[45] First among these tax advantages are "flow-through shares" that enable investors to deduct up to 150 percent of their investment costs.[46] In this respect, Quebec is even more generous than the federal government or other Canadian provinces. Another tax measure that deprives the government of substantial revenues is the tax credit relating to resources that allows companies to deduct their exploration expenses.

Nor are mine operators forgotten. They, too, can benefit from an impressive roster of advantages such as the refundable tax credit for resources, the refundable tax credit for exploration expenses, the credit for allocation of resources, the credit for the cost of bringing an ore body into production, the allowance for equipment to treat mine tailings, the capital tax deduction, the credit on duties refundable for losses, fiscal incentives for starting a mining company, fuel-tax reimbursements, and tax exemptions.[47] The IRIS report also lists the tax credit for research and development wages, fiscal expenditures related to reimbursement of the fuel tax, fiscal expenditures related to the corporate tax regime, the tax credit for research, the tax credit for pre-competitive research, the tax credit for fees and payments to research consortia, the additional tax credit for scientific research and experimental development, and the tax credit for jobs created in designated regions.[48]

Quebec's lax fiscal supervision may lead to misuse of these advantages not merely for tax avoidance, which is legal, but for tax evasion, which is not. This would mean that exploration companies would no longer have to probe the subsoil to find lucrative ore deposits, nor would they be creating any of those famous jobs. Instead, they could get rich just by speculating – harking back to practices of the early twentieth century – or they could simply provide shareholders with significant tax deductions for doing nothing at all. Doubts are reinforced by the obscure names of Quebec exploration companies such as 173714 Canada Inc., 2329-1677 Québec Inc., 3421856 Canada Inc., or 170364 Canada Inc. Some of these entities may have only a single shareholder.[49]

Since the beginning of the decade, the level of tax advantages granted to mineral companies has never declined: in its budget speech of March 30, 2004, the Quebec government extended indefinitely the full range of tax advantages available to them under the flow-through shares program.[50] The 2012 budget further extended the flow-through share program.[51]

Yet the government is aware of the risks of tax incentives: in a document on tax evasion drawn up by the Quebec ministry of finance in 2005, the government recognized abusive reliance on tax credits as one of the chief ways of evading tax.[52]

Public Investment in the Mining Sector

In January 2008, the president of the metalworkers' federation of Quebec's Confederation of National Trade Unions (FM-CSN) remarked: "Quebec is tied hand and foot to the mining companies."[53] In terms of favours granted to the mining industry, the government does not stop at tax breaks.

A host of government bodies, each endowed with budgets in the tens or even hundreds of millions of dollars, supports the mining companies active in Quebec in a multiplicity of ways. They transfer public funds to these corporations at high speed, whether the companies are merely involved in exploration or are actually operating a mine. The money may be used to create a few jobs, but above all it enables the company to turn a profit and gain shareholder confidence. The accumulated profits from company activities, which are substantial in the mining sector, are then siphoned off to a handful of corporate executives, shareholders, or speculators. These same profits are tax deductible, which brings us back to square one.

Who are these public entities? Among them, we find:

- **Ressources Québec**, a subsidiary of Investissement Québec, established in the March 2012 budget to consolidate the government's investment in the mining development and hydrocarbon sectors.[54]

- The **Diversification of Exploration Investment Partnership** (Sidex), whose mission is to "invest in companies engaged in mineral exploration in Quebec." Sidex manages a venture capital

A Case Study

budget of \$50 million provided by the Quebec government (70 percent) and the Quebec Federation of Labour (30 percent).[55] It invests directly in the equity of companies and acts as a lever to obtain additional private investments.[56] In other words, it acts to build confidence as an institutional guarantor for other investors, not primarily Quebeckers or even necessarily Canadians concerned about the security of their investments.

- The **Mining Industry Development and Investment Companies** (Sociétés de développement des entreprises minières et d'exploration, Sodemex, and Sodemex II) are public venture capital companies belonging to Quebec's Caisse de dépôt et placement. They provide financing for exploration companies whose market capitalization is less than \$125 million[57] and participate in company equity with a view to maintaining the share prices of junior exploration companies.[58]

- The **Société québécoise d'exploration minière** (SOQUEM Inc.), now a subsidiary of Ressources Québec, "annually devotes more than \$10 million, with its partners, to off-mine-site exploration in Quebec," representing "about 10% of all exploration investments within Quebec."[59]

- The **Société de recherche et développement minier** (SOREDEM), a non-profit organization made up of mining companies, with the mandate to support the development of new technologies for underground mines. The society operates on a contractual basis and receives about \$180,000 annually from the Quebec government to carry out its research projects.[60]

- The **Société de développement de la Baie-James** (SDBJ) has a mining-industry investment fund of more than \$7 million.[61]

- **Investissement Québec** provides consultation on investment credit financing and investment guarantees and lends to Quebec and international businesses.[62]

The opacity of Quebec's public investment companies makes them look almost like caricatures of government agencies in so-called narco-states. The SOQUEM website, for example, is remarkably spare, providing no data on the sums invested by the company or on any current project. However, the website does tell us that SOQUEM is a wholly owned subsidiary of Investissement Québec. This has been the case since Investissement Québec merged with the Société générale de financement (SGF) in April 2011; until then, SOQUEM belonged to the SGF, a venture capital company whose objective was to "attract investment that will spur growth in Québec." SOQUEM's new owner, Investissement Québec, defines itself as "both a financial institution and an economic development agency,"[63] entirely at the service of the private sector. It provides advice, particularly in such areas as tax credits and investment guarantees, and grants loans to Quebec and international corporations. Investissement Québec welcomes mining companies by advising them on the most effective ways to avoid income tax. Investissement Québec also offers institutional financial support that ensures the indispensable confidence of private sector corporate shareholders. "Our team of specialists can help you: acquire sound industry intelligence; forge productive strategic alliances with local and international partners; find the ideal site that suits your exact needs; benefit from competitive fiscal incentives; secure the right financial solutions, including: loans, loan guarantees and working capital."[64] The only figures to appear in Investissement Québec's annual reports are listed by sector or region, not by firm. It is impossible to determine what sums of money and what services have been provided, and to whom. Only news releases allow the public to know that the public agency invested $50 million in the giant aluminum producer Alcoa[65] and loaned $175 million to Rio Tinto Alcan.[66]

As for Sodemex, it is financed by the Caisse de dépôt et placement du Québec and SOQUEM. Citizens trying to understand where public money is going must learn to orient themselves in a labyrinth of subsidiaries and intercompany holdings. Quebec's publicly owned corporations are the deep-pocket partners that exploration companies desperately need to finance their surveys and attract other investors. The public corporations provide initial venture capital to junior exploration companies. If a highly subsidized junior then discovers a profitable ore deposit, it will generally be bought by a larger firm – a major – with access to large amounts of capital and the ability to develop and operate a mine.[67]

In Quebec, government corporations find themselves advising private firms on how they can take maximum advantage of the province's de facto status as a mineral-state tax haven. Confirming the complexity and efficiency of Quebec's financial activity in the sector, a report jointly published by the Pembina Institute and MiningWatch Canada, entitled *Looking Beneath the Surface: An Estimate of the Value of Public Support for the Metal Industry in Canada*, reveals that Quebec is "unique among Canada's provinces and territories in that it provides direct equity assistance to the mining industry."[68] The report states that "Quebec provides the highest level of financial and fiscal support to the metal mining industry among all of the provinces and territories studied."[69] The study, carried out in 2002, noted how difficult it was to obtain detailed data on governmental expenditures in the mining sector. Little appears to have changed since.

To this incomparable public financial and logistical support must be added a group of government programs, administered by the MRNF, that are designed to provide direct financial and logistical assistance for mining exploration and pre-exploratory preparation: valuation expenses, subsidies to universities, repayment guarantees, interest payment on loans, manpower-training subsidies, and exchange-rate guarantees. The MRNF also provides basic financial assistance to build mining infrastructures. Both upstream and downstream services are made available to the mining industry: the MRNF conducts exploration activities ($385 million spent in 2007)[70] and maintains geoscientific databases that help prepare the ground for exploration companies. (According to the 2009 "Mineral Strategy," "target areas identified by Géologie Québec help to direct mining exploration companies to the most promising regions.")[71] The MRNF also restores abandoned mine sites. From 2007 to 2009, known expenditures in these programs amounted to $53.4 million. However, amounts allocated by the government to many programs that support the mining industry are not made public, which means that, as with the royalties paid by mining companies, total amounts cannot be known. Programs on which full information is not publicly available include the Explor-action program, the FAIRE program (Fonds pour l'accroissement de l'investissement privé et la relance de l'emploi – volet minier), the Programme d'assistance financière aux études technico-économiques et à l'innovation technologique, the Programme de bourses d'étude de l'industrie minière, the Programme d'aide aux régions ressources, and the Programme d'assistance financière pour travaux d'évaluation de gisements miniers.[72] The Pembina Institute–MiningWatch Canada report also includes, as a form of government support to the industry, the free access provided to Quebec's water resources.[73] We can appreci-ate the generosity involved when we consider the fact that large-scale gold mines use more than 100 litres of water per second.[74]

The COREM consortium is an instructive example of govern-ment support. COREM is "a consortium of applied research for the processing and transformation of mineral substances" that carries out "pre-competitive research" (a combination of fundamental and corporate research) for the benefit of the mining industry. Its members include mineral firms such as Iamgold, Agnico-Eagle, Rio Tinto Alcan, and Xstrata,[75] and the Quebec government, represented by the MRNF, is represented on the Pre-Competitive Research Committee.[76] COREM's board of directors also includes university researchers.[77] These connections between academics and the mining industry provide a clue to the nature of the research carried out in the academic world; we may wonder to what extent university professors are producing knowledge for the well-being of all when they are partners with an industry that has demonstrated its contempt for the common good on every continent.

In November 2008, the government established the Mining Heritage Fund with a commitment to endow it with $20 million a year.[78] The fund, which is supported by royalties paid by mining companies operating in Quebec, provides funding for COREM and SOREDEM. In this way, the few millions collected from mining companies in the form of taxes flow directly back to the companies in a perfect loop.

The Quebec Mining Act

Mining companies are extremely sensitive about the legitimacy of their presence in the territories they exploit. Since in many cases they cannot impose their will by force, their preferred option is to invest in countries that provide legal protection for the social and ecological destruction that will inevitably accompany their exploration activities and their operations if they open a mine.

As in most Canadian provinces, Quebec's mining legislation is based on practically unlimited subsoil access rights. After all, this is the cornerstone of Canada's famous mining-industry expertise. The customary rights of Canada's indigenous peoples with respect to their lands have long since given way to laws governing access to the subsoil, and these laws are exclusively designed to facilitate the work of private prospectors and mining companies.

The *Mining Act*[79] currently in force in Quebec is based on the principle of free access to resources, known as free mining. This principle, originating in nineteenth-century laws enacted in California during the gold rush, is still the basis of Quebec's mining law in 2012. Free mining guarantees prospectors the right to access most of a territory, the right to appropriate its underground mineral resources, the right to carry out exploration work, and the right to exploit any potentially profitable deposit.[80] The free-mining principle is based on the idea that mining is the best possible use for any given piece of land. This premise, directly inherited from the nineteenth-century West, explains why Quebec's mining law gives priority to mining activities over the creation of new protected areas such as parks or conservation areas.[81]

Thus the free-mining principle threatens individual, community, and collective rights over territory and environment. The existing *Mining Act* is often in conflict with other laws such as the *Sustainable Development Act, Civil Code of Quebec, Environment Quality Act, Quebec Charter of Human Rights and Freedoms*, and the *Canadian Charter of Rights and Freedoms*; it also frequently contradicts the constitutional rights of Aboriginal peoples in Canada.[82] Quebec activists belonging to the Coalition Québec Meilleure Mine point out that a mining company can apply for many different kinds of leasehold arrangements, depending on the stage it has reached in an exploration or exploitation project, but that all of these leases establish the priority of mining over almost any other use of the land.[83] For example, it is impossible to protect an area once it has been "claimed" by a company that wants to explore its underground (subsoil) resources.

In a report submitted to the MRNF during public consultations on the government's "mineral strategy," Ecojustice, a non-profit organization of lawyers and scientists, severely criticized the opaque manner in which the existing *Mining Act* gives priority to the rights of the mining industry. In particular, the act does not require that the holder of an exploration permit inform property owners of its existence.[84] Mining titles (the lands claimed by mining companies with a view to exploration) can be acquired via the Internet with a simple click.[85] More than 85 percent of the province's territory is available for such claims:[86] "To this effect, the principle of *transparency and access to information* should be incorporated into a new *Mining Act*. In fact, this principle is not at all required in the current law, and this has generated frustration among private property owners, municipalities, and First Nations. None of the above are ever informed or forewarned of the acquisition of a land claim by a third party on their land or territory."[87]

A company claiming a territory belonging to a municipality is not required to consult local authorities. When the company claims a zone on privately owned land, it is not obliged to obtain the consent of the owners – who may discover overnight that a mining company is suddenly (and legally) operating on their property. According to Section 235 of the existing *Mining Act*, the holder of a mining title may acquire "by expropriation, any property permitting access to or necessary for the performance of exploration work or mining operations."[88] The act however says nothing about compensation for expropriation.[89] In general, the owner has no alternative but to leave: any legal procedure to protect or reclaim property would require far too great an expenditure of money and time. To protect themselves against such threats, citizens have now taken to acquiring claims on their own property – which may cost them thousands of dollars over the years – in order to stop mining companies from obtaining the rights to the subsoil of their homes.[90]

The mining industry responds to its many critics with the kind of neo-liberal rhetoric that shows little regard for facts. In a May 8, 2008, letter to Montreal's *Le Devoir*, the director of the Quebec Mineral Exploration Association, Jean-Pierre Thomassin, asserted that the concept of free mining "demonstrated no pro-industry bias. In Quebec, any citizen may obtain a mining lease … The law gives an opportunity to everyone. Free mining is democratic and fair …"[91] According to Thomassin's theory, Quebec has become a gigantic casino where anyone can "try his luck." But the larger the company, the better the luck, or so it seems: a claim "can be renewed indefinitely, on condition that exploration costs are incurred ... However, the cost of exploration work that is supposed to be carried out on a given site can be attributed to other sites and applied to other renewal periods. Large and medium-sized mining companies use these laws to maintain their right to claims that have not been worked over long periods of time."[92] Given that large mine operators active in Quebec, from ArcelorMittal to Xstrata, are based in Toronto or in other countries, Quebec's economic sovereignty in a sector as vital as that of mining would appear to be quite limited.

In the name of the "democratic" principles praised by Thomassin, Quebeckers might want to demand the right to scrutinize the activities of the mining industry, the second most-waste-generating in North America after industrial agriculture.[93]

In areas where the existing *Mining Act* provides for the possibility of imposing some limitations on industry activities, the government appears unable to enforce its own laws. For example, MRNF inspectors are theoretically able to access mining sites in order to make sure the law is being respected. However, investigation by Quebec's auditor general revealed that "there was a serious lack of organization in the inspection activities."[94] In other words, even when the law appears to provide for supervisory mechanisms, the authorities do not necessarily apply them. In addition, in his report the auditor general emphasizes that the ministry of the environment and MRNF barely consult each other when it comes to enforcing the laws governing mining companies. And in any case, laxism prevails where environmental issues are concerned. Ecojustice reports: "no mining exploration project and only a minority of mining exploitation projects are subject to a public environmental impact assessment evaluation,"[95] though even exploration can have long-lasting impacts on the environment.[96]

In these circumstances, many Quebec citizens may feel that documentary filmmaker Richard Desjardins was right when he told journalist Yves Chartrand of *Rue Frontenac* that the *Mining Act* should be called the Act *for* Mining.[97] Close examination of existing legislation confirms that Quebec deserves its status as champion among mining jurisdictions. It also confirms that the mission of the Quebec government is to serve up Quebec's mineral wealth on a silver platter to the first investor to come along, who is generally a foreign investor. As for the regime that grants mineral rights on municipal or private lands – and on the lands of the Innu, Cree, or Algonquin – through the simple click of a mouse from an office in a Bay Street skyscraper, this is perfectly in tune with the colonizing spirit that underlies the economic system in every Canadian province.

Playing this game and using "good governance" principles, the government continues to gain time and postpone a genuine public analysis and reform of the legal framework governing the mining sector. While citizens continue to protest in public consultations, mining companies continue to exploit mineral resources, rake in the profits, and leave persistently negative long-term socio-economic consequences.

The Quebec Mineral State: A More Profitable Colony than All the Rest

In terms of attractive mining legislation, Quebec is a worthy rival to the resource-rich nations of the South where, because of their promise of record profits, Canadian investors often turn their hungry gaze.[98]

The Quebec mining haven warmly welcomes investors. For their operations in Quebec, these investors use the Toronto Stock Exchange with its ultra-permissive information disclosure regulations, just as they do for operations in Africa and Latin America; they also benefit from the many fiscal, financial, and legal advantages enacted at the federal level. The great majority of profits end up in the pockets of a handful of shareholders or administrators who can shelter their fortunes in tax havens. The Quebec government, in the person of minister of natural resources Serge Simard, spells it out clearly: "The reason Quebec gives mining companies so many advantages is to invite them to 'come and make money'."[99]

According to a document published by the influential Quebec engineering firm SNC-Lavalin, when deciding to invest in a given region, the mining industry seeks the following conditions: "clear, simple, and transparent mining legislation; a relatively rapid and transparent project approval process; free repatriation of profits and free foreign currency convertibility; a discreet governmental role in mining activities; an attractive geological potential; available and easily accessible geological information."[100]

Mining companies also require an infrastructure network that provides easy access to mineral deposits and cheap, abundant energy. Quebec appears to satisfy all these criteria, and this must be what Serge Simard meant when he told journalist Chartrand that the province has been recognized as "the world's most favourable place for investment."[101] Documentary filmmaker Richard Desjardins reaches the same conclusion. In an interview with *RueFrontenac.com*, he insisted that the MRNF must stop being a simple "transmission belt" conveying the interests of the mining sector to political authorities. He is right on target: the existing *Mining Act* "gives mining companies an unacceptable legislative power. The result is a banana-republic economy or worse. There are African countries that insist on more money than we do for their natural resources."[102]

Quebec has done more than just behave like a country willing to have its resources plundered: it also provided the inspiration and test bench for policies that the North would later apply to the South. Quebec invites the highest-bidding foreign investor to set up shop and loot its resources, exactly as resource-rich developing countries on which the World Bank or CIDA have imposed their famous "mining codes" today invite mining companies to "invest" in their mining resources. In Quebec, free-mining principles also apply to the plunder of most non-renewable resources, as was demonstrated by the recent rush on natural-gas exploitation – a sector that will continue to be regulated by the *Mining Act* until a specific *Hydrocarbons Act* is adopted (this was originally announced for 2011 but has now been postponed until at least 2014).[103]

According to Gordon Laxer, co-director of the University of Alberta's Parkland Institute, "a colony or a satellite state is a people who lose control of their resources to a foreign power."[104] A nation's economic sovereignty depends on its ability to control the management of its natural resources. Having sold control of its immense mineral resources to foreign transnationals, Quebec cannot ensure that the profits generated by their operations will be distributed to Quebeckers; instead, it allows foreign private interests, rather than Quebec citizens, to capitalize on our resources. Even more alarming, the examples of the pharmaceutical industry[105] and the wind-power industry[106] suggest that the same logic is being extended to the entire Quebec economy. How did it come to this?

Noir Quebec: A Century of Ecological Crime and Dispossession of Aboriginal Peoples

The mining industry's record in Quebec is a dismal one, comparable to the appalling record of mining companies in other Canadian provinces and to Canadian companies' controversial exploitation of the African and Latin American continents. The mining expertise developed in Quebec over the past century has given rise to a long series of environ-mental and human catastrophes. Today, having learned nothing from a development model that creates devastation, Quebec is preparing to apply a new, even more predatory version to areas still untouched by industrial development. Plan Nord, a project to open Northern Quebec to massive mining development, is likely to create environmental problems on an equally massive scale.[107] Even if development under Plan Nord puts into effect the "progress" that has been achieved in solid and liquid waste treatment,[108] such "progress" will be characterized by constantly shifting scientific parameters. And in any case, the dangers that the pollution caused by mining activity represent cannot really be measured, because mining involves destruction of ecosystems, extensive modification of the land's physical or natural features, an enormous demand for water resources, contamination of the air and surface and underground water by heavy metal, contamination of surface water by acid mine drainage, toxic particle emissions, production of waste matter that will disfigure the land for decades,[109] redefinition of energy production on a regional scale, and intensification of global warming (the mining industry is viewed as one of the world's largest emitters of greenhouse gases).

Applying this development model will entail serious consequences. For Quebec's Aboriginal and other populations, who are already suffering from pathologies linked to toxic substances in the environment, there is reason to fear the worst. North Americans will long suffer from the destruction to be carried out in the name of over-consumption, greed, and the market. In the judgment of future generations, there is little doubt that our societies will be found guilty of "ecological crime" on a world scale.

Tailings: The Price of Prosperity

Even if, overnight, the mining industry were to acquire through some alchemist's operation the ability to work without destroying the environment, ecosystems and the health of nearby populations, would still be threatened for decades by "tailings" – the dumping grounds

A Case Study

where the waste produced by mining operations is stored. Many of these dumps are now the responsibility of the government following the (often suspiciously well-timed) bankruptcies of mine operators. As usual, the Quebec taxpayer ends up footing the bill.

In 2007, Quebec officially acknowledged fifteen hundred hectares of tailings in need of remediation in Abitibi-Témiscamingue alone; in 2011, 1,199 hectares of tailings were listed for all regions of the province.[110] Major problems of tailings include the leaching of mineral acids (resulting from oxidization of the sulphur compounds unearthed by extraction on contact with the air or with surface or underground water), as well as the dispersal in the environment of highly toxic pollutants such as cyanide, arsenic, and mercury. Water becomes contaminated in the course of runoff or when it seeps through tailings or other mine installations. This contaminated, acidic water then flows into neighbouring water systems, leading to massive die-off of aquatic life; its toxicity can be fatal up to several kilometres away.[111] The problem of acid mine drainage is not limited to abandoned mines; it also affects those in operation.[112] In addition to acid mine drainage, "wind and water erosion have an impact far from the sites where residues are concentrated" – another unmonitored danger.[113]

The quantity of waste produced by mining companies is phenomenal. "An 'average' Canadian metal mine rejects 42% of the total mined material immediately as waste rock, 52% from the mill as tailings, 4% from the smelter as slag, with the remaining 2% comprising the 'values' for which the ore was mined."[114] In large-scale open-pit mines, daily mineral waste production is calculated in the tens or even hundreds of metric tons.[115]

Mine tailings are a poisoned inheritance. For Canadian taxpayers, the bill for decades of "laissez-faire" in this field will likely be huge. In 1994, the Mining Association of Canada itself estimated the cost of abandoned mine remediation in Canada at a total of $6 billion.[116] By

March 31, 2011, a total of 679 mine sites were listed in the inventory of the Quebec government's environmental liabilities, for a total of $891.6 million.[117] The health and environmental damage caused by the mining industry can only be assessed in the long term. The average mine is in operation for only a few years but the waste products left over after it is dismantled can have long-lasting consequences. According to Carol Ptacek of the University of Waterloo, "there are over 10,000 abandoned mine sites in Canada which have the potential to release unacceptable concentrations of metals to groundwater and surface waters for many decades to centuries after mining activities cease."[118] In some cases, according to the auditor general of Canada, time is running out and environmental catastrophe may occur if nothing is done.[119] In a 2002 report on abandoned mines in the North, she asserts that "in many cases, long-term site management will be needed because complete and definitive cleanup will not be possible."[120] Moreover, we do not really understand how long it takes for flora and fauna to be contaminated; a substantial part of the Canadian hydrographic system ultimately may be polluted. [121]

The effects of this progressive contamination may also be brutally amplified by accidents. When dikes built to contain mining wastes are breached, for example, a region's entire river system can be contaminated. A dam failure in a tailing pond at the former Opemiska mine near Chapais in June 2008 quickly sent an estimated one million cubic metres of water and 40,000 to 60,000 cubic metres of sediment flowing downstream from the site and caused copper, iron, and zinc pollution of a nearby stream, eventually affecting the Chibougamau River and the town's two thousand inhabitants.[122]

Given the scale of current mining projects (such as the Osisko project at Malartic, to which we will turn our attention below), there is ample reason for concern about the legacy we bequeath to future generations. Although Quebec's existing *Mining Act* stipulates that the operating company must meet 70 percent of estimated remediation costs, the province's auditor general has shown that companies' real responsibilities are strictly limited, since they provide for remediation of only part of contaminated areas, fail to honour financial commitments, and deal with officials who do not oversee mining sites and do not insist that payments be made on time.[123] Given these many worrying anomalies, the promise found in Bill 14, the 2009 "Mineral Strategy" to force companies to assume 100 percent of remediation costs, appears insufficient. It does not guarantee Quebec citizens that they will not be charged for the future remediation of present and future exploitation sites.

As usual, the mining sector, speaking through the Quebec Mining Association, makes every effort to assure us of its good intentions: "For the past fifteen years, the modern mining industry has ensured the restoration of mining sites where activities have ceased."[124] Given the Quebec government's reluctance to regulate its mining industry, Quebeckers can do little more than hope that these declarations lead to genuine and enforceable advances in remediation guarantees.

The problems of remediation are so serious that, even in the very accommodating "Mineral Strategy" document, the government recognizes the situation is catastrophic: "Mining lease holders have an obligation to rehabilitate mine sites after a mine closes. Despite this obligation and the increased awareness of mining companies, improvements to procedures for ensuring mine site rehabilitation are needed in order to avoid situations where the government again finds itself responsible for sites and their rehabilitation costs."[125]

The Quebec auditor general in 2009 wrote that it would cost $264 million to restore the 345 sites for which the government was responsible.[126] In September 2005, the government announced it was earmarking $7 million for the restoration of abandoned mining sites – a pittance compared with the hundreds of millions later unblocked by

Investissement Québec to shore up companies hit by the collapse of the real-estate speculation bubble. Faced with a long-term ecological crisis or a short-term economic crisis, the Charest government made its choice about where to channel Quebec's public funds.

Asbestos: Defending the Indefensible

In a May 2008 letter to the Canadian government, occupational-hygiene expert Trevor Ogden noted: "Canada has a pretty bleak reputation in most of the health science world."[127] In fact, asbestos is an issue that reveals Canada's hidden face, one that is at odds with the "good guy" image the country likes to project at home and abroad.[128]

Most of the asbestos mined in Canada is extracted in the Thetford Mines area of Quebec. Asbestos was once the pride of the Quebec mining industry, but its glory days are over, and the industry's future in Quebec is no longer assured.

Once hailed as a "miracle substance," asbestos was valued for its fire-resistance properties and used as insulation in the mid-twentieth century by the automobile industry in clutches and brakes and in the construction industry for its ability to insulate electrical wiring. After many studies proving that asbestos is highly toxic and causes deadly illnesses such as pulmonary fibrosis (also known as asbestosis), lung and bronchial cancer, and mesothelioma,[129] its use is now forbidden in most Western countries. The World Health Organization has declared that all varieties of asbestos are carcinogenic for human beings and that "stopping the use of asbestos now will only result in a decrease in the number of asbestos-related deaths after a number of decades."[130]

Canada took due notice of these health concerns, and asbestos today is not commonly used in Canada.[131] In 2010, however, Canada remained the world's fifth largest asbestos producer,[132] and although the two Canadian mines producing asbestos, both located in Quebec, suspended production at the end of 2011, in July 2012 the Quebec government stepped in to keep the industry alive by agreeing to lend the Jeffrey Mine $58 million to restart and expand. The loan was opposed by the Canadian Cancer Society on the grounds that it "would help propagate the world epidemic of cancers caused by asbestos."[133]

If this substance is to be avoided because of its health risks, what were the 100,000 metric tons produced in Canada in 2010[134] being used for? The answer: "Fully 96% of the asbestos that is produced in Canada is for export, primarily to developing countries such as India, Indonesia, and Thailand, where it is mainly turned into asbestos cement for construction."[135] There, populations unprotected by Canadian health regulations handle asbestos or come into daily contact with it, mainly because weather-resistant asbestos cement is used to construct water conduits.

With astonishing cynicism, against the international movement to ban asbestos and flying in the face of all the evidence, the Canadian and Quebec governments support the extraction and sale of a known carcinogen. Both levels of government finance the Asbestos Institute,[136] a lobby group composed of representatives of the Quebec government, the mining industry, and some trade unions, that was renamed the Chrysotile Institute in 2004 as part of a new marketing strategy. The institute does not hesitate to censor the reports of respected national and international scientific organizations for whom chrysotile asbestos is a deadly carcinogen.[137] It even launched a SLAPP libel suit against researcher Marc Hindry and his thesis director, François Desriaux, of the French asbestos victims' defence organization ANDEVA (Association nationale de défense des victimes de l'amiante), for a publication entitled *L'amiante au Canada: une industrie meurtrière et moribonde* ("Asbestos in Canada: a deadly and dying industry"). Confronted with fierce resistance by the defendants, the institute withdrew its suit in March 2009; according to ANDEVA, this was an "admission of guilt in the form of a withdrawal."[138] Hindry's report describes the diplomatic last stand of a government that is completely isolated and uses "methods that are unworthy of it." In a striking example of "dirty politics," in 2007 Canada even tried to "obstruct the posting of warning notices on asbestos shipments to Asian countries."[139]

Perhaps the height of cynicism is Canada's insistence on refusing to allow chrysotile asbestos to be included on the list of potentially toxic substances as stipulated by the Rotterdam Convention.[140] To justify this position, it is claimed that the chrysotile variant of asbestos produced in Quebec is less carcinogenic and thus not dangerous if used in controlled conditions.[141] At the meeting of the Rotterdam Convention in Rome in October 2009, bringing together the representatives of 126 countries, Canada stood alone in its stubborn refusal. Canadian representatives did not attend negotiating sessions; according to observers, this destroyed the conference and created a precedent that endangers its founding principles.[142] The obstinacy of Canadian representatives touched off strong reactions. Gopal Krishna of India's Ban Asbestos Network stated that the Canadians "in their naked lust for profit, are willing to sacrifice whatever reputation Canada has as a civilized nation."[143] Shrugging off international criticism, Canada, true to form, played for time by commissioning a study by a Health Canada subcommittee. At the 2011 meeting in Geneva, Canada again blocked the listing of chrysotile asbestos as a hazardous substance, a position opposed by dozens of scientists, environmental groups, and NGOs of all kinds.[144]

Quebec has never faltered in its role as provider of public funds to the asbestos industry, which has received both direct financing and loan guarantees, particularly from the Caisse de dépôt et placement du Québec. The federal government has also been supportive, and together the two levels of government are said to have provided asbestos mining firms with hundreds of millions of dollars since the late 1980s.[145]

While tax dollars have flowed generously into the accounts of the mining companies, mountains of waste have accumulated in Quebec's Eastern Townships region around giant open-pit mines. Today the rate of mesothelioma in Quebec is among the world's highest.[146] The results of a study published in 2007 in the *International Journal of Occupational and Environmental Health* revealed that earth, air, and dust samples from twenty-six homes in the Thetford Mines region indicated a high cancer risk to residents, particularly children.[147] As if to demonstrate that awareness of feminist concerns has not yet completely penetrated the higher spheres of government, the then minister responsible for the Chaudière-Appalaches region, Laurent Lessard, attempted to discredit the article by describing it as a "women's piece."[148]

This is the story behind profits in the mining sector. Public institutions provide millions of dollars to fund polluting mine operations that in turn cause the early deaths of hundreds of miners and put future generations at risk around the great craters and tailings created by the industry. Every year until 2011, thousands of metric tons of asbestos were exported to countries whose low safety standards ensure the profits of Quebec companies.[149]

To put an end to legitimate questions about what the government and mine operators are doing in their name, the government uses taxpayers' money to mislead them about the real dangers of asbestos mining and use. Taxpayers also provide indirect funding for libel suits against the voices that challenge the corporate line, since the legal expenses of companies that launch the suits are tax deductible.

The bankruptcies of LAB Chrysotile in 2007 and the Bell mine in 2008 appeared to signal the beginning of the true end for this "dirty business." However, given the Quebec government's unyielding commitment to the position that asbestos may be safely used, and given its objective, identified in the 2009 "Mineral Strategy," to "contribute financially to promoting the use of chrysotile,"[150] it seems that asbestos may still have good days ahead. At the very least, whatever the future of the asbestos industry, Quebec taxpayers can look forward to paying the rehabilitation costs entailed by the closing of these mines – costs that will certainly be enormous whenever the mines close for good.

Oujé-Bougoumou: Surrounded by "Kill Zones"

The Cree village of Oujé-Bougoumou is located 850 kilometres north of Montreal, in Eenou Astchee country (traditional lands of the Cree). The story of the people of Oujé-Bougoumou since the arrival of European settlers is a litany of abuse involving repeated expropriations (seven times in fifty years) and environmental and cultural destruction. The suffering visited on the Cree people in the twentieth century is part of the ongoing continent-wide genocide of the North American Indians, the ultimate aim being to "empty" the territory of its original inhabitants, whatever the price to be paid.[151] According to the Oujé-Bougoumou community website, the forced relocations were brought about by collusion between mining companies and the Quebec and Canadian governments, and were part of a deliberate policy to make the people of Oujé-Bougoumou disappear.[152] Since 1989, the six-hundred-strong community has been located on the banks of Lake Opemisca.

A dozen mines in operation since the 1950s on Oujé-Bougoumou lands, combined with the clear-cutting of the boreal forest, have destroyed wildlife habitat and the Cree way of life. Every departing mine operator has left behind immense tailings sites, some of which are extremely toxic (as demonstrated by the accident at Chapais in June 2008).[153]

Studies on the danger to populations from exposure to the toxic substances in mine waste are rare. It took the ingenuity of Christopher Covel, a graduate student in geology from New Hampshire who lived in the Oujé-Bougoumou community in March 2000, to reveal the potential risks of the widespread contamination of ecosystems in Eenou Astchee lands. Alarmed by the deformed fish without any eyes frequently caught by the Cree in the region's lakes and by stories of incurable disease, the young scientist decided to carry out extensive analyses of the air and water at Oujé-Bougoumou.[154]

At least three abandoned mines are located close to Cree lands. Around these sites, Covel discovered large "kill zones," spaces in which both plant and animal life is impossible because of the toxicity of the environment. The film *Heavy Metal*, a documentary by Cree film-maker Neil Diamond and Jean-Pierre Maher, shows the empty spaces expressing the desolation of this tormented land. Samples taken from the sedimentary basin and from riverbeds in the immediate area of the mines have given rise to a chilling verdict: they reveal concentrations of arsenic, chromium, cadmium, cyanide, and zinc up to two thousand times above normal. These contaminants flow into the river system of the Cree lands before emptying into James Bay. High concentrations of heavy metals from mining operations and waste products were also discovered in nearby lakes, in air samples, in fish, and in the hair of the local population. Although it was accredited by the United States Environmental Protection Agency, the Covel report was received with skepticism by the Quebec government, which of course is committed to the cause of the mining industry.

Before the report's explosive findings could reach Montreal, the industry had set its propaganda machine in motion. In 2002, a Montreal press conference at which Christopher Covel and representatives of the Cree Nation were scheduled to speak had to be cancelled.[155] A subsequent study by government-appointed "experts" then attempted to discredit the work of the American researcher. High-handed and yet uneasy in front of filmmaker Neil Diamond's camera, Eric Dewailly, a public-health specialist representing the government case, claimed that "this sort of testing reveals the contents of your shampoo rather than those of your hair."

Malartic: What Goes Around Comes Around

The Abitibi region of Quebec continues to serve up its resources to the mining industry on a silver platter. With the price of gold, copper, and zinc reaching record levels, mining companies are returning to dig deep into Abitibi subsoil, even when the quantities of ore to be found are minimal. Low-grade, high-tonnage deposits that require immense crater-like open-pit mines are the new model for an industry that can no longer find easy access to metals now that many ore-bearing veins are exhausted. But the impact of open-pit exploitation on the environment and local populations is far greater than that of underground mine operations. In the case of gold, the sodium cyanide lixiviation process makes it profitable to exploit ore bodies where metal concentrations are no higher than 0.02 or 0.03 percent. The process generates thousands of metric tons per day of waste contaminated with cyanide, a notorious poison. Use of cyanide by the mining industry is known to produce chronic local contamination and has exposed entire regions to environmental disasters caused by dramatic accidents.[156]

Open-pit extraction processes, such as the exploitation of the Alberta oil sands, reflect the mad rush for increasingly rare resources in a world where, thanks to hyper-consumption, the need for raw materials keeps on growing. Along with globalization, megalomaniacal operating methods are spreading from North to South and back again. To preserve its image at all costs, the industry continues to boast of how clean its techniques are. Mining companies, once the flagships of industry, now present themselves as technological flagships. These enterprises of devastation are even awarded the "sustainable development" label, whose value is diluted further each day.

One example of a recent open-pit mining project is the Osisko gold mine at Malartic, in Abitibi. (Others are Joanna at Rouyn-Noranda and Royal Nickel at Amos.) When the Osisko mine was announced, it was estimated that the project would involve digging a crater that in its final size would be 2 kilometres long, 780 metres wide, and 400 metres deep at the south end of the small town of Malartic;[157] that the mine would use 11 metric tons of cyanide, 25 million litres of water, and 30 metric tons of other chemicals every day; that it would generate some 55,000 metric tons of sterile waste; and that each ton of ore treated would yield approximately one gram of gold.[158]

The Abitibi region has already experienced the impact of the mining industry on its environment. Encircled by six immense tailing sites from nearly a century of mining operations, the city of Rouyn-Noranda is a perfect symbol of the negative environmental consequences of Quebec's mining industry.

However, promises of job creation and clean mining,[159] actively supported by the processes of manufacturing consent to which Quebec's mainstream media are tireless contributors,[160] convinced a significant fraction of Osisko's population to support the project. A psychological state reminiscent of Tunisian author Albert Memmi's portrait of the alienated colonial subject[161] seems to induce part of the Quebec population to accept a life of dependence on foreign capital, which flows in and out depending on the fluctuations of stock prices. Toronto-based shareholders stand most to gain from the mine, which gives no indication of generating any of the diversified economic activity it claims to stimulate. As Gilles Chapadeau, a union representative for the Quebec Federation of Labour (FTQ), noted in 2007, "the region is not profiting fully from the mining boom."[162] If mining were really capable of bringing lasting prosperity to the Abitibi region, its inhabitants would not be reduced to begging for a handful of jobs in order to survive, after ninety years of intensive mine operations.[163] Fifteen years from now, when the ore body is exhausted, the mine operator will move on to a more profitable environment, leaving hundreds of people to go back on welfare again to survive.

Like the villagers of Sadiola in Mali,[164] the people of Malartic were suddenly presented with an open-pit mining project. The project developer, Toronto-based Osisko, was able to take maximum advantage of the existing Quebec *Mining Act* to carry out its prospecting activities in the town centre. In Sadiola, it quickly became apparent that open-pit gold extraction was catastrophic for the environment and for the health of local residents,[165] and Abitibi is now being given a dose of the same medicine. The Osisko mine was given the green light by the government. Two hundred homes and five public institutions were "displaced" (read: destroyed),[166] and the mine began operations in May 2011.[167]

Before deciding to authorize the project, and given the substantial concerns raised by the local population, the Quebec government dispatched its consultative agency, the Bureau d'audiences publiques sur l'environnement (BAPE, or Public Environmental Hearing Office). In the name of pluralism, the agency invited all parties to attend hearings from which "recommendations" would be drawn up to guide the government in its decision-making process.

Once again, the scheme dovetails perfectly with the strategy of "good governance":[168] a style of administering public affairs that is designed to gain time in order to wear down organized opposition to a project.

On paper, the BAPE gives the local population an opportunity to be consulted, so that its "concerns and opinions are taken into account in the governmental decision-making process." However, the BAPE is a "quasi-legal" agency,[169] hardly a reassuring fact considering the "costs, the deadlines, the stress, and the undermining of the quality of life that legal procedures imply."[170] The agency's hearings at Malartic followed this pattern: tight deadlines were imposed, and no systematic financial

A Case Study

assistance was made available to citizens to help with procedures requiring the intervention of a cohort of experts. People directly threatened by the project exhausted themselves in preparing their case, while the mining company's financial resources gave it the advantage of coming to the hearings in the best possible conditions of preparation. BAPE hearings, in which the media play a prominent role, are now at risk of being transformed into a publicity platform.

Pierre André, a geographer who has been a substitute commissioner on the BAPE since 2002, stated in an April 2009 lecture at the Université de Montréal that the existence of the BAPE is vital to validating the decision-making process.[171] If this is true, then the BAPE is really a tool enabling the government to legitimize the operations of private companies by presenting decisions as the natural outcome of the democratic process. The Quebec government appears to be an expert in the perverse misuse of state institutions. A letter from a group of experts in public consultations (among them many ex-BAPE commissioners), published in *Le Devoir* on September 17, 2010, confirms the view that the BAPE has been gradually stripped of its purpose, with more and more restrictions being imposed on its original mandate to organize consultations. As an example, the experts cited the very short time given the BAPE to study the issue of shale-gas extraction and said they were worried about "the BAPE's loss of independence, or at least the subservience of the commission when giving an opinion on projects supported, if not already decided on, by the government."[172]

At Malartic, everything appeared to favour the company long before the decision was made known. Six months before the decision was given out, Osisko had already invested $350 million, houses had already been removed, and construction of the new residential area was well under way. The BAPE looked more and more like an elaborate masquerade in which the local population was encouraged to believe it could influence the final decision, while the only players whose opinions carried any weight with Cabinet were private mining firms. In July 2009, it came as no surprise that the BAPE approved the project.

Meanwhile, Osisko had instituted its own consultation process two years earlier in order to "maintain open communication and transparency as the project progresses."[173] The process drew its inspiration from the directives of the International Finance Corporation, a subsidiary of the World Bank. Osisko was applying, in Abitibi, methods that have been sharply criticized in the South.

Abitibi has often been described as a "resource region," and with the Osisko project, the meaning of this term is now apparent: it is a synonym for "colony." Local observers of the mining sector, such as geologist Jean Descarreaux, are quick to identify the colonial dynamic at work: "We're living in occupied territory," he says.[174] According to economist Marc-Urbain Proulx, the trend is to increasing concentration of capital. In an alarming article on the state of Quebec's regional economy, he suggests that "Quebec's regions are producing more and more wealth, but they are reaping fewer and fewer of the financial benefits." [175]

As the prices of raw materials fell in the 1990s, Canadian mining firms looking for profitable ventures exported their methods to the South. The companies' assets included expert skills in destroying the environment, wildlife habitat, and the socio-cultural balance of Aboriginal communities. These skills were highly useful, since at practically every latitude, mines tend to be located on Aboriginal lands.

The open-pit "supermines" currently in the exploration phase or under development in the South are the logical consequence of the export of Canadian know-how abroad. Having fully developed their techniques in Africa and Latin America over the past twenty years, mining companies today are reinvesting in Quebec, bringing their devastating methods home. For the inhabitants of Malartic, and the rest of Quebec, it looks like what goes around comes around.

Quebec's New Gold Rush: "Le Plan Nord"

The Quebec Liberal government's latest colonial project – Plan Nord – will facilitate the looting of the unexploited mineral and hydroelectric resources of Quebec's Far North, building on the solid foundations set down by the Quebec mineral state. Plan Nord inaugurates an era of the final destruction of boreal forest and Aboriginal territory.

"We are going to push back the limits of our last frontier," declared Jean Charest in a speech at Lévis in September 2008 to a group of Liberal supporters, at which he unveiled the new plan for the sell-off of Quebec's natural resources.[176] The energy and mineral potential of the project is described as immense: four thousand megawatts of hydro and wind power, along with uranium, nickel, platinum, palladium, gold, iron, copper, zinc, and diamond deposits.

Mining companies are already licking their lips, preparing for a new gold rush that everyone knows will be generously financed out of public funds. A close reading of the annual reports of the MRNF reveals that the Nord-du-Québec region has already experienced an invasion by junior mining companies. From 2002 to 2007, the number of exploration projects almost tripled, leaping from 90 to more than 250. Quebec taxpayers will be footing the bill to provide access to these far-flung territories. How else to interpret the recent earmarking of $106 million for construction of fifteen airports in Nunavik and on the North Shore?[177] True to form, the government justifies the expenditure by promising that Aboriginal peoples will have a better future and that resources will be exploited in a way that respects the environment. Catchphrases such as "partnerships with the First Nations" or the ever-popular "sustainable development" are put forward. But the true reasons for these publicly funded infrastructure projects are to be found elsewhere: the airports serve regions that look promising for mining, or where intense mining activity has already taken place in recent years (such as the Labrador and Ungava Trough in Nunavut).[178] The government confirms this direction in its 2009 "Mineral Strategy," allocating $350 million for the improvement or construction of new highways and airports over the next five years,[179] and in 2011 with the transport plan for Plan Nord, which includes infrastructure projects such as airports, highways, ports, and railways.[180] It will invest $1.191 billion in the development of this infrastructure between 2011 and 2016. [181]

The Assembly of First Nations of Quebec and Labrador (AFNQL) did not mince words when Chief Ghislain Picard asserted, in response to the Plan Nord: "For the time being, words are meaningless."[182] The First Nations will be the first victims of exploration in the North, particularly the Innu of Nitassinan, the Cree who live along the Rupert, and the Inuit who live along the entire Northern Quebec coastline.

The aspirations of the Innu of Quebec and Labrador should win the support of all Quebeckers who favour true sovereignty: "As peoples, and distinct nations, we have the right to self-determination, including the inherent right to self-government," explained Chief Picard.[183] Already, in 2008, he had called on the Charest government to "make a difference, to turn talk into action, to put an end to the colonialist attitude which still prevails in the relationship with the First Nations."[184]

The question of the First Nations is rarely raised in public debate in Quebec. But, by putting their lands at the service of foreign mining companies, and selling "clean energy to our American neighbors" at bargain prices,[185] the government has transformed Quebec into a simple protectorate, and has made it possible to continue with the destruction of First Nations traditional habitat and culture. Corruption being one of the world's most widely shared vices, there will always be a decorative group of Aboriginal representatives to legitimize the pursuit of the Quebec and Canadian colonial enterprise. It may be argued, however, that the July 2012 signing of a government agreement in the Eeyou Istchee James Bay territory between the Crees of Eeyou Istchee and the government of Quebec is a step forward. The Canadian Boreal Initiative sees the agreement as "an innovative model for indigenous governance across Canada's Boreal Forest."[186] In most cases, though, the intense positive media exposure given to such announcements that showcase "community representatives" is calculated to give Quebeckers a clear conscience.

Despite Jean Charest's explicit reference to Adélard Godbout, the Quebec premier who created Hydro-Québec, and to Jean Lesage's slogan "*Maîtres chez nous*" (Masters in our own house), it is hard to imagine how the Plan Nord devised by his government, focused on providing a maximum of corporate profits and a minimum of benefits for the First Nations and other Quebeckers, will allow citizens to exert long term control over the extraction of their natural wealth.

Mining companies' energy needs are immense, which brings Hydro-Québec into the picture. Hydro-Québec is skilled in presenting itself as a "green" alternative to fossil fuels. But hydroelectric dams operating far from Montreal and Quebec City, hidden from inquiring eyes, are actually generating environmental disasters on a continental scale. Moreover, although it is a state-owned corporation, and thus the only force that might offset the private companies that own most of Quebec's economic resources, Hydro-Québec's role in Northern Quebec actually seems to consist in blazing a trail for mining companies.

Two Hydro-Québec projects are designed to meet mine operators' expanding demand for cheap energy: the Romaine River project on the Lower North Shore of the St. Lawrence and the project to finalize the Rupert River dam. Once these projects have been carried out, all of Quebec's great rivers will have been harnessed, and the destruction of their natural cycles will be complete.

The Eastmain-1-A Project on the Rupert River has diverted 71 percent of the river's flow.[187] The project, scheduled for completion by the end of 2012,[188] involves routing the diverted water through a series of spillways and tunnels; 188 square kilometres have been flooded,[189] leading to the eviction of the Cree populations living in the region. Public investment in the project totals $5 billion.[190]

The Rupert River diversion project will launch a sequence of destruction that makes the word "sustainable" highly inappropriate. The long-term effects of such infrastructure changes on ecosystems, human beings, fauna, and flora are well known.[191] One example is the production of methyl-mercury, a toxic substance that poisons fish and ultimately humans, as a consequence of the creation of reservoirs behind power dams.[192] The mining boom that the government expects to launch with Plan Nord will dramatically increase the number of exploration companies operating in the region; in itself this is expected to cause damage leading to "major environmental impacts."[193] Mining companies are getting ready to act: "71% of new mining claims issued in 2008 were for Northern Quebec."[194]

The plan to colonize Quebec's Far North is the continuation of a development model that shows no consideration for impacts known to be catastrophic for the environment and for the populations directly involved. As usual, the dividends paid to shareholders in their California monster houses, their second homes in Switzerland, or their Florida condos will bear no trace of these externalities.

Uranium: A Planet-Wide Cataclysm Foretold

After twenty years in the doldrums, the price of uranium began to rise in 2003, heading for the stratosphere in 2007. By 2012, it had settled to a steady rise, fluctuating 2 to 3 percent each month. The civilian use of uranium, in particular, has been stimulated by "the growth of world demand for electricity and the need to reduce greenhouse gas emissions."[195] According to Geneva-based Gonet Bank, "28 reactors are under construction in 12 countries, in addition to 62 reactors in the planning stage and 160 as proposals."[196] Between 2003 and 2007, the price of uranium-308 (an oxidized form of uranium that is easily transported) leapt from $10 to $140 a pound, keeping pace with the surge in crude oil prices. Fears of impending peak oil are a source of hope for uranium-mine operators, who believe uranium will become the primary energy source in the future. The price of uranium-308 nevertheless fell to US$40 in early 2010, forcing many mining projects to be put on hold, and the Fukushima disaster in 2011 has caused a widespread retreat from nuclear energy in many developed nations, most notably Germany. By mid-2012, the commodity price of uranium-308 was US$49 a pound.[197] However, there is no sign of any second thoughts about nuclear reactors currently being built or planned in developing economies such as those of China and India, for example. [198]

In Canada, uranium mines have been operating for decades in Saskatchewan, Ontario, and the Northwest Territories. Canadian uranium may well have been used to build the atomic bombs dropped on Hiroshima and Nagasaki.[199] Canadian uranium was also extensively used in building up the existing American nuclear arsenal.[200] Though it is not widely known, Canada is the world's second-largest producer of uranium (more than 20 percent of world production)[201] and clearly intends to profit from the current uranium ore boom to develop its huge potential.

In Quebec, despite the absence of a uranium mining tradition, the Plan Nord is also motivated by the newly "greened" status of nuclear energy. Deposits in the Otish Mountains near the Rupert basin, along the North Shore (around the Baie Johan-Beetz-Aguanish area and in the Sept-Îles Nord sector close to the Romaine basin), and in the eastern part of Nunavut, have already revealed their mining potential and will be actively explored.[202] Exploration companies have also invaded the Outaouais region, filing hundreds of mining claims over the past four years.[203] This action has angered many local property owners who, discovering the absolute permissiveness of the existing *Mining Act* and the free-mining rights it confers on companies, have set up coalitions to oppose exploration (and eventually extraction) on their property. During the summer of 2010, a wide coalition of these property owners set up a permanent camp in front of the Quebec National Assembly, asking for a moratorium on uranium exploration and exploitation similar to those already established in other provinces and territories such as British Columbia, Nova Scotia, and Northern Labrador.[204] These groups are attempting to alert the population to the largely unrecognized consequences of uranium extraction and use. The mining lobby, meanwhile, has not hesitated to use the legal weapons at its disposal. In Ontario, Robert Lovelace, spokesman of the native inhabitants of the traditional lands of the Ardoch Algonquin First Nation, was condemned to six months in jail and a $25,000 fine for demonstrating peacefully against uranium-mining companies.[205] Six members of the Kitchenuhmaykoosib Inninuwug community, near Big Trout Lake in Northern Ontario, were also jailed for peacefully opposing the activities of Platinex Inc., a junior exploration firm.[206] An appeal court later reversed both decisions.[207]

The record of the uranium-mining industry explains why protest-ors are so determined despite the dangers they face. Uranium extraction has caused the worst disasters in Canada's mining history. In fact, the extraction phase is the riskiest of all the processes involved in uranium production.[208] Many pathologies have been diagnosed among miners: they are affected by radiation from uranium and its by-products; they ingest uranium by mouth or through their lungs; and they inhale radon, a gas generally present with uranium and known to cause lung cancer.[209]

Just as gold is extracted from low-grade, high-tonnage deposits, uranium is commonly exploited in ore bodies where the concentration is low. In Quebec, these concentrations are particularly low, typically in the range of 0.02 percent: this means 1,000 metric tons of ore are needed in order to get 2 metric tons of uranium, leaving behind 998 metric tons of waste.[210] Only uranium is extracted from the ore, while other radioactive by-products of the natural decomposition of uranium (radium, polonium, and thorium) are rejected and accumulate in tailing ponds. Uranium tailings also include heavy metals and toxic substances released by reactive agents such as sulphuric acid and ammonium chloride used during extraction.[211] These metals constitute a long-term danger for wildlife, vegetation, and the neighbouring populations. The half-life of uranium-238, the most abundant form (isotope) in the natural state, is four and a half billion years, and it takes several hundred thousand years for the radioactivity of thorium, radium, polonium, and lead to reduce significantly. This means that by extracting these minerals from the ground in massive quantities, humanity is indulging in one of the most hazardous experiments it has ever attempted.

Uranium, an award-winning documentary film by Magnus Isacsson, paints a horrifying picture of the history of uranium mining in Canada. Mining wastes from the twelve mines that operated at the peak of mining (1954 to 1958) near Elliot Lake, Ontario, have contaminated nearby river systems.[212] Water and fish in the region are unfit for consumption. Pollution dealt a final – and fatal – blow to the way of life of the Aboriginal community living along the Serpent River, the Jebwee, who were strangers to such destructive methods of development.[213] According to the Ontario Workers' Compensation Board, 116 claims for lung cancer among miners at Elliot Lake were processed in the 1990s.[214]

The Jebwee are not the only ones to have suffered the consequences of uranium mining. The waters of the Serpent River drain into Lake Huron, meaning that the entire St. Lawrence valley may be affected. Radioactive contaminants tend to be detected where they are least expected. In 1975, St. Mary's School in Port Hope, Ontario, had to be evacuated due to high levels of radon gas in the cafeteria. Large amounts of radioactive waste had been used to build the school and other buildings in the area.[215]

Uranium mining in Saskatchewan has laid waste to an entire region in the north of the province. More than ninety radioactive leaks were recorded between 1981 and 1989, each one an environmental disaster whose long-term impact on the ecosystem is not known. In 1983, six months after the opening of the Key Lake mine, 100,000 million litres of wastewater contaminated with radium, nickel, uranium, zinc, and arsenic were spilled into the environment.[216] Not long before that, the administrators of the Key Lake Mining Corporation (KLMC) had hailed the mine as the cutting edge of technology, the world's safest uranium mine. According to experts at the U.S. Institute for Energy and Environmental Research, effective monitoring of the impact of these wastes, whose radioactivity will not decline significantly for thousands of years, seems unlikely.[217]

Evidence of the disastrous impact of the uranium-mining industry on the environment will not stop companies from exploring for the mineral. Nuclear-energy generation also produces huge quantities of waste, the safe storage of which has raised issues of public interest worldwide. Memories of Chernobyl may be fading, but the risk of nuclear accidents and the tragedies that accompany them must not be forgotten.[218] The uranium to be produced in Quebec, despite the rhetoric with which it is enshrouded by the government and the mining industry, will be no exception to the rule. Moreover, there is every possibility that it will be used to manufacture nuclear weapons. Once uranium has been produced and sold, it is impossible to determine whether it will be used for civilian or military purposes.[219]

Most Quebeckers, the majority of whom consider themselves to be pacifists, and most Canadians, for that matter, would be fiercely opposed to massive government support for the uranium-mining industry if we knew more about it.

A Case Study

Conclusion: The Perfect Mineral State

When it comes to the mining industry, no other government in the world goes as far as Quebec's in providing a climate favourable to care-free and profitable operations.[220] The Quebec mineral state is in fact seen as a "standard" that the industry would like to see replicated worldwide. Journalist Diane Francis relayed this message in the *Financial Post*: describing what she considers a near-ideal business environment, she called on "every single province and territory [to] emulate Quebec's lead so that the country can take advantage of the 'supercycle' in commodities, thanks to Asia's industrialization, that will continue to keep prices high for possibly a generation or more."[221] Francis did not limit herself to Quebec, which makes perfect sense since, at the time she was writing (in 2008), seven Canadian provinces were listed among the world's top ten mining-friendly regions, according to the Fraser Institute.[222]

It is easy to understand why the world's mining industry would like to see the Quebec model widely adopted, particularly in terms of taxation, environmental regulation, and government support. In an auditor's report commissioned from the Quebec firm SNC-Lavalin (hardly a disinterested party because of the engineering and technical support it provides to the mining industry) on the reform of the Congolese mining code, we learn that "Quebec's expertise in mineral-resource management is internationally recognized and is often called upon by African countries at the government-to-government level, or through the intermediary of Quebec attorneys."[223] When the mining codes of countries with a confirmed geological potential come up for revision (an ongoing task undertaken jointly by the World Bank and CIDA in many African and Latin American countries over the past twenty years), Quebec legislation is used as a source of inspiration.

In this context, we are logically forced to consider the issue of corruption in relation to a part of Quebec's political class. It is certainly odd, to say the least, that political players in Quebec hand over so many advantages to the extractive industry without requiring a more substantial return for Quebec citizens.

It also must be pointed out that whatever its position as a Canadian leader, the Quebec mineral state could not exist in its unchallenged subordination of the public interest to mining interests if the mineral state structure had not been pre-established at the federal level, and if the public interest of Canada itself had not already been subordinated to the interests of the mining sector. Many of the characteristics of the Quebec system can be found at the federal level, both in terms of tax incentives such as flow-through shares and through direct financial support for the sector. From the environmental standpoint in general, and specifically in terms of the destruction of habitat and of Aboriginal cultures, dozens of instances similar to Oujé-Bougoumou can be found elsewhere in Canada. Others are under threat, such as at Thunder Bay.[224] It is no accident that Canada (along with New Zealand and the United States) is one of the few countries that initially refused to sign the UN Declaration on the Rights of Indigenous Peoples. Quebec can be seen as a microcosm of a much broader Canadian practice.

In Quebec, the government acts as neither regulator nor operator, but as promoter and service provider for the mining industry – just as countries of the South, under the tutelage of the World Bank, the IMF, and the WTO, have seen their (frequently corrupted) presidents reduced through the "good governance" game to the role of brokers touting their nations' resources and inviting foreign investors to pillage them. With jurisdictional rules that allow its territory to be fragmented, gaping tax breaks, and a lineup of public corporations that provide direct assistance and counselling to help firms maximize their profits, Quebec has historically offered a dream environment for the corporations that have come to the province to profit from its remarkable geological potential. Extractive-sector corporations are designated as "partners" of a government that does little more than manage the public relations spin on the "disagreeable" consequences of mineral extraction.

Like Quebec, Canada as a whole looks on complacently as the small amount of economic sovereignty of which it might still boast erodes ever further. Politically, even though its territory is rich in natural resources, Canada neither claims nor possesses any strategic reserve for its resources. An important change occurred in the past decade. According to data provided by Statistics Canada, "foreign-controlled mining assets jumped from $10 billion in 2005 to $54 billion in 2006. So, foreign control of Canadian mining actually rose from 12% to 48%."[225] At the same time, the country exports 65 percent of its petroleum and natural gas to the United States.[226] Inco, Falconbridge, and Noranda, giants of the Canadian mining industry, have been sold to foreign interests. Canada has abandoned its sovereignty, thrown its jurisdiction open to the international extractive industry, and transformed itself into a paradise for the extractive sector and a hell for ordinary citizens and for all those concerned with the common good.

CONCLUSION

Some Issues We Need to Address

Whether they like it or not, the vast majority of Canadians participate in the global financial adventurism indulged in by their extractive industries with the support of their government.

According to the Toronto Stock Exchange, some $439 billion changed hands in the mining sector in Toronto in 2011[1] – a figure that does not take into account assets that may be invested beyond Canada's borders, or especially, assets sheltered in tax havens.[2] Financial institutions, insurance companies, private and public funds, and other institutional investors to whom Canadians entrust their savings invest a sizeable portion of these funds in an industry that has come in for serious international criticism. In Africa, Latin America, Asia, and Eastern Europe, strong criticisms have been made of mining and oil companies that win concessions in ways over which citizens feel they have no control. From their bases in Canada, these companies enjoy virtual immunity from the consequences of the many misdeeds, or even crimes, of which they are accused beyond our borders. And here in Canada, those who raise critical questions about the extractive industry's record may at any moment be subject to a SLAPP (strategic lawsuit against public participation).

How did it come to this? To answer this question, we need to look at our collective past. We need to remember that, historically, development in Canada was driven by stock-market speculation. Investors in Canadian grain, lumber, railways, and mines were betting that the value of the shares they owned in companies that exploited (or coveted) Canadian resources would increase, and their gamble determined when the exploitation of Canadian resources would take place.

In this context, our settler ancestors did not come to create a specific nation, even less to establish a sovereign republic: they came to strip a territory of its resources. Moreover, they undertook this project as agents of the great monopolies (the Hudson's Bay Company, the Northwest Company, and other iconic members of the Beaver Club) whose interests determined how the colony developed, when and where new towns were established, and when and where land was conceded.

In general, this project was carried out with complete disregard for Aboriginal peoples. As Robin Fisher observes in his book *Contact and Conflict*, from the moment European colonists began to take an interest in gold mines in the western part of the country, First Nations lost the one and only function conferred on them by our colonial economy up to that point: "The reciprocity of interest between Indians and Europeans broke down because settlers came not so much to accommodate to the frontier as to re-create the metropolis. Vancouver Island and British Columbia were changing from colonies of exploitation, which made use of indigenous manpower, to colonies of settlement, where the Indians became at best irrelevant, and at worst an obstacle, to the designs of the Europeans."[3]

Reserves were created in which to corral these undesirable people, and the model worked so well that South African government officials took the Aboriginal reserves of Western Canada as a reference point when they came to design the repressive apparatus of the apartheid regime. Between 1948 (when the National Party took power in Johannesburg) and the early 1960s, representatives of Canada and the province of Manitoba proudly showed South African visitors the Canadian colonialist achievement. Documents from the Public Archives in

Ottawa indicate that in 1962, the federal government was still "eager to help" the visiting South African commissioner.[4]

Shaped by resource exploitation, Canadian institutions still reflect it today. Everything here was arranged to suit the interests of the powerful, to facilitate the operations of the largest firms, and to help them in their determination to seize whole categories of resources.

The earliest Toronto stock exchanges had no other purpose than to provide a framework for the financial flows defining Canada's vocation. London had originally been the place where people transacted land-based loans, negotiated property titles, speculated on mining resources, and issued bonds for the railways linking these commodities to international markets; beginning in the mid-1850s, Toronto offered to replace Montreal as the centre toward which speculative funds might converge. Crimes, lies, abuse, and greed were the fundamental characteristics of Toronto's intense stock-exchange activity, focused on promises of riches to come and the profits investors might earn from them.

The history of the Quebec and Ontario mining codes shows how laws have been specifically designed, up to the present day, to provide industry with free access to resources. Political bodies purposely designed to serve industry needs established the large-scale land appropriation system known as the claim system. They provided tax holidays and ensured no royalties would be paid to governments, gave large and regular subsidies, formally spelled out the right to pollute, and ignored the issue of how territories would be rehabilitated once they had been emptied of their wealth.

In the mercantilist context defined by the stock exchange, Canada developed to the point where today it has become a springboard for exploration and industrial projects to be carried out abroad – projects that are often vigorously condemned for their negative environmental, social, cultural, political, and social impacts by communities who do not understand how any form of economic "growth" could justify the damage they entail. This is the economic "know-how" that Canada is attempting to globalize today.

In a forthcoming work, we analyze the connections between Canada's extractive industry and Canada's contribution to the creation of contemporary tax havens in the Caribbean. The frenetic activity of speculators on the Toronto Stock Exchange, and the crimes and abuse it engendered, took place during the period of Canada's first expansionist ambitions, which initially concerned the West Indies and more generally the Caribbean. The Canadian banking sector experienced spectacular growth in this part of the world, and this led to the establishment of the first business districts of the area's "governments of convenience," which would eventually develop into some of the planet's most controversial tax havens. Today, our government even shares official diplomatic responsibilities with these offshore jurisdictions.[5] The inscrutable international financial system of which they are a part goes far to explain the drastic cuts carried out in the public finances of countries in the South, to the benefit of Northern actors who, along with elected dictators and complicit government officials in the South, reap the fruits of the system's corruption.

Through international institutions such as the World Bank and the International Monetary Fund, where it unquestionably carries weight, Canada has used its influence to spread its mining-industry model to countries of the South.[6] There can be little doubt that the Canadian government has acted within these institutions to favour the appearance in the South, such as metastases, of virtually identical, ultra-permissive mining codes that are curiously reminiscent of those enacted in Canadian history. In the South, just as in Canada, government decrees have allowed tax holidays and environmental laxism, and under cover of what is euphemistically known as good governance, national technocracies have developed to welcome foreign corporations and legalize their plundering. These are countries that suffer from chronic debt problems, and for years, every possible step has been taken to ensure their economic dependency.

Canada has used public funds to provide financial support for such international processes of colonial exploitation. One example – the Moanda Leasehold project in Congo-Kinshasa – epitomizes the kind of free-trade projects we usually associate with nineteenth-century European colonialism and its brutal disregard for local populations and their environment. This mining project, which would involve making over a huge area to foreign interests for a century to allow them to exploit power plants and natural resources for export purposes, is promoted by Canadian capital and elites as a flagship of economic cooperation and international development.[7]

When we consider these facts, it becomes easier to understand that if we require Canada to rein in its speculative stock markets, control the frightening excesses of the extractive industry, make this industry accountable to Canadian courts for the serious abuses of which it is accused in countries where corruption rules and justice is dead; if we ask Canada to break its ties with dictatorships that are complicit in exploiting resources, abolish its links with tax havens, publicly apologize to populations that have been harmed, set up programs to make reparations, and vigorously regulate the extractive industry to ensure minimal compliance with the principles that Canada claims to honour (as a UN agency, the Committee on the Elimination of Racial Discrimination, has explicitly asked it to do);[8] then we are expecting Canada to act as it has never acted in the past, and to put itself in opposition to the historical dynamic by which it was created as a country.

Canada began as a colony, its legal and regulatory framework conceived, planned, and developed to suit the great extractive monopolies belonging to a financial oligarchy, first within, and then beyond its borders. At every stage of Canada's socio-economic history, it has always been speculation on the value of land and its resources – and the unbridled exploitation of those resources – that positioned the country in webs of international trade.

After having been the object of speculation on international markets (the wood and railway "bubbles" of the mid-nineteenth century London Stock Exchange come to mind), Canada became the subject of its own colonial-style exploitation, providing local and international speculators with a political and legal environment that encouraged the generation of rapid profits on its mineral resources. That many of those early Canadian speculators were also in charge of the country's legislation and economic policies simply demonstrates that for some of our founding fathers, politics was the continuation of speculation by other means. As a colony, Canada was a mineral-producing state that was completely dedicated to its extractive industry, just as narco-states are completely dedicated to letting drug traffickers produce and sell drugs. Everything here was politically designed and developed to suit the great exploitation monopolies of a financial oligarchy. Then, because the spirit of the times required it, timidly and with many delays, Canada eventually achieved a certain form of sovereignty (through laws voted in London), without ceasing to be a monarchy and without our ceasing to be what we still are today: subjects.

More recently, by providing legal and political support to extractive sector corporations with disputed practices worldwide, Canada has become the springboard of an industry that has always remained colonial in its conceptions of economic activity and profit-making.

Perhaps it is time to reread Canada's history with an eye to this subtextual meta-narrative of colonial continuity. From its days as a colony of the British Empire, to the establishment of its own Dominion from Sea to Sea, to its participation in other countries' civil wars, to its all-out defence of the interests of the extractive industry in international institutions, Canada has reinvented itself time and again only to better serve the same interests: those of the speculators and exploiters of the resources of the world's land.

What then are we? As the "settlers" of the Canadian economy, throughout history we have acted primarily as agents of colonial exploitation rather than as "citizens" shaping a country through the exercise of our will. Moving further and further away from our historical memory of the metropolis, and thus from any historical awareness of what we are, we have come to believe in the originality of the world that was constituted for us. From one generation to the next, we have unconsciously handed down the habits and customs befitting colonial agents. Influenced by the ideology and management typical of former colonial jurisdictions, we have progressively developed euphemisms to describe ourselves: we say "middle class" to designate the settlers that we remain, and "elite" or "ruling class" to denote our colonizers with their often-sombre past.

As for the colonized, we no longer mention them. Canada's indigenous peoples are treated like a bad memory that won't go away and that we would like to handle with increasing doses of combined alcohol and repression. (Although Canada finally signed the UN Declaration on the Rights of Indigenous Peoples in November 2010, it was careful to specify that the declaration would not change Canadian laws.)[9]

Aboriginal peoples stood historically apart from the colonizers by virtue of their organic connection to place. They could not conceive of land as something to be used, exploited, and finally exhausted; they lived on it as in their element, and considered themselves a part of it. They looked on in horror as the settlers – agents of colonization intent on appropriating the gigantic profits created by the settlers' work – decimated the buffalo population, laid waste any territory thought to contain oil, emptied the soil of whatever metals it held, and diverted entire rivers to provide the energy to fuel runaway consumption. And all of it accompanied by effigies of God and legal texts to justify this frenzied and shameful agitation.

So it went until it all became a matter of vanity. Images of the Mounties, hockey cards, and plastic figurines of Iroquois stand as emblems of our "victory" over (respectively) the land, the climate, and the colonized, and have convinced us that this victory belongs to us. How we have loved Canada ever since. But we required the word "Canada" to stand only for certain things: a soundtrack to go with the images, a toothbrush logo, a backpack label, the name of a hockey team, a tall tale told around a campfire, or a brand of beer.

We feel pride in our national symbols, but take no responsibility for what they represent. Things are different when we are confronted with the fact that these syllables – "Ca-na-da" – do not have the same resonance to a person who has had no running water and no house ever since the time a Canadian planted a flag on his land, informing him at gunpoint: "This is my plane – this is my mine – this is my water, and this is my lawyer telling you that you've been here illegally ever since I bought you."

Things are different, too, when people in other countries confront us with the less-than-charming behaviour of our fellow citizens. In Latin America, people shout names at us. Africa thinks of us as passive accomplices supporting acts of atrocious barbarity. We are seen as imperialists in Asia and mafiosi in the Caribbean. Europeans laugh at our humanist pretensions. Chastened and confused, we continue to wave our maple leaf flag each July 1 in Ottawa, in the spirit described by Georges Perec in *Things*:

> It now seemed to them that before – and each day, that
> *before* receded further into the past, as if their anterior
> life was falling slowly into the domain of legend, of the
> unreal, or of the shapeless – before, they had had at least

a passion for possessing. Often it was wanting that had been all their existence. They had felt drawn towards the future, impatient, consumed with desire.

And then what? What had they done? What had happened?

Something resembling a quiet and very gentle tragedy was entering the heart of their decelerating lives. They were adrift in the rubble of a very ancient dream, lost amidst unrecognizable ruins.[10]

For the first time in history, we are feeling the pressure of world opinion. We have discovered that we too can play the villain's role. This is not the propaganda about ourselves to which we have been accustomed, and as self-respecting liberal democrats, this is not the self-image we like to carry around. So we turn to national roundtables of experts. We tell our naughty colonizers that we are angry with them. We threaten them with opinion polls. We send the prime minister preprinted post-cards in support of issues instead of talking about them, reminding him at the same time that we remain tourists in the colony's political life.

The time has come for Canadians to lay claim to a great democratic model. A tiny voice within us has begun to say: Faced with everything they're saying about you in the world, you need to give up your comfortable role as a settler and become a citizen. Open yourself to politics instead of viewing it as a tiresome electoral chore. Find the critical tools you need to think about the world. Be a step ahead of those who speak on your behalf, instead of following them. Do not allow your government to make you feel ashamed. Refute their sophistries instead of adopting them. Do something forceful instead of being satisfied with parroting colonial justifications.

What is to be done? We can begin by coordinating our efforts. There is no lack of potential.

Because emancipation is something for which each one of us has a personal responsibility, as citizens we need to provide ourselves with information through a large number of independent networks. The information we need ranges from case studies to overviews and includes analysis of the financial interests that govern us. Interdisciplinarity is essential, for to understand Canada and its foreign connections, we need to think in a unified way about issues of geopolitics, public-health, finance, history, sociology, taxation, law, and current affairs.

The establishment attack on information is so vigorous today that it is a clear indication of the value of this information, which we must not underestimate. Direct interventions and the use of alternative media can be multiplied to seek out perspectives other than the corporate viewpoint of our mainstream media.

Collecting and disseminating this alternative information is also the task of communities or diasporas concerned with the consequences of Canadian extractive industry operations. Many ties remain to be created between those who feel the impact of mining projects abroad and diaspora communities in Canada.

Approaching members of Parliament with critical ideas – instead of leaving the field to experts appointed from within the charmed circle of "governance" – can sometimes lead to promising outcomes.

Before us lies the major political task of building on the useful concept of "ethical" or "responsible" investment, even if some of the financial products claiming to comply with such standards do so in a purely formal manner. The underlying political principle is crucial: that people assume responsibility for the way their own collective savings, both public and private, are used, based on considerations that are not purely monetary.

Sustained political and legal support is required to help researchers, intellectuals, activists, and other citizens facing corporate lawsuits (SLAPPs) intended to silence them. Similar movements could also be established to support legal action in Canada against companies that are active in the South and against whom many serious allegations have been made.

These are the considerations that underlie our collective responsibilities at the beginning of the twenty-first century.

Endnotes

Introduction
Canada: Home to a Dangerous Industry

1   "Uranium in Canada," World Nuclear Association (London), May 2012, http://
    www.world-nuclear.org/info/inf49.html; and "Canada Still One of World's Largest
    Exporters of Chrysotile Asbestos," joint statement of the Canadian Public Health
    Association, Canadian Medical Association, and National Specialty Society for
    Canadian Medicine, Canadian Public Health Association (Ottawa), June 30, 2010,
    http://www.cpha.ca/uploads/media/asbestos_f.pdf.

2   Camille De Vitry, *Le Prix de l'or*, documentary film (France : Les Productions
    Cam, 2004), and *L'or nègre* (Lyon: Éditions Tahin Party, 2009).

3   "Canadian Gold Mining Interests Involved in Police Shootings in Ghana,
    West Africa" (Ottawa: MiningWatch Canada, December 30, 1999), http://www.
    miningwatch.ca/canadian-gold-mining-interests-involved-police-shootings-
    ghana-west-africa.

4   Christophe Lutundula, Rapport des travaux de la commission spéciale chargée
    de l'examen de la validité des conventions à caractère économique et financier
    conclues pendant les guerres de 1996–1997 et de 1998, 1ere partie (Kinshasa:
    Assemblée Nationale, République démocratique du Congo, 2003), www.con-
    gonline.com/documents/Rapport_Lutundula_pillage_2006.pdf. This report
    was classified top secret when signed between 1996 and 2003, but was leaked
    in 2006. See Freddy Mulongo, « Où est le rapport Lutundula sur le pillage des
    ressources ? » report broadcast October 15, 2009, Réveil-FM, http://reveil-fm.
    com/index.php/2009/10/15/527-fde.

5   Ian Smillie, Lansana Gberie, and Ralph Hazleton, *The Heart of the Matter: Sierra
    Leone, Diamonds, and Human Security* (Ottawa: Partnership Africa Canada,
    January 2000), http://pacweb.org/Documents/diamonds_KP/heart_of_the_
    matter-full-2000-01-eng.pdf.

6   Dominic Johnson, *Les Sables mouvants. L'exploration du pétrole dans le Graben
    et le conflit congolais* (Goma : Pole Institute, March 2003), 9, www.pole-institute.
    org/documents/heritagefr.pdf; African Unification Front, "Canadian Mercenary
    Corporation Strikes Oil in Uganda: Oil Is Potential Source of Conflict in Great
    Lakes Region," 1998, http://www.africanfront.org/234.php; Lisa Rimli, « Krieg-

swirtschaft in Friedenszeiten, Die private Sicherheits-industrie in Angola», in Dario Azzellini und Boris Kanzleiter, *Das Unternehmen Krieg, Paramilitärs, Warlords, und Privatarmeen als Akteure der neuen Kriegsordnung* (Berlin: Assoziation A, 2003), 163–64; and Laurence Mazure, «Lucrative reconversion des mercenaires sudafricains», *Le Monde diplomatique* (Paris), October 1996, 22–23, http://www. monde-diplomatique.fr/1996/10/MAZURE/7295.

7 Alain Deneault with Delphine Abadie and William Sacher, *Noir Canada : Pillage, corruption, et criminalité en Afrique* (Montréal : Éditions Écosociété, 2008).

8 The NGO Working Group on the Export Development Corporation [Export Development Canada], *Reckless Lending: How Canada's Export Development Corporation Puts People and Environment at Risk*, vol. 2 (Ottawa: Halifax Initiative, May 15, 2001), http://www.halifaxinitiative.org/content/reckless-lending-volume-ii.

9 Canadian International Development Agency (CIDA), "Project Profile: Senegal Railway Sector," *Infrastructure Services Performance Review: Summary of Results* (Gatineau: n.d.), 11, http://www.acdi- http://www.acdi-cida.gc.ca/INET/IMAGES. NSF/vLUImages/Performancereview5/$file/ISPR_E_Results.pdf.

10 Millenia Hope Biopharma, "Heenan Blaikie, Jean Chretien Team with Millenia Hope in a Crusade against Malaria," news release, July 11, 2006, http://www. biospace.com/News/heenan-blaikie-jean-chretien-team-with-millenia/23887.

11 Based on five International Rescue Committee studies, the IRC estimates in excess of 5.4 million deaths between August 1998 and April 2007. See Benjamin Coghlan, Pascal Njoy, Flavien Mulumba, Colleen Hardy, Valerie Nkamgang Bemo, Tony Stewart, Jennifer Lewis, and Richard Brennan, *Mortality in the Democratic Republic of Congo: An Ongoing Crisis* (New York: International Rescue Committee, 2007), ii.

12 Lutundula 2003; Mulongo 2009.

13 United Nations Panel of Experts on the Illegal Exploitation of Natural Resources and Other Forms of Wealth of the Democratic Republic of Congo, final report, S/2002/1146, October 16, 2002, para. 131, http://www.victorbout.com/ Documents/S_2002_1146_Congo.pdf.

14 Barrick Gold, "Barrick Announces Inaugural Members of Corporate Social Responsibility Advisory Board," news release, March 2, 2012, http://www.barrick. com/Theme/Barrick/files/docs_pressrelease/2012/Barrick-Announces-Inaugural-Members-of-CSR-Advisory-Board.pdf.

15 Randall Oliphant, president and chief executive officer of Barrick Gold, speech presented at annual meeting to shareholders, Toronto, May 8, 2001, http://www. barrick.com/Theme/Barrick/files/docs_presentations/pr5_8_2001_alanan.pdf.

16 Douglas Goold and Andrew Willis, *The Bre-X Fraud* (Toronto: McClelland & Stewart, 1997), 96.

17 Joe Clark and Associates, "Who We Are," http://www.maureenmcteer.com/who-we-are/joe-clark, consulted June 19, 2012.

18 Chen-I Lin and Allison Schuster, "Hydroelectricity Investment in Democratic Republic of the Congo: The Grand Inga," paper prepared for civil and environmental engineering (Lin) and political science (Schuster) departments, Tufts University, March 2009, http://wikis.uit.tufts.edu/confluence/display/aquapedia/Hydroelectricty+Investment+in+the+Democratic+Republic+of+the+Congo+-+The+Grand+Inga; and « Avant-projet international Moanda, site promotionnel », http://s4.e-monsite.com/2011/05/27/72955536plagiat-1-pdf.pdf.

19 "Gabon: The Power to Diversify," special advertising section, *OMNIA International* (Paris and Geneva), n.d., S5, http://www.timeincnewsgroupcustompub.com/sections/061225_Gabon.pdf.

20 Karyn Keenan, *Canadian Mining: Still Unaccountable*, NACLA report on the Americas, May–June 2010, https://nacla.org/sites/default/files/A043030031_8.pdf.

21 Brett Popplewell, "Canadian Firms Face Abuse Allegations," *The Star* (Toronto), November 22, 2009, http://www.thestar.com/news/canada/article/729147--canadian-mining-firms-face-abuse-allegations.

22 Janet Bagnall, "Canadian Mining Companies, Behaving Badly: Liberal Bill Would Try to Rein in Some Ruthless International," *The Gazette* (Montreal), February 5, 2010, http://www2.canada.com/montrealgazette/news/yourbusiness/story.html?id=d50c75d5-31f4-43d7-934a-4123fda6c8d4.

23 Fernando Cabrera Diaz, "El Salvador Government Considers Ban on Mining as Permit Freeze Leads to CAFTA Arbitration," September 2, 2009, http://www.iisd.org/itn/2009/08/31/el-salvador-government-considers-ban-on-mining-as-permit-freeze-leads-to-cafta-arbitration/.

24 *OECD Guidelines for Multinational Enterprises*, 2008, http://www.oecd.org/dataoecd/56/36/1922428.pdf; Cameron French, "Guatemalan Groups File Complaint on Goldcorp Mine: Community Groups Allege Water Contamination, Illness," *Reuters*, December 9, 2009, http://www.reuters.com/article/idAFN0923516520091209.

25 Rory Carroll, "Gold Giant Faces Honduras Inquiry into Alleged Heavy Metal Pollution: Villagers and NGOs Have Accused Goldcorp of Poisoning People and Livestock by Contaminating the Siria Valley," *The Guardian* (London), December 31, 2009, http://www.guardian.co.uk/environment/2009/dec/31/goldcorp-honduras-pollution-allegations?INTCMP=SRCH.

26 MiningWatch Canada, report from the March 20–27, 2010, fact-finding delegation to Chiapis, Mexico, to investigate the assassination of Mariano Abarca Roblero and the activities of Blackfire Exploration Ltd., 2, http://www.miningwatch.ca/sites/miningwatch.ca/files/Chiapas_delegation_report_exec_sum_web.pdf.

27 Karyn Keenan, *Canadian Mining: Still Unaccountable*, NACLA report on the Americas, May–June 2010, https://nacla.org/sites/default/files/A043030031_8.pdf.

28 Asad Ismi, "Profiting from Repression: Canadian Investment in and Trade with Colombia," *Americas Update*, November 2000, http://www.asadismi.ws/colombiareport.html.

29 Deneault, Abadie, and Sacher 2008.

30 Yves Engler, *The Black Book on Canadian Foreign Policy* (Black Point, NS: Fernwood Publishing and Vancouver: RED Publishing, 2009).

31 Joan Baxter, *Dust from Our Eyes: An Unblinkered Look at Africa* (Hamilton, ON: Wolsak and Wynn, 2008).

32 MiningWatch Canada, "Canadian Gold Mining Interests Involved in Police Shootings in Ghana, West Africa," December 30, 1999, http://www.miningwatch. ca/canadian-gold-mining-interests-involved-police-shootings-ghana-west-africa.

33 *British North America Act of 1867.* See *Constitution Act, 1867,* 30 & 31 Victoria, c. 3 (U.K.), R.S.C. 1985, App. II, No. 11, http://laws.justice.gc.ca/eng/Const/page-1.html.

34 Alain Deneault, *Offshore: Tax Havens and the Rule of Global Crime,* translated by George Holoch (New York: New Press, 2012).

35 The mining and quarrying sector (excluding oil and gas) paid corporate taxes in 2010 to the value of \$1.129 billion, according to Statistics Canada, Table 1-9, "Summary Table – Corporate Income Taxes Paid by Industries," *Financial and Taxation Statistics for Enterprises,* Catalogue 61-219-X 35 (Ottawa: Statistics Canada, 2010), 35, http://www.statcan.gc.ca/pub/61-219-x/61-219-x2010000-eng.pdf.

36 Alain Deneault and Aline Tremblay, *Mapping Financial Secrecy, report on Canada* (London: Tax Justice Network, October 2011), http://www.secrecyjurisdictions. com/PDF/Canada.pdf.

37 The World Bank, "Canada and the World Bank Group," 2011, http://web.worldbank. org/WBSITE/EXTERNAL/COUNTRIES/CANADAEXTN/0,,contentMDK:207 18286~menuPK:1879418~pagePK:1497618~piPK:217854~theSitePK:519567,00. html; and Government of Canada, *report on operations under the Bretton Woods and related agreements,* http://www.fin.gc.ca/bretwood/bretwd99_1-eng.asp.

The Argument
Canada: Tax Haven for the World's Extractive Sector

1 TMX Group, "A Capital Opportunity: Mining," slide presentation, slide 22, http:// www.tmx.com/en/pdf/Mining_Presentation.pdf, consulted August 17, 2012.

2 Ibid., slide 17.

3 Ibid., slide 20.

4 Ibid.

5 Department of Foreign Affairs and International Trade (DFAIT), "Building the Canadian Advantage: A Corporate Social Responsibility (CSR) Strategy for the Canadian International Extractive Sector," March 2009, http://www.international.gc.ca/trade-agreements-accords-commerciaux/ds/csr-strategy-rse-stategie. aspx?lang=eng&view=d.

6 TMX Group, "A Capital Opportunity: Mining," slide 13.

7 Douglas Goold and Andrew Willis, *The Bre-X Fraud* (Toronto: McClelland & Stewart, 1997).

8   *R. v. Felderhof*, 2007 ONCJ 345 (CanLII), http://canlii.ca/t/1sbq4.

9   National Instrument 43-101 *Standards of Disclosure for Mineral Projects* (NI 43-101), http://www.osc.gov.on.ca/en/15019.htm.

10 Canadian Institute of Mining, Metallurgy, and Petroleum (CIM), "CIM Mineral Property Valuation Committee (CIMVal)," *Standards and Guidelines for Resources and Reserves*, August 17, 2012, http://web.cim.org/standards/MenuPage. cfm?sections=214&menu=279.

11 *TSX Venture Exchange Corporate Finance Manual*, Appendix 3F, June 14, 2010, http://www.tmx.com/en/pdf/Appendix3F.pdf.

12 John M. Sibley, "Mineral Project Disclosure Standards: An Assessment of Recent Canadian Experience," *Journal of Energy and Natural Resources* 20, no. 364 (2002): 369.

13 Scott Wright, "Junior Golds 101," *Zeal Intelligence*, February 25, 2005, www.zealllc. com/2005/juniors.htm.

14 Ibid.

15 A. C. Noble, "Geologic Resources vs. Ore Reserves," *Mining Engineering* (February 1993): 173–78, quoted in T. R. Ellis, D. M. Abbott Jr., and H. J. Sandri, "Trends in the Regulation of Mineral Deposit Valuation," paper presented at Society of Mining, Metallurgy, and Exploration (SME) annual meeting, Denver, CO, March 1–3, 1999, 2, www.mineralsappraisers.org/99-029.pdf.

16 Virginia Heffernan, "Mineral Property Valuation: International Movement to Standardize Property Evaluation Gathers Momentum," *Engineering and Mining Journal, Mining Media* (August 2004): 21–26 at 21, www.geopen.com/samples/ vh_propertyvaluationaugust2004.pdf.

17 Thierry Michel, *Katanga Business,* documentary film press kit (Belgium : Les Films de la Passerelle, Les Films d'Ici, and RTBF, 2009), http://www.clorofilm. ro/userfiles/Katanga_Dossier_de_presse_EN.pdf2; documentary film available at http://www.youtube.com/watch?v=io1cVXwOhJo.

18 National Instrument 43-101 *Standards of Disclosure for Mineral Projects* (NI 43-101), http://www.osc.gov.on.ca/en/15019.htm.

19 Heffernan 2004, 22, 24.

20 Alain Deneault with Delphine Abadie and William Sacher, *Noir Canada : Pillage, corruption, et criminalité en Afrique* (Montréal : Éditions Écosociété, 2008).

21 Claude Lamoureux, keynote speech presented at "Transparency and Corporate Integrity," the Canadian Institute of Chartered Accountants (CICA) National Financial Reporting conference, Toronto, September 11, 2007, http://docs.otpp. com/CICA_ClaudeLamoureux_Sep07.pdf.

22 William J. McNally and Brian F. Smith, "Do Insiders Play by the Rules?", *Canadian Public Policies – Analyse de politiques* XXIX no. 2 (2003): 125–44 at 137, http:// investorvoice.ca/Research/Laurier_IT_2003.pdf.

23 *Sarbanes-Oxley Act* of 2002, Pub.L. 107-204, 116 Stat. 745, enacted July 29, 2002, http://www.gpo.gov/fdsys/pkg/PLAW-107publ204/content-detail.html.

24 Toronto Stock Exchange Committee on Corporate Governance in Canada, *Where Were the Directors? Guidelines for Improved Corporate Governance in Canada*, 1994, http://www.ecgi.org/codes/documents/dey.pdf.

25 Stéphane Rousseau, « La gouvernance d'entreprise en droit canadien, convergence, et divergence », in *La gouvernance juridique et fiscale des organisations*, edited by Jean-Luc Rossignol, 91–113 (Paris : Lavoisier, 2010), 101, our translation.

26 Ibid., 105, our translation; and Denizon, "How to Reduce Costs When Complying with SOX 404," posted May 2, 2012, http://www.denizon.com/governance/how-to-reduce-costs-when-complying-with-sox-404/.

27 Multilateral Instrument 52-111 *Reporting on Internal Control over Financial Reporting* (MI 52-111), February 9, 2007, http://www.osc.gov.on.ca/en/13558.htm.

28 Canadian Securities Administrators Notice 52-313 *Status of Proposed Multilateral Instrument 52-111 Reporting on Internal Control over Financial Reporting and Proposed Amended and Restated Multilateral Instrument 52-109 Certification of Disclosure in Issuers' Annual and Interim Filings*, March 10, 2006, http://www.osc.gov.on.ca/en/SecuritiesLaw_csa_20060310_52-313_status-52-111.jsp.

29 Defined in sec. 3.1 and 3.4 of National Instrument 58-201 *Corporate Governance Guidelines*, http://www.osc.gov.on.ca/en/SecuritiesLaw_rule_20050617_58-201_corp-gov-guidelines.jsp NI 58-201. The definition for "independence" appears in sec. 2.1.

30 Rousseau 2010, 102, our translation.

31 Ibid., 108, our translation.

32 Association pour la taxation des transactions financières et pour l'action citoyenne (ATTAC), *La Bourse contre la vie : Dérive et excroissance des marchés financiers* (Montréal : Éditions MultiMondes, 2010), 73, 74, 112, our translation.

33 Ibid., 74, our translation.

34 Patrick Chabal and Jean-Pascal Daloz, *L'Afrique est partie! Du désordre comme instrument politique* (Paris : Economica, 1998).

35 Béatrice Hibou, « Le 'capital social' de l'État falsificateur », in *La criminalisation de l'État en Afrique*, edited by Jean-François Bayart, Stephen Ellis, and Béatrice Hibou, 106–58 (Brussels : Éditions Complexe, 1997), 136, our translation.

36 National Roundtables on Corporate Social Responsibility (CSR) and the Canadian Extractive Industry in Developing Countries, Advisory Group Report, March 29, 2007, http://www.pdac.ca/pdac/misc/pdf/070329-advisory-group-report-eng.pdf.

37 Janis Sarra and Vivian Kung, "Corporate Governance in the Canadian Resource and Energy Sectors," *Alberta Law Review* 43, no. 4 (2006): 905–61 at 961.

38 National Instrument 51-102 *Continuous Disclosure Obligations* (NI 51-102), November 18, 2011, http://www.osc.gov.on.ca/en/13342.htm.

39 Canadian Securities Administrators Staff Notice 51-333 *Environmental Reporting Guidance*, October 27, 2010, 3, 5, http://www.osc.gov.on.ca/documents/en/Securities-Category5/csa_20101027_51-333_environmental-reporting.pdf.

40   Claire Woodside, *Lifting the Veil: Exploring the Transparency of Canadian Companies* (Ottawa: Publish What You Pay – Canada, 2009), 14, http://www.pacweb. org/Documents/PWYP/Lifting_the_veil-Nov2009.pdf.

41   National Instrument 43-101 *Standards of Disclosure for Mineral Projects.*

42   National Instrument 51-101 *Standards of Disclosure for Oil and Gas Activities* (NI 51-101), December 24, 2010, http://www.osc.gov.on.ca/en/13338.htm.

43   Canadian Securities Administrators Staff Notice 51-333 *Environmental Reporting Guidance*, October 27, 2010, http://www.osc.gov.on.ca/en/29620.htm; and Derek Wong, "New Environmental Disclosure Guidance from Canadian Regulators," November 10, 2010, http://www.carbon49.com/2010/11/new-environmental-disclosure-guidance-from canadian-regulators/.

44   NI 51-102, Form 2, *Annual Information Form* (AIF), sec. 5.1(4), quoted in Woodside 2009, 27.

45   Mary Kimani, "L'industrie minière africaine : Les États cherchent à négocier des contrats équitables," *Afrique Renouveau* 23, no. 1 (2009): 4–5, http://www.un.org/ fr/africarenewal/vol23no1/ar-23no1-fr.pdf.

46   Gaétan Breton, « Des comptes et des contes », *À Babord* (Montréal) 26 (October–November 2008): 12, our translation, http://www.ababord.org/spip.php?article741.

47   Libération Afrique, "European Parliament Supports Mandatory Reporting by Oil, Gas, and Mining Companies for Each Country of Operation," November 14, 2007, http://www.liberationafrique.org/spip.php?article2022.

48   Woodside 2009, 17.

49   Alain Deneault, *Offshore: Tax Havens and the Rule of Global Crime*, translated by George Holoch (New York: New Press, 2012).

50   *Congo Conflict Minerals Act of 2009* (CCMA), S. 819, United States Congress, http://www.gpo.gov/fdsys/pkg/BILLS-111s891is/pdf/BILLS-111s891is.pdf.

51   *CCMA*, sec. 4(d)(2)(C).

52   *The Dodd-Frank Wall Street Reform and Consumer Protection Act* (*Dodd-Frank*), Public Law 111-203, sec. 1502, United States Congress, January 5, 2010, http://www. gpo.gov/fdsys/pkg/BILLS-111hr4173enr/pdf/BILLS-111hr4173enr.pdf.

53   *CCMA*, sec. 4(3).

54   *Dodd-Frank*, sec. 1504.

55   Dominic Johnson, "Who's in Charge? Putting the Mineral Trade in Eastern DRC under International Control: An Overview," in *Blood Minerals: The Criminalization of the Mining Industry in Eastern DRC*, 22–45 (Goma: Pole Institute, August 2010), 44, http://www.friendsofthecongo.org/pdf/blood_minerals_pole_aug2010. pdf.

56   Thierry Michel, *Katanga Business,* documentary film press kit (Belgium : Les Films de la Passerelle, Les Films d'Ici, and RTBF, 2009), http://www.clorofilm. ro/userfiles/Katanga_Dossier_de_presse_EN.pdf2; documentary film available at http://www.youtube.com/watch?v=i01eVXwOhJo.

57 Sarah McHaney and Peter Veit, "Stopping the Resource Wars in Africa" (Washington: World Resources Institute, August 10, 2009), http://www.wri.org/stories/2009/08/stopping-resource-wars-africa.

58 Alberto Acosta, "La Maldición de la Abundancia" (Quito : Abya-Yala, 2009), available at http://www.abyayala.org/informacion.php?CODLIBRO=1809&FAC_CODIGO=.

59 Lutundula 2003.

60 Erik Kennes, « Du Zaïre à la République démocratique du Congo : Une analyse de la guerre de l'Est », special issue on Femmes d'Afrique, L'Afrique politique (1998) : 175–204 (Paris : Karthala, 1998), 203n111.

61 Nestor Kisenga, « Mines : des milliards de boni pour le 'quatrième pillage' », Congolite, July 25, 2006, http://www.congolite.ca/economy61.htm, quoted in Deneault, Abadie, and Sacher 2008, 82, our translation.

62 Lutundula 2003; United Nations High Commissioner for Human Rights, Democratic Republic of Congo, 1993–2003, report of the mapping exercise documenting the most serious violations of human rights and international humanitarian law committed within the territory of the Democratic Republic of the Congo between March 1993 and June 2003 (unofficial translation from French original), August 2010, sec. 774, http://www.ohchr.org/Documents/Countries/ZR/DRC_MAPPING_REPORT_FINAL_EN.pdf; All-Party Parliamentary Group on the Great Lakes Region of Africa 2003; Sénat belge, Rapport : Commission d'enquête parlementaire chargée d'enquêter sur l'exploitation et le commerce légaux et illégaux de richesses naturelles dans la région des Grands Lacs au vu de la situation conflictuelle actuelle et de l'implication de la Belgique, document législatif no. 2-942/1, session de 2002–2003 (Brussels : Sénat de Belgique, February 20, 2003), http://www.senate.be/www/?MIval=/publications/viewPub&COLL=S&LEG=2&NR=942&PUID=33578926&LANG=fr; Laurence Juma, "The War in Congo: Transnational Conflict Networks and the Failure of Internationalism," Gonzaga Journal of International Law 10, no. 2 (2006): 97, http://www.gonzagajil.org/pdf/volume10/Juma/Juma.pdf.

63 Ian Smillie, Lansana Gberie, and Ralph Hazleton, The Heart of the Matter: Sierra Leone, Diamonds, and Human Security (Ottawa: Partnership Africa Canada, January 2000), http://pacweb.org/Documents/diamonds_KP/heart_of_the_matter-full-2000-01-eng.pdf.

64 Dominic Johnson, Les Sables mouvants : L'exploration du pétrole dans le Graben et le conflit congolais, edited by Aloys Tegera with the assistance of Mikolo Sofia (Goma : Pole Institute, March 2003), www.pole-institute.org/documents/heritagefr.pdf; and Laurence Mazure, « Lucrative reconversion des mercenaires sudafricains », Le Monde diplomatique (Paris), October 1996, 22–23, http://www.monde-diplomatique.fr/1996/10/MAZURE/7295.

65 Canada Revenue Agency, "Flow-Through Shares," 2008, http://www.cra-arc.gc.ca/tx/bsnss/tpcs/fts-paa/menu-eng.html.

66 MRNF, "Flow-Through Shares," http://www.mrnf.gouv.qc.ca/english/mines/fiscal/
fiscal-incentives-shares.jsp, consulted August 17, 2012.

67 Canada Department of Finance, *The 2008 Budget Plan: Responsible Leadership*,
February 26, 2008, 160, http://www.budget.gc.ca/2008/pdf/plan-eng.pdf.

68 Lutundula 2003.

69 Tables based on reports of the Canada Pension Plan Investment Board and the
Caisse de depot et placement du Québec, showing Canadian public fund investments in Africa over the past ten years, are available at www.imperialcanada.ca.

70 TMX, "Mining Sector Sheet," 2012, 1, http://www.tmx.com/en/pdf/Mining_Sec-
tor_Sheet.pdf.

71 TMX Group, "A Capital Opportunity: Mining," slide presentation, Africa, slide
30; Latin America, slide 32; Europe and United States, slide 23, http://www.tmx.
com/en/pdf/Mining_Presentation.pdf, consulted August 3, 2012.

72 DFAIT 2009.

73 Karyn Keenan, "Bringing Canadian Mining to Justice," *Pambazuka News* 536
(June 22, 2011), http://pambazuka.org/en/category/features/74254.

74 Amnesty International Canada and eight other groups, open letter on the United
Nations Declaration on the Rights of Indigenous Peoples, August 9, 2007, http://
www.ubcic.bc.ca/News_Releases/UBCICNews08090701.htm#axzz22OpSQWbw;
and Amnesty International Canada, " 'Lost year' for the Rights of Indigenous
Peoples Worldwide: Canada Must Stop Stalling on Vital United Nations Declaration," news release, June 28, 2007, http://www.eniar.org/news/un42.html.

75 Asad Ismi, "Profiting from Repression: Canadian Investment in and Trade with
Colombia," *Americas Update*, November 2000, http://www.asadismi.ws/colom-
biareport.html.

76 Ibid.

77 Canadian Space Agency, "Geology," 2006, http://www.asc-csa.gc.ca/eng/satellites/
radarsat1/geology.asp; International Development Research Centre (IDRC),
"Sharing Canada's Eye in the Sky: RADARSAT," http://web.idrc.ca/en/ev-2684-
201-1-DO_TOPIC.html, consulted June 19, 2012.

78 Thomas Akabzaa, "Ghana : La législation minière et les bénéfices nets de la mise
en valeur de ce secteur pour le pays," in *Enjeux des nouvelles réglementations
minières en Afrique*, edited by Bonnie Campbell, 28–33 (Göteborg : Nordiska
Afrikainstitutet, 2004).

79 Márk Curtis and Tundu Lissu, *A Golden Opportunity. How Tanzania Is Failing
to Benefit from Gold Mining*, Christian Council of Tanzania (CCT), National
Council of Muslims in Tanzania (BAKWATA), and Tanzania Episcopal Conference (TEC), March 2008, 7, http://tanzania-network.de/download/Themen/
Oekonomie/2008_gold_mining_report.pdf.

80 Marie Mazalto, "Réforme de la législation minière et rôle des institutions mul-
tilatérales de financement dans le développement du secteur minier en RDS,"
paper presented at the L'exploitation des ressources naturelles en situation de

conflits: Responsabilités internationales et perspectives de solutions en République démocratique du Congo conference, Université du Québec à Montréal, April 2, 2004, 9, http://www.ieim.uqam.ca/IMG/pdf/MMazalto-presentation.pdf.

81 Peter Diekmeyer, "Diekmeyer Report: Managing International Mining Political Risk," *CIM Magazine*, 2009, http://www.peterdiekmeyer.com/091120.html.

82 Fidy Rajaonson and Aryanne Besner Quintal, "Madagascar a mauvaise mine," *Quartier Libre* (Montréal) 16, no. 13 (March 11, 2009), http://quartierlibre.ca/archives0810/Madagascar-a-mauvaise-mine.

83 Canadian Network on Corporate Accountability (CNCA), *Dirty Businesses, Dirty Practices: How the Federal Government Supports Canadian Mining, Oil, and Gas Companies Abroad* (Ottawa: May 2007), 1.2, http://cnca-rcrce.ca/wp-content/uploads/CNCA-DirtyPractices-may2007.pdf.

84 Canada Investment Fund for Africa (CIFA), *Final Closing of US$212 Million Canada Investment Fund for Africa,* Actis and Cordiant Investor Group Report, July 28, 2006, http://www.cifafund.ca/en/news/2006/CIFA_Final_Closing_July_28_2006.pdf.

85 Canadian International Development Agency (CIDA), "Evaluation of the CIDA Industrial Cooperation (CIDA-INC) Program," 2008, http://www.acdi-index

86 pro.gc.ca/acdi-cida/acdi-cida.nsf/eng/NAT-2792834-JYW.

87 Ludi Joseph, "Canada and IFC Establish New Technical Assistance Trust Fund," International Finance Corporation, July 8, 2004, http://www.ifc.org/ifcext/pressroom/ifcpressroom.nsf/PressRelease?openform&BBED10DADBAC86128525697 7004C5DBA, no longer available.

88 CNCA 2007; Pierre Beaudet, *Qui aide qui ? Une brève histoire de la solidarité internationale au Québec* (Montréal : Boréal, 2009).

89 Canadian International Development Agency (CIDA), "Minister Oda Announces Initiatives to Increase the Benefits of Natural Resource Management for People in Africa and South America," news release, September 29, 2011, http://www.acdi-cida.gc.ca/acdi-cida/ACDI-CIDA.nsf/eng/CAR-929105317-KGD.

90 Stephen Eldon Kerr, "CIDA Under-Fire for Partnering with Mining Company," *Alternatives International Journal*, March 30, 2012, http://www.alterinter.org/article3786.html.

91 Frédéric Lambolez and Jean-Marie Pernelle, *Je veux ma part de terre*, documentary film (France : La Réunion, 2011); Enquêteprod.com, "Je Veux Ma Part de Terre – Repérages à Madagascar," May 4, 2009, http://www.enqueteprod.com/fr/actualites/reperages-et-tournages/57-je-veux-ma-part-de-terre-reperages-madagascar; Ehoalaport.com, "Sur Rio Tinto QMM," 2012, http://www.ehoalaport.com/index.php?option=com_content&view=article&id=118&Itemid=73; Industry Canada, "QIT-Fer et Titane inc. – Complete Profile," Canadian Company Capabilities, Ottawa, 2011, http://www.ic.gc.ca/app/ccc/srch/nvgt.do?sbPrtl=&prtl=1&estblmntNo=131297470124&profile=cmpltPrfl&profileId=2052&app=sold&lang=eng.

92 United Nations High Commissioner for Human Rights 2010; and United Nations Committee on the Elimination of Racial Discrimination (CERD), "Concluding Observations for Canada," UN Doc. CERD/C/CAN/CO/18, May 25, 2007, http://www2.ohchr.org/english/bodies/cerd/docs/CERD.C.CAN.CO.18.doc.

93 United Nations High Commissioner for Human Rights 2010.

94 Ibid., para. 774.

95 Ibid., para. 778 and 867–69.

96 Ibid., para. 774, n1403.

97 Erik Kennes, « Le secteur minier au Congo : Déconnexion et descente aux enfers », in L'Afrique des grands lacs, Annuaire 1999–2000, edited by Filip Reyntjens and Stefaan Marysse, 299–342 (Paris : L'Harmattan, 2000), 316.

98 Adam Hochschild, "Heart of Sadness: Congo," Amnesty International, Fall 2003, http://www.thirdworldtraveler.com/Africa/Heart_Sadness_Congo.html; Marie-France Cros and François Misser, Géopolitique du Congo (RDC) (Brussels : Éditions Complexe, 2006), 15.

99 United Nations High Commissioner for Human Rights 2010, sec. 775.

100 United Nations Panel of Experts 2002, para. 131.

101 Ibid.

102 Ibid., para. 170.

103 Ibid.

104 Ibid., Annex III; see also Toby A. A. Heaps, "Canadian Companies in the Congo and the OECD Guidelines," Corporate Knights, June 5, 2006, http://www.corporateknights.com/article/canadian-companies-congo-and-oecd-guidelines?page=show.

105 OECD Guidelines for Multinational Enterprises, 2008, http://www.oecd.org/dataoecd/56/36/1922428.pdf.

106 Lutundula 2003.

107 All-Party Parliamentary Group on the Great Lakes Region of Africa, Illegal Minerals and Conflicts, parliamentary briefing, London: UK Parliament, 2003, http://www.appggreatlakes.org/index.php/appg-reports-mainmenu-35/briefing-papers-mainmenu-34/18-illegal-minerals-and-conflict.

108 Sénat belge 2003.

109 Audiencia nacional de España, Administración de Justicia, Juzgado Central de Instrucción N° 4, Reino de España, Sumario 3 / 2,008, Madrid, February 6, 2008, http://www.veritasrwandaforum.org/dosier/resol_auto_esp_06022008.pdf; Mbaya J. Kankwenda, L'économie politique de la prédation au Congo-Kinshasa : Des origines à nos jours 1885–2003 (Kinshasa, Montreal, and Washington : ICREDES [l'Institut Congolais de Recherche en Développement et Études Stratégiques], 2005); Amnesty International, Democratic Republic of Congo: Arming the East, AFR 62/006/2005, July 5, 2005, http://www.amnesty.org/en/library/asset/AFR62/006/2005/fr/08df105c-d4d2-11dd-8a23-d58a49c0d652/afr620062005en.pdf; Global Witness, Faced With a Gun, What Can You Do? War and the Militarisation of Mining in Eastern Congo (London: July 2009), http://www.globalwitness.

org/sites/default/files/pdfs/report_en_final_0.pdf; Human Rights Watch 2003; Pierre Baracyetse, "L'Enjeu géopolitique des société minières internationales en République démocratique du Congo (ex-Zaïre)" (Buzet, Belgique: SOS Rwanda-Burundi, 1999), http://www.freespeechatrisk.ca/wp-content/uploads/2010/08/ ENJEU%20GEOPOLITIQUE%20Baracyetse.pdf; Keith Harmon Snow, "Covert Actions in Africa: A Smoking Gun in Washington," special congressional hearing on Africa, Subcommittee on International Operations and Human Rights, Committee on International Relations, House of Representatives, Washington, April 6, 2001, http://allthingspass.com/journalism.php?catid=10; Keith Harmon Snow and David Barouski, "Behind the Numbers: Suffering in the Congo," Zmag, March 5, 2006, http://allthingspass.com/uploads/html-151Suffering%20in%20 Congo.htm; Joan Baxter, Dust from Our Eyes: An Unblinkered Look at Africa (Hamilton, ON: Wolsak and Wynn, 2008); Marie-France Cros and François Misser, Géopolitique du Congo (RDC) (Brussels : Éditions Complexe, 2006), 15; Colette Braeckman, Les nouveaux prédateurs : Politiques des puissances en Afrique centrale, 2nd ed. (Brussels : Aden, 2009); Madelaine Drohan, Making a Killing: How and Why Corporations Use Armed Force to Do Business (Toronto: Random House, 2003); Yves Engler, The Black Book of Canadian Foreign Policy (Black Point, NS: Fernwood Publishing and Vancouver: RED Publishing, 2009); Adam Hochschild, "Heart of Sadness: Congo," Amnesty International, Fall 2003, http://www.thirdworldtraveler.com/Africa/Heart_Sadness_Congo.html; Dominic Johnson, Les Sables mouvants, L'exploration du pétrole dans le Graben et le conflit congolais, edited by Aloys Tegera with the assistance of Mikolo Sofia (Goma : Pole Institute, March 2003), www.pole-institute.org/documents/heritagefr.pdf; Dominic Johnson, "Killing the Economy in the Name of Peace: The New US 'Conflict Minerals' Legislation for the DRC" (Goma: Pole Institute, July 19, 2010), http://www.pole-institute.org/site%20web/echos/echo138.htm; Dominic Johnson, "Who's in Charge? Putting the Mineral Trade in Eastern DRC under International Control: An Overview," in Blood Minerals: The Criminalization of the Mining Industry in Eastern DRC, 22–45 (Goma: Pole Institute, August 2010), http:// www.friendsofthecongo.org/pdf/blood_minerals_pole_aug2010.pdf; Dominic Johnson and Aloys Tegera, Rules for Sale: Formal and Informal Cross-Border Trade in Eastern DRC (Goma: Pole Institute, May 2007), www.pole-institute. org/documents/regard19_anglais.pdf; Kennes 1998; Kennes 2000; John Lasker, "Digging for Gold, Mining Corruption," published in Canada in Canadian Dimension, October 29, 2009, http://canadiandimension.com/articles/2565/, and in the United States as "Canadian Company Eyes Gold in DRC," Global Policy Forum, August 20, 2009, http://www.globalpolicy.org/security-council/dark-side-of-natural-resources/minerals-in-conflict/48091.html; Wayne Madsen, Genocide and Covert Operation in Africa, 1993–1999 (Lewiston, NY; Queenston, ON; and Lampeter, UK: Edwin Mellen Press, 1999); Wayne Madsen, "Genocide and Covert Operations in Africa 1993–1999: Prepared Testimony and Statement of Wayne Madsen," special congressional hearing on Africa, subcommittee on international operations and human rights, committee on international relations, House of Representatives, Washington, May 17, 2001, http://allthingspass.com/journalism.

php?jid=23; Honoré Ngbanda Nzambo, *Crimes organisés en Afrique centrale : Révélations sur les réseaux rwandais et occidentaux* (Paris : Éditions Duboiris, 2004); Denis Tougas, "Les transnationales minières à l'assaut du Zaïre comme du Congo," *Info-Zaïre* (Montréal) Entraide missionnaire 127 (May 23, 1997): 8.

110 OECD Guidelines 2008.

111 United Nations High Commissioner for Human Rights 2010.

112 Brett Popplewell, "Canadian Firms Face Abuse Allegations," *The Star* (Toronto), November 22, 2009, http://www.thestar.com/news/canada/article/729147--canadian-mining-firms-face-abuse-allegations.

113 Foreign Affairs and International Trade Canada, *Canada's National Contact Point (NCP), annual report 2005*, updated January 5, 2009, http://www.international.gc.ca/trade-agreements-accords-commerciaux/ncp-pcn/report2005-rapport2005.aspx?lang=eng&view=d.

114 Global Witness, *Digging in Corruption: Fraud, Abuse, and Exploitation in Katanga's Copper and Cobalt Mines* (London: July 2006), 51, http://www.globalwitness.org/sites/default/files/import/kat-doc-engl-lowres.pdf.

115 Jean-Marc Larouche and Anne-Marie Voisard, "Dossier : Responsabilité sociale et éthique de la recherche : *Noir Canada* : Une recherche socialement responsable," *Éthique publique* 12, no. 1 (2010) : 105–21, http://ethiquepublique.revues.org/249.

116 Gérard Prunier, *Africa's World War: Congo, the Rwandan Genocide, and the Making of a Continental Catastrophe* (New York: Oxford University Press, 2008).

117 Ibid., 281, n446.

118 Madelaine Drohan, *Making a Killing: How and Why Corporations Use Armed Force to Do Business* (Toronto: Vintage Canada, 2003), 321.

119 CERD 2007, para. 17.

120 Ibid.

121 Ibid.

122 Aboriginal Affairs and Northern Development Canada, "Canada Endorses the United Nations Declaration on the Rights of Indigenous Peoples," news release, November 12, 2010, http://www.aadnc-aandc.gc.ca/eng/1292354321165.

123 See, for example, People's International Health Tribunal, Guatemala 2012, documentary film, posted July 18, 2012, http://www.youtube.com/watch?v=aAJdmMfaoHk; Paul Carlucci, "In Ghana, A Mining Activist Fights the Gold Goliaths," *The Star* (Toronto), April 7, 2012, http://www.thestar.com/news/world/article/1157071--in-ghana-a-mining-activist-fights-the-gold-goliaths?bn=1; Josh Tapper, "Massive Mongolian Mine Raises Environmental Fears," *The Star* (Toronto), April 10, 2012, http://www.thestar.com/news/world/article/1159478--massive-mongolian-mine-raises-environmental-fears.

124 Drohan 2003, 321.

125 Canadian Centre for International Justice (CCIJ), "Anvil Mining," 2012, http://www.ccij.ca/programs/cases/index.php?WEBYEP_DI=14; and Hélène Dragatsi, *Criminal Liability of Canadian Corporations for International Crimes* (Toronto: Carswell, 2011).

126 Deneault, Abadie, and Sacher 2008, 334.

127 *Alien Tort Statute*, 28 U.S.C., c. 85, sec. 1350, also called the *Alien Tort Claims Act*, http://www.law.cornell.edu/uscode/text/28/1350.

128 John Ruggie, "Obstacles to Justice and Redress for Victims of Corporate Human Rights Abuse," Oxford Pro Bono Publico, University of Oxford, November 3, 2008, 36, http://www.reports-and-materials.org/Oxford-Pro-Bono-Publico-submission-to-Ruggie-3-Nov-2008.pdf.

129 Mark Hamblett, "Alien Tort Action Survives Concerns of U.S., Canada," *New York Law Journal* (September 2, 2005), http://www.law.com/jsp/law/international/LawArticleIntl.jsp?id=900005545145. See also Ruti Teitel, « L' 'alien tort' et l'état de droit mondial », *Revue internationale des sciences sociales* 3, no. 185 (2005): 597–607, http://www.cairn.info/revue-internationale-des-sciences-sociales-2005-3-page-597.htm.

130 Hamblett 2005.

131 *Sudan Peace Act*, Pub. L. No. 107-245, 116 Stat. 1504 (2002).

132 James W. Buckee, president and chief executive officer, Talisman Resources, "A Discussion with Dr. Jim Buckee," in *2002 Corporate Responsibility Report*, March 4, 2003, 3, http://www.talisman-energy.com/upload/report_link/4/02/tlm02cr.pdf.

133 *Crimes against Humanity and War Crimes Act*, S.C. 2000, c. 24, in effect June 29, 2000, http://canlii.ca/t/7vw9.

134 CIDA, "Minister Oda Announces Initiatives to Increase the Benefits of Natural Resource Management for People in Africa and South America," news release, September 29, 2011, http://www.acdi-cida.gc.ca/acdi-cida/ACDI-CIDA.nsf/eng/CAR-929105317-KGD.

135 Export Development Canada (EDC), "Political Risk Insurance for Companies with Overseas Assets," http://www.edc.ca/EN/Our-Solutions/Insurance/Documents/brochure-political-risk-insurance-assets.pdf, consulted August 19, 2012.

136 Canada Investment Fund for Africa (CIFA), *Final Closing of US$212 Million Canada Investment Fund for Africa,* Actis and Cordiant Investor Group Report, July 28, 2006, http://www.cifafund.ca/en/news/2006/CIFA_Final_Closing_July_28_2006.pdf.

137 Michelle Collins, " 'Gender Equality,' 'Child Soldiers,' and 'Humanitarian Law' Are Axed from Foreign Policy Language," *Embassy* (Ottawa), July 29, 2009, http://www.embassymag.ca/page/view/foreignpolicy-7-29-2009.

138 Ibid.

139 United Nations Sub-Commission on the Promotion and Protection of Human Rights, report of the United Nations High Commissioner on Human Rights on the responsibilities of transnational corporations and related business enterprises

with regard to human rights, E/CN.4/2005/91 (New York: Commission on Human Rights, Economic, and Social Council, February 15, 2005), http://daccess-dds-ny.un.org/doc/UNDOC/GEN/G05/110/27/PDF/G0511027.pdf?OpenElement.

140 Les Whittington and Brett Popplewell, "Miner Accused of 'Aggressive' Tactics," *The Star* (Toronto), November 25, 2009, http://www.thestar.com/news/investigations/article/730442--miner-accused-of-aggressive-tactics.

141 *Recherches Internationales Québec v. Cambior Inc.,* [1998] Q.J.No. 2554, a decision of Justice Maughan of the Quebec Superior Court (Class Action), District of Montreal, August 14, 1998.

142 Jean-Moïse Djoli, "La question congolaise (R.D. Congo) et les responsabilités canadiennes," April 2009, http://fr.groups.yahoo.com/group/CongoElite/message/161.

143 *Anvil Mining Ltd. c. Association canadienne contre l'impunité (ACCI) c. Anvil Mining Ltd.,* 2012 QCCA 117, overturning *Association canadienne contre l'impunité (ACCI) c. Anvil Mining Ltd.,* 2011 QCCS 1966 (CanLII), http://canlii.ca/t/fl6jl.

144 Amnesty International, "Court Decision in Kilwa Massacre Case Denies Right to Remedy for Victims of Corporate Human Rights Abuses," AMR 20/002/2012, February 1, 2012, http://www.amnesty.org/en/library/asset/AMR20/002/2012/en/56ff3c1f-dbd6-483f-8eb2-bce8abf9a7ea/amr200022012en.pdf.

145 Canadian Centre for International Justice (CCIJ), "Anvil Mining," 2012, http://www.ccij.ca/programs/cases/index.php?WEBYEP_DI=14; and Hélène Dragatsi, *Criminal Liability of Canadian Corporations for International Crimes* (Toronto: Carswell, 2011).

146 Radio-Canada – Ontario, "Mines – Guatémala : la femme d'un militant tué poursuit Hudbay Minerals au Canada," report broadcast on December 2, 2010, http://www.radio-canada.ca/regions/Ontario/2010/12/02/001-hudbay-minerals-poursuite-adolfo-ich-chaman.shtml.

147 TMX Exchange Bulletin, "TSX Delisting Review – Copper Mesa Mining Corporation (CUX)," January 19, 2010, http://tmx.com/en/news_events/exchange_bulletins/bulletins/1-19-2010_TSX-ReviewCUX.html.

148 *Ramírez v. Copper Mesa & TSX,* "Ecuadorians Lose Appeal in Lawsuit against Canadian Mining Company and TSX: Canadian Law Continues to Fail Communities Harmed by Canadian Mining Overseas," 2012, http://ramirezversuscoppermesa.com/; and Radio-Canada – Ontario 2010.

149 *Bil'In (Village Council) c. Green Park International Inc.,* 2009 QCCS 4151, September 18, 2009, http://www.jugements.qc.ca/php/decision.php?liste=62445458&doc=1F9CE82C85BCE3E7A88BCAFAA6B8FBC727D7D2097D2024DA22DEE17A1161D4F2&page=1; Radio-Canada – International, "Colonisation en Cisjordanie, des Palestiniens de Bil'in déboutés," report broadcast on September 21, 2009, http://www.radio-canada.ca/nouvelles/International/2009/09/21/008-Palestiniens_Bilin_deboutes.shtml; Denis Barrette and Diane Lamoureux, "Bil'in : un village qui refuse de se taire," *Relations* (Montréal) 736 (November 2009), http://cjf.qc.ca/fr/relations/article.php?ida=1075.

150 Gregoire C. N. Webber, "Canada," in *Obstacles to Justice and Redress for Victims of Corporate Human Rights Abuse*, edited by John Ruggie, 35–46 (Oxford: Oxford Pro Bono Publico, University of Oxford, November 3, 2008), 35, http://www.reports-and-materials.org/Oxford-Pro-Bono-Publico-submission-to-Ruggie-3-Nov-2008.pdf.

151 *Frontenac Ventures Corporation v. Ardoch Algonquin First* Nation, 91 OR (3d) 1, 295 DLR (4th) 108, 239 OAC 257, http://canlii.ca/t/1z9q1. See also Ann Bigué and Marc-Alexandre Hudon, « Jurisprudence récente concernant les droits des Autochtones dans le cadre de la *Loi sur les mines (Ontario)* et de sa réforme », McCarthy Tétrault, August 23, 2008, our translation, http://www.mccarthy.ca/fr/article_detail.aspx?id=4134#.

152 Canadian Park and Wilderness Society (CPAWS), "Aboriginal Leaders Face Jail Time in Spreading Disputes over First Nations Rights and Mining Claims," Ottawa, January 28, 2008, http://cpaws.org/news/aboriginal-leaders-face-jail-time-in-spreading-disputes-over-first-nations-; Bigué and Hudon 2008.

153 CPAWS 2008.

154 Mines and Communities, "Romanian Campaigners Chalk Up Final Victory," December 10, 2008, http://www.minesandcommunities.org//article.php?a=8969; Save Rosia Montana, "About Us" and "Media Kit," 2012, http://rosiamontana.org/en/categorii.shtml?cmd[321]=c-1-32836&cmd[316]=x-322-32846&x=32846&set[319]=selected-32836&set[321]=selected-32846; Gabriel Resources, "Gabriel Provides Clarification on Bucharest Court of Appeal Ruling in Environmental Impact Assessment Case," news release, July 6, 2009, http://www.infomine.com/index/pr/Pa775155.PDF; NGO.RO, "EIA Chronology of the Rosia Montana mine proposal," working paper, March 2008, http://www.ngo.ro/img_upload/17ef04f0530a65b2f4e73d9a4b5d99ea/EIAcronology_updateMarch08.pdf.

155 Alburnus Maior–Independent Centre for the Development of Environmental Resources, joint press statement, Cluj-Napoca, Romania, June 23, 2010, http://rosiamontana.org/en/index.shtml?cmd%5b314%5d=x-314-37031&cmd%5b316%5d=x-322-37031&cmd%5b300%5d=x-299-37031.

156 Rocío Barahona and Benjamín Ramos, *El legado del CAFTA DR : Millonaria demanda de Pacific Rim al Estado Salvadoreño*, Centro de Investigación sobre Inversión y Comercio (CEICOM), June 2009, http://www.omal.info/www/IMG/pdf/INVESTIGACION_ESPECIAL_DE_COYUNTURA_DEMANDA_PACIFIC_RIM.pdf.

157 Isabelle Rey-Lefebvre, « Suez remporte la bataille de l'eau en Argentine », *Le Monde* (Paris), August 4, 2010, our translation, http://issuu.com/snoopedk/docs/le-monde---jeudi-5-aout-2010-.

158 "Exigen el cierre inmediato de Minera San Xavier," *La Jornada*, July 22, 2010, http://www.conflictosmineros.net/contenidos/23-mexico/5731-exigen-el-cierre-inmediato-de-minera-san-xavier.

159 Greg Palast, *The Best Democracy Money Can Buy: The Truth about Corporate Cons, Globalization, and High-Finance Fraudsters* (New York: Plume Books, 2002), 313–17.

160 Deneault, Abadie, and Sacher 2008.

161 *Barrick Gold Corporation c. Éditions Écosociété inc.*, 2011 QCCS 4232, August 12, 2012.

162 *Barrick Gold Corporation c. Éditions Écosociété inc.*, 2011 QCCS 6758, December 1, 2011.

163 An appeal to the Supreme Court of Canada was dismissed on March 25, 2012; see *Éditions Écosociété Inc. v. Banro Corp.*, 2012 SCC 18.

164 Drohan 2003, 322.

165 Mario Pelletier, *La Caisse dans tous ses états. L'histoire mouvementée de la Caisse de dépôt et placement du Québec* (Montréal : Carte blanche, 2009).

166 Pierre Trudel, *Ouvert le samedi*, report broadcast on Radio-Canada, May 23, 2009, http://www.radio-canada.ca/emissions/ouvert_le_samedi/2010-2011/chronique. asp?idChronique=81387.

167 Ecojustice, "About Ecojustice," 2012, http://www.ecojustice.ca/about.

168 Kevin Libin, "Academics Fear Speaking Freely in Canada: Political Scientists Worried about 'Legal Jeopardy', " *National Post* (Don Mills, ON), August 23, 2008, A8, http://search.proquest.com/docview/330935023?accountid=13800.

169 Roderick Macdonald, Daniel Jutras, and Pierre Noreau, *Les poursuites stratégiques contre la mobilisation publique – les poursuites-bâillons (SLAPP).* Rapport du comité au ministre de la Justice, Montreal, March 15, 2007, 1, our translation, http:// www.justice.gouv.qc.ca/francais/publications/rapports/pdf/slapp.pdf.

170 *Quebec Code of Civil Procedure*, R.S.Q., c. C-25, as amended by Bill 9, *An Act to amend the Code of Civil Procedure to prevent improper use of the courts and promote freedom of expression and citizen participation in public*, S.Q., 2009, c. 12, in effect June 9, 2009, http://www2.publicationsduquebec.gouv.qc.ca/dynam-icSearch/telecharge.php?type=5&file=2000C46A.PDF, consulted August 2, 2012; Normand Landry, *SLAPP : Bâillonnement et répression judiciaire du discours politique* (Montréal : Éditions Écosociété, 2012).

171 Ronald Daniels, *Canada in the 21st Century. Institutions and Growth – Framework Policy as a Tool of Competitive Advantage for Canada* (Ottawa: Industry Canada, December 1998), http://www.ic.gc.ca/eic/site/eas-aes.nsf/eng/ra01739.html.

172 De Beers Canada, "History," *Inside De Beers Canada*, 2009, http://www.debeer-scanada.com/files_3/history.php.

173 Royal Ontario Museum, "The Nature of Diamonds Opens at the ROM on October 25, 2008," news release, July 28, 2008, http://www.rom.on.ca/news/releases/public. php?mediakey=02fnwhxgag.

174 Nigel Worden, *The Making of Modern South Africa: Conquest, Apartheid, Democracy*, 5th ed. (Oxford: Wiley, 2012), 44.

175 Stuart Tannock, *Mining Capital and the Corporatization of Public Education in Toronto: Building a Global City or Building a Globally Ignorant City?*, independent research study, May 2009, 2, http://burningbillboard.org/wp-content/2009/08/Mining-and-Education-in-Toronto-2009-Report.pdf.

176 Ontario Ministry of Education and Training, *The Ontario Curriculum, Grades 1–8: Science and Technology* (Toronto: 2007), 93.

177 Tannock 2009, 15.

178 Tannock 2009, 11.

179 Tannock 2009, 24, citing Roger Moody, *The Risks We Run: Mining, Communities and Political Risk Insurance* (Utrecht: International Books, 2005); No Dirty Gold, "Buyat Bay, Indonesia," 2004, http://www.nodirtygold.org/buyat_bay_indonesia.cfm; EarthWorks, "Expert Study Shows Buyat Bay, Indonesia, Polluted," 2004, www.earthworksaction.org/PR20041110buyatbay.cfm; Alburnus Maior et al. "Opposition Surges to Romanian Gold Project Propaganda," news release, January 23, 2007, http://miningwatch.ca/index.php?/Gabriel_Resources/alburnusmaior; Save Rosia Montana 2009.

180 Tannock 2009, 21.

181 Ibid., 22.

182 Ibid., 23.

183 Martin Frigon, *Mirage of El Dorado*, produced by Lucie Pageau, press kit (Paris : Productions Multi-Monde, 2008), http://pmm.qc.ca/eldorado/media/English/Brief%20synopsis%20MIRAGE%20OF%20EL%20DORADO.pdf; documentary film available at http://www.youtube.com/watch?v=LoTk_qeWUWQ.

184 (Mulroney, Munk) Barrick Gold, "Board of Directors," 2012, http://www.barrick.com/Company/CorporateGovernance/BoardofDirectors/default.aspx; (Bush) "Barrick responds to Pascua-Lama Chain Email," June 2006, http://www.barrick.com/CorporateResponsibility/PascuaLama/BarrickRespondsbrtoChainEmail/default.aspx; (Desmarais) Bloomberg Businessweek, "Executive Profile: Paul G. Desmarais, Sr., P.C., C.C., O.Q.," http://investing.businessweek.com/research/stocks/people/person.asp?personId=22074061&ticker=PARG:SW&previousCapId=519888&previousTitle=Bertelsmann%20AG, consulted August 19, 2012.

185 Tannock 2009, 22.

186 Institute for the Study of International Development, McGill University, "Public-Private Partnerships for Sustainable Development: Toward a Framework for Resource Extraction Industries," Resources Extraction conference, Montreal, March 29–31, 2012, http://www.mcgill.ca/isid/events/resource-extraction-conference.

187 Tannock 2009, 20, 25.

188 Third World Network-Africa et al., "Africans Join Civil Society Groups Condemning World Bank," November 29, 2004, http://www.minesandcommunities.org//article.php?a=1678, quoted in Tannock 2009, 24.

189 Dennis Tessier, *The Challenge of the Mines: The Role of Stakeholder Engagement in the Sustainable Development of Tanzania's Gold Mining Sector. A Case Study of Shinyanga*, University of Western Ontario and University of Dar es Salaam Institute of Development Studies, 2005?, 99, http://www.miningwatch.ca/sites/www.miningwatch.ca/files/The_Challenge_of_the_Mines_0.pdf.

190 Council on Ethics (Norway), *The Government Pension Fund*, global report to the ministry of finance, recommendation of August 14, 2008, http://www.regjeringen.no/upload/FIN/etikk/recommendation_barrick.pdf.

191 United Nations Commission on Human Rights 2002, 113.

192 CNCA 2007.

193 Marty Logan, "Corruption: Canada Backs Firm Banned by World Bank," Inter Press Service (Johannesburg), July 30, 2004, http://www.halifaxinitiative.org/fr/node/846.

194 BBC News, "Lesotho Court Suspends Bribery Fine," December 11, 2002, http://news.bbc.co.uk/2/hi/business/2566311.stm.

195 Stephen Kerr and Kelly Holloway, "The Men Who Moil for Gold," *The Varsity and the Atkinsonian* (University of Toronto), special investigative report, April 15, 2002, http://www.miningwatch.ca/sites/www.miningwatch.ca/files/Bulyanhulu.pdf.

196 The NGO Working Group on the Export Development Corporation [Export Development Canada], *Reckless Lending: How Canada's Export Development Corporation Puts People and Environment at Risk*, vol. 2 (Ottawa: Halifax Initiative, May 15, 2001), http://www.halifaxinitiative.org/content/reckless-lending-volume-ii.

197 Canadian International Development Agency (CIDA), "Project Profile: Senegal Railway Sector," *Infrastructure Services Performance Review: Summary of Results* (Gatineau: n.d.), 11, http://www.acdi- http://www.acdi-cida.gc.ca/INET/IMAGES.NSF/vLUImages/Performancereviews5/$file/ISPR_E_Results.pdf.

198 Barrick Gold, "Board of Directors," 2012, http://www.barrick.com/Company/CorporateGovernance/BoardofDirectors/default.aspx.

199 Joe Clark and Associates, "Who We Are," 2012, http://www.maureenmcteer.com/who-we-are/joe-clark.

200 Jean Chrétien's daughter France is married to Desmarais's son André; see Peter C. Newman, "Paul Desmarais: King of the Establishment," in *Heroes: Canadian Champions, Dark Horses, and Icons*, Part 3: Business (Toronto: HarperCollins, 2010).

201 Peter Koven, " 'Incredible Synergies' in Cliffs-Consolidated Thompson deal: Tobin," *Financial Post* (Toronto), January 12, 2011, http://www.financialpost.com/related/topics/Incredible+synergies+Cliffs+Consolidated+Thompson+deal+Tobin/4099458/story.html; and Cliffs Natural Resources Inc., "Steel Starts Here," corporate mergers and acquisitions factsheet, Cleveland, OH, June 10, 2011, http://www.cliffsnaturalresources.com/EN/aboutus/globalbizdev/Documents/MandAFactSheet.pdf.

202 Joe Clark and Associates 2012; Carter Center, "Preliminary Statement of Carter Center on the Democratic Republic of Congo July 30, 2006, Elections," August 1, 2006, http://www.cartercenter.org/news/documents/doc2445.html.

203 Renaud Vivien, Yvonne Ngoyi, Victor Nzuzi, Dani Ndombele, José Mukadi, and Luc Mukendi, "L'ingérence sournoise du FMI et de la Banque mondiale en République démocratique du Congo," Comité pour l'annulation de la dette du Tiers-Monde, *La Libre Belgique* (Brussels), October 7, 2009, http://www.lalibre. be/debats/opinions/article/533922/l-ingerence-sournoise-du-fmi-au-congo.html.

204 Delphine Abadie, « Le Canada en République Démocratique du Congo : 'ô mes amis, il n'y a nul ami ...' », (Brussels : Comité pour l'annulation de la dette du Tiers-Monde, August 2, 2010), http://www.cadtm.org/Le-Canada-en-Republique.

205 Ivanhoe Energy, "Ivanhoe Energy Appoints Jean Chretien, Former Canadian Prime Minister, as Senior International Adviser," news release, July 8, 2009, http:// www.ivanhoeenergy.com/en/news/ie-2009-07-08.pdf; Presse Canadienne, « En bref – Jean Chrétien chez Ivanhoe Energy », *Le Devoir* (Montréal), July 9, 2009, http://www.ledevoir.com/2009/07/09/258341.html.

206 Deneault, Abadie, and Sacher 2008.

207 Mines and Communities 2009.

208 Agence France-Presse, "« Niger : Robert Fowler, porté disparu depuis lundi, était en mission selon l'ONU », December 19, 2008, our translation, http://www. avmaroc.com/print/niger-robert-fowler-actualite-a151649-d.html.

209 Radio-Canada International, « Mystérieuse visite canadienne impromptu », report broadcast December 19, 2008, http://www.radio-canada.ca/nouvelles/ International/2008/12/19/003-niger_diplomates.shtml?ref=rss; Ludovic Hirtzmann, « Niger : deux diplomates canadiens restent introuvables », *Le Figaro* (Paris), December 24, 2008, http://www.lefigaro.fr/international/2008/12/24/01003-20081224ARTFIG00267-niger-deux-diplomates-canadiens-restent-introuvables-. php; Matthew Russell Lee, "Fowler's Niger Companion Guay Active in Mining, UN Stonewalls on Their Mission," *Inner City Press*, December 18, 2008, www. innercitypress.com/un3fowler121808.html.

210 Matthew Russell Lee, "Fowler's Niger Companion Guay Active in Mining, UN Stonewalls on Their Mission," *Inner City Press*, December 18, 2008, www.innercitypress.com/un3fowler121808.html.

211 Robert Fowler, *A Season in Hell: My 130 Days in the Sahara with Al Qaeda* (Toronto: HarperCollins Canada, 2011).

212 Craig Wong, "Barrick Launches New Corporate Social Responsibility Advisory Board," *The Canadian Press*, March 2, 2012, http://www.globalnews.ca/barrick+launches+new+corporate+social+responsibility+advisory+board/6442592981/story.html Barrick Gold, "Barrick Announces Inaugural Members of Corporate Social Responsibility Advisory Board," news release, March 2, 2012, http://www.barrick.com/Theme/Barrick/files/docs_pressrelease/2012/Barrick-Announces-Inaugural-Members-of-CSR-Advisory-Board.pdf.

213 Ryan Dube, "Sólida presencia diplomática beneficia a mineras, afirma Iamgold," *Business News Americas*, June 25, 2010, our translation, http://www.bnamericas.com/news/mineria/Solida_presencia_diplomatica_beneficia_a_mineras,_afirma_Iamgold.

214 Frigon 2008.

215 Hugo Lavoie, « Une mine d'or canadienne contestée au Guatemala », report broadcast on *Dimanche Magazine*, Radio-Canada – Montréal, February 13, 2005, our translation, http://www.radio-canada.ca/actualite/v2/dimanchemag/niveau2_2059.shtml.

216 Faustin Kuediasala, « Tourbillon sur le PEG 2 : KMT et TFM plombent les négociations du Club de Paris », *Le Potentiel* (Kinshasa), November 21, 2009, http://www.lepotentiel.com/afficher_article.php?id_article=89094&id_edition=4841.

217 Department of Foreign Affairs and International Trade (DFAIT), "Initial Environmental Assessment (EA) of the Canada-Peru Foreign Investment Protection and Promotion Agreement (FIPA)," 2005, 6, http://www.international.gc.ca/trade-agreements-accords-commerciaux/agr-acc/peru-perou/report-rapport.aspx?view=d.

218 Gerelyn Valle Cabanillas, "La minería y su repercusión económica en el Perú," paper prepared for Prof. Jorge Córdova in the department of macroeconomics, facultad de ciencias administrativas y recursos humanos, Universidad de San Martín de Porres, Lima, Peru, 2009, http://www.monografias.com/trabajos60/repercusion-economica-mineria/repercusion-economica-mineria2.shtml.

219 José de Echave, "Mines et conflits sociaux : de la nécessité de développer une approche de défense des droits," paper presented at Colloque sur les enjeux et impacts des investissements canadiens à l'étranger ("Industries extractives, industries destructives? Enjeux et impacts des investissements canadiens à l'étranger"), Montréal, November 13, 2006.

220 Ibid.

221 Ibid.

222 DFAIT 2005.

223 "Canadá es ejemplo de minería, según Correa," *Hoy.com* (Quito), February 21, 2009, http://www.hoy.com.ec/noticias-ecuador/canada-es-ejemplo-de-mineria-segun-correa-335129.html.

224 Jaona Ravaloson, « Dessous et enjeux de la crise politique à Madagascar » *Le Devoir* (Montréal), April 22, 2009, our translation, http://www.ledevoir.com/international/actualites-internationales/246836/dessous-et-enjeux-de-la-crise-politique-a-madagascar.

225 Marie-Ève Proulx, "L'Afrique : des opportunités d'affaires pour le Canada," *24 heures* (Montréal), October 7, 2009, 16, our translation, http://www.24hmontreal.canoe.ca/24hmontreal/actualites/archives/2009/10/20091006-180935.html.

226 National Roundtables on Corporate Social Responsibility (CSR) and the Canadian Extractive Industry in Developing Countries, Advisory Group Report, March 29, 2007, http://www.pdac.ca/pdac/misc/pdf/070329-advisory-group-report-eng.pdf.

227 Claude Lévesque, « Les minières canadiennes à l'étranger. Un ombudsman pour les ressortissants étrangers? » *Le Devoir* (Montréal), November 18, 2006, A6.

228 DFAIT 2009.

229 Jack H. Morris, *Going for Gold: The History of Newmont Mining Corporation* (Tuscaloosa, AL: University of Alabama Press, 2010), 172; Diane Francis, "Barrick's Swell Soiree," *National Post* (Toronto), June 10, 2008; David Leigh and Rob Evans, "Biography: Adnan Khashoggi," *The Guardian* (London), June 8, 2007, http://www.guardian.co.uk/world/2007/jun/08/bae52.

230 Fran Abrams, Andrew Buncombe, Steve Boggan, and Mark Stucke, "Who Is Tony Buckingham? And Why Does Everyone Want to Talk to Him?", *The Independent* (London), May 13, 1998, http://www.independent.co.uk/news/who-is-tony-buck-ingham-and-why-does-everyone-want-to-talk-to-him-1159724.html; Simon Goodley, "Profile: Tony Buckingham, chief executive of Heritage Oil," *The Guardian* (London), November 13, 2011, http://www.guardian.co.uk/business/2011/nov/13/heritage-oil-chief-tony-buckingham.

231 DFAIT 2009.

232 Brett Popplewell, "Canadian Firms Face Abuse Allegations," *The Star* (Toronto), November 22, 2009, http://www.thestar.com/news/canada/article/729147--cana-dian-mining-firms-face-abuse-allegations.

233 Ibid.

234 Ibid.

235 Ruggie 2008, 36.

236 DFAIT 2009.

237 Parliament of Canada, *Corporate Accountability of Mining, Oil, and Gas Corpora-tions in Developing Countries Act*, Bill C-300, Second Session, Fortieth Parliament, 57–58 Elizabeth II, 2009, http://www.parl.gc.ca/HousePublications/Publication.aspx?Docid=3658424&file=4%2ft_blank.

238 Popplewell 2009.

239 Canada Newswire, "Bill C-300: Narrow Defeat Despite Widespread Support for Mining Accountability and Human Rights," October 28, 2010, http://cnw.ca/5qXuv.

240 François Cardinal, « Honte au Canada », *La Presse* (Montréal), October 29, 2010, http://www.lapresse.ca/debats/editoriaux/francois-cardinal/201010/28/01-4337160-honte-au-canada.php.

241 Edward Said, *Representations of the Intellectual*, The 1993 Reith Lectures (New York: Vintage Books, 1994), 77.

242 House of Commons, Bill C-438, *An Act Respecting the Extraterritorial Activities of Canadian Businesses and Entities, Establishing the Canadian Extraterritorial Activities Review Commission and Making Consequential Amendments to Other Acts*, 2009, http://parl.gc.ca/content/hoc/Bills/402/Private/C-438/C-438_1/C-438_1.PDF.

243 Parliament of Canada, Bill C-323, *An Act to Amend the Federal Courts Act (International Promotion and Protection of Human Rights)*, private member's bill, First Session, Forty-First Parliament, introduced October 5, 2011, http://www.parl.gc.ca/LegisInfo/BillDetails.aspx?billId=5138027&Mode=1&Language=E.

244 Tables based on reports of the Canada Pension Plan Investment Board and the Caisse de depot et placement du Québec, showing Canadian public fund investments in Africa over the past ten years, are available at www.imperialcanada.ca.

245 Council on Ethics 2008.

246 MiningWatch Canada, "Norwegian Pension Fund Excludes Barrick Gold on Ethical Grounds," February 2, 2009, http://www.miningwatch.ca/norwegian-pension-fund-excludes-barrick-gold-ethical-grounds.

The History
Stock Market Speculation: Historical Wellspring of the Canadian Economy, or How Toronto Became the Place Where the Mining Sector Goes for Capital

1 Max Weber, "Stock and Commodity Exchanges" ("Die Börse"), translated by Steven Lestition, *Theory and Society* 29, no. 3 (June 2000): 305–38, originally published 1894.

2 James West, "The TSX Venture Exchange: The Greatest Stock Market on Earth," *Gold World*, July 24, 2007, http://www.goldworld.com/articles/tsx-venture-exchange/152.

3 *Superbrands Canada* magazine published between 2004 and 2008. It is now defunct.

4 Weber [1894] 2000, tr. Lestition, 316–17.

5 Max Weber, *The Protestant Ethic and the Spirit of Capitalism*, translated by Talcott Parsons (North Chelmsford, MA: Courier Dover Publications, 2003; originally published 1920), 53.

6 Pierre-Joseph Proudhon, *Manuel du spéculateur à la bourse : Une anthologie* (Alfortville, France : Éditions Ère, 2009; originally published 1856), 71, our translation.

7 Proudhon (1856) 2009, 58–59, our translation.

8 Edward Chancellor, *Devil Take the Hindmost: A History of Financial Speculation* (New York: Plume, 2000), xi.

9 Fyodor Dostoevsky, *The Gambler*, translated by C. J. Hogarth (Rockville, MD: Wildside Press, 2003, originally published 1915), 14. Also available on Project Gutenberg, http://www.gutenberg.org/files/2197/2197-h/2197-h.htm.

10   Anatole Browde, "Settling the Canadian Colonies: A Comparison of Two Nine-teenth-Century Land Companies," *The Business History Review* 76, no. 2 (Summer 2002): 299–335, http://www.jstor.org/stable/4127841.

11   Chancellor 2000, 100.

12   Ibid., 100–14.

13   Pierre Alexandre, *Dans les coulisses de Wall Street : De l'euphorie aux larmes* (Paris : Fayard, 2002), 91.

14   Chancellor 2000, 101.

15   Ibid., 131.

16   Ibid., 142.

17   Ibid., 152.

18   Graham D. Taylor and Peter A. Baskerville, *A Concise History of Business in Canada* (Toronto, Oxford, and New York: Oxford University Press, 1994), 255.

19   Christopher Armstrong, *Blue Skies and Boiler Rooms: Buying and Selling Securities in Canada, 1870–1940* (Toronto: University of Toronto Press, 1997), 6–7.

20   Gordon Wills, "The Stock Exchange and the Street," *Canadian Banker* 58 (Spring 1951), 120, quoted in Armstrong 1997, 12.

21   George Fetherling, *Gold Diggers of 1929: Canada and the Great Stock Market Crash* (Toronto: MacMillan, 1979; repr. Toronto: Wiley, 2004), 24.

22   Armstrong 1997, 48.

23   Gustavus Myers, *A History of Canadian Wealth* (Toronto: James Lorimer, 1975, originally published 1914).

24   Stanley B. Ryerson, *Unequal Union: Confederation and the Roots of Conflict in the Canadas, 1815–1873* (New York: International Publishers, 1968), 252.

25   John Dwyer, *Business History: Canada in the Global Community*, 2nd ed. (North York: Captus Press, 2000), 188.

26   Myers 1975, 165, 178.

27   Frank Leonard, *A Thousand Blunders: The Grand Trunk Pacific Railway and Northern British Columbia* (Vancouver: University of British Columbia Press, 1996); and Leslie Thomas Fournier, *Railway Nationalization in Canada: The Problem of the Canadian National Railw*ays (Toronto: Macmillan, 1935; repr. North Stratford, NH: Ayer Co. Pub., 1981).

28   Fournier 1935, 102–103.

29   Armstrong 1997, 307.

30   Fetherling 2004, 26.

31   Armstrong 1997, 117.

32   Ibid., 7.

33   Ibid., chap. 4.

34   Sasha Yusufali, "Toronto Stock Exchange," *The Canadian Encyclopedia*, http://www.thecanadianencyclopedia.com/articles/toronto-stock-exchange, consulted August 15, 2012.

35 Armstrong 1997, 49.

36 Ibid., 57.

37 John Maynard Keynes, *The General Theory of Employment, Interest, and Money* (New York: Harcourt, Brace, 1936; Basingstoke, England: Palgrave Macmillan, 2006), 142.

38 Taylor and Baskerville 1994, 288.

39 Ibid., 255–58.

40 Isaac W. C. Solloway, *Speculators and Politicians* (Toronto: Political and Economic Publishing, 1933).

41 Fetherling 2004, 34.

42 Georg Simmel, *The Philosophy of Money*, 3rd ed., translated by Tom Bottomore and David Frisby (London and New York: Routledge, 2004; originally published 1900), 294.

43 Fetherling 2004, 55.

44 Roland Parenteau, « Les idées économiques et sociales de Bourassa », in *La pensée de Henri Bourassa*, 166–79 (Montréal : L'Action nationale, 1954), 174–75, http://bibnum2.banq.qc.ca/bna/actionnationale/src/1954/01/11/1954-01-11.pdf.

45 Armstrong 1997, 124.

46 Provincial Archives of British Columbia, AG Corr., file S-209-1-G, report on the *Security Frauds Prevention Act* by H. G. Garrett, February 18, 1981, quoted in Armstrong 1997, 170.

47 Armstrong 1997, 126.

48 Ibid., 255.

49 Ibid., 227.

50 *Financial Post* (Toronto), March 18, 1939, quoted in Armstrong 1997, 272–73.

51 *Financial Post* (Toronto), April 8, 1939, quoted in Armstrong 1997, 273.

52 Christopher Armstrong, *Moose Pastures and Mergers: The Ontario Securities Commission and the Regulation of Shares Markets in Canada, 1940–1980* (Toronto: University of Toronto Press, 2001), 144.

53 Ibid., 119.

54 Ibid.

55 Ibid.

56 Ibid., 148.

57 Ibid.

58 Joel Seligman, *The Transformation of Wall Street: A History of the Securities and Exchange Commission and Modern Corporate Finance*, rev. ed. (Boston, 1995), 622, quoted in Armstrong 2001, 17.

59 Provincial Archives of Ontario, AG 4-02, file 122.13, Memorandum from Lennox to Roberts, August 5, 1958, quoted in Armstrong 2001, 148.

60 Armstrong 2001, 17–18.

61 TSE, Historical files, A-1, "TSE-SSME Amalgamation," in "History of the Development of Listing Standards on the TSE," n.d. [1964], quoted in Armstrong 2001, 113.

62 *Financial Post* (Toronto), November 22, 1952, quoted in Armstrong 2001, 118.

63 E. K. Cork, *Finance in the Mining Industry: A Staff Study for the Royal Commission on Banking and Finance*, n.p., n.d. (1964), quoted in Armstrong 2001, 227.

64 John Hagan and Patricia Parker, "White-Collar Crime and Punishment: Class Structure and Legal Sanctioning of Securities Violations," in *White-Collar Crime: Classic and Contemporary Views*, edited by Gilbert Geis, Robert F. Meier, and Lawrence M. Salinger, 259–70 (New York: Free Press, 1995); reprinted from *American Sociological Review* 50 (1985): 302–316 at 333.

65 Ibid., 330.

66 Alain Deneault with Delphine Abadie and William Sacher, *Noir Canada : Pillage, corruption, et criminalité en Afrique* (Montréal : Éditions Écosociété, 2008), 72.

67 Hagan and Parker 1995, 346.

68 R. T. Naylor, *Wages of Crime: Black Markets, Illegal Finance, and the Underworld Economy*, rev. ed. (Montreal and Kingston: McGill-Queen's University Press, 2004), 212; Denis Robert and Ernest Backes, *Révélation$* (Paris : Les Arènes, 2001), 96.

69 David Cruise and Alison Griffiths, *Fleecing the Lamb: The Inside Story of the Vancouver Stock Exchange* (Vancouver and Toronto: Douglas & McIntyre, 1991), xii.

70 *Forbes*, April 27, 1981, quoted in Cruise and Griffiths 1991, ix.

71 William P. Barrett, "Blame Canada: SEC Says Vancouver Stock Promoter Tried Another Fast One," *Forbes*, January 26, 2011, http://www.forbes.com/sites/williampbarrett/2011/01/26/blame-canada-sec-says-vancouver-stock-promoter-tried-another-fast-one/.

72 Benjamin Beit-Hallahmi, "Scientology: Religion or Racket?", *Marburg Journal of Religion* 8, no. 1 (2003): 7, http://www.uni-marburg.de/fb03/ivk/mjr/pdfs/2003/articles/breit2003.pdf.

73 Cruise and Griffiths 1991, 40.

74 Robert and Backes 2001, 289, our translation.

75 Craig Wong, "Barrick 'Threatened and Coerced' Bre-X during Talks over Busang, Court Hears," *Canadian Press*, December 7, 2004; *Le Devoir* (Montréal), « Barrick aurait tenté de contraindre Bre-X au cours de pourparlers » December 8, 2004, http://www.ledevoir.com/economie/actualites-economiques/70290/barrick-aurait-tente-de-contraindre-bre-x-au-cours-de-pourparlers.

76 *R. v. Felderhof*, 2007 ONCJ 345, 224 CCC (3d) 97, 75 WCB (2d) 46, July 31, 2007, http://canlii.ca/t/1sbq4.

77 Douglas Hunter, *The Bubble and the Bear: How Nortel Burst the Canadian Dream* (Toronto: Doubleday Canada, 2002), 6–7.

78 François Morin, *Le nouveau mur de l'argent : Essai sur la finance globalisée* (Paris : Seuil, 2006), 244, our translation.

79 Jean-Luc Gréau, *Le capitalisme malade de sa finance : Des années d'expansion aux années de stagnation* (Paris : Gallimard, 1998); Jean-Luc Gréau, *L'avenir du capitalisme* (Paris : Gallimard, 2005); Jean-Luc Gréau, *La trahison des économistes* (Paris : Gallimard, 2008).

80 François Desjardins, « Bourse de Toronto : La CMVO souhaite plus de rigueur de la part des sociétés étrangères », *Le Devoir* (Montréal), March 22, 2012, http://www.ledevoir.ca/economie/actualites-economiques/345618/bourse-de-toronto-la-cmvo-souhaite-plus-de-rigueur-de-la-part-des-societes-etrangeres.

81 Ontario Securities Commission (OSC), OSC Staff Notice 51-719 *Emerging Markets Issuer Review*, March 20, 2012, http://www.osc.gov.on.ca/documents/en/Securities-Category5/sn_20120320_51-719_emerging-markets.pdf.

82 Peter Koven, "Kinross Faces New $4-Billion Class-Action Lawsuit," *Financial Post*, March 13, 2012, http://business.financialpost.com/2012/03/13/kinross-faces-new-4-billion-class-action/.

83 Morin 2006, 62, our translation.

A Case Study
Quebec Colonial Ltd.

1 Sylvain Larocque, « Charest veut stimuler l'entrepreneurship des chercheurs », *La Presse* (Montréal), May 18, 2009, http://affaires.lapresse.ca/economie/quebec/200905/18/01-857566-charest-veut-stimuler-lentrepreneurship-des-chercheurs.php.

2 In 2010, the mining and quarrying sector (excluding oil and gas) earned revenues of $32.76 billion, according to Statistics Canada, Table 1-1, "Summary Table – Operating Revenue by Industries," *Financial and Taxation Statistics for Enterprises*, Catalogue 61-219-X (Ottawa: Statistics Canada, 2010), 19, http://www.statcan.gc.ca/pub/61-219-x/61-219-x2010000-eng.pdf; and Fraser Institute, *Annual Survey of Mining Companies* 2008–2009, 2009–2010, 2010–2011, and 2011–2012 (Calgary).

3 Laura Handal, « Le soutien à l'industrie minière : Quels bénéfices pour les contribuables? » research report (Montréal : Institut de recherche et d'informations socio-économiques [IRIS], April 29, 2010), 16–17, http://www.iris-recherche.qc.ca/publications/le_soutien_a_lindustrie_miniere_quels.

4 Canada Department of Finance, *Canada at the IMF and World Bank Group 2011, report on operations under the Bretton Woods and Related Agreements Act*, F1-28/2011E-PDF (Ottawa: Public Works and Government Services Canada, 2012), http://www.fin.gc.ca/bretwood/pdf/bretwd11-eng.pdf.

5　Marie Mazalto, "La réforme du secteur minier en République démocratique du Congo : enjeux de gouvernance et perspectives de reconstruction," *Afrique contemporaine* 3, no. 227 (2008): 53–80, http://www.cairn.info/revue-afrique-contemporaine-2008-3-page-53.htm.

6　See page 6 of PwC (PricewaterhouseCoopers), *Mine: The Growing Disconnect,* review of global trends in the mining industry – 2012, edited by Tim Goldsmith, Stuart Absolom, and Ananth Rajaratnam, http://download.pwc.com/gx/mining/pwc-mine-2012.pdf.

7　André Lavoie, « Une période d'expansion sans precedent », *CIM Magazine* 3, no. 8 (December–January 2008–2009), our translation, http://www.cim.org/bulletin/bulletinlive/articles.cfm?Issue_ID=161&Type=1&row=4&Segment_ID=77.

8　MRNF, Plan Nord, "Building Northern Quebec Together: The Project of a Generation," Government of Quebec, 2012, http://plannord.gouv.qc.ca/english/index.asp.

9　Leslie Roberts, *Noranda* (Toronto: Clarke Irwin & Company, 1956).

10　Xstrata, "Takeover Documents," 2006, http://www.xstrata.com/publications/acquisitionsandoffers/falconbridge/.

11　See Gabriel Girard-Bernier, "Rule of Law" of the Mining Monopolies," *TML Daily* 155 (August 10, 2009), http://www.cpcml.ca/Tmld2009/D39155.htm; and United Steel Workers District 5, *Development with Vision, director's report 2011* (Montreal : December 8, 2011), 3, http://www.usw.ca/districts/5/publications?id=0009.

12　Gérard Filion, « Réforme des lois et des mœurs électorales », editorial, *Le Devoir* (Montréal), August 8, 1956, our translation.

13　Canadian Museum of Civilization, "Quebec: The Common Front," *Canadian Labour History, 1850–1999*, web page posted (1999) 2010, http://www.civilization.ca/cmc/exhibitions/hist/labour/labh39e.shtml.

14　Pierre Godin, *René Lévesque, héros malgré lui (1960–1976)* (Montréal : Boréal, 1997), 59, our translation.

15　Radio-Canada Archives, "Maîtres chez nous," video clip, October 22, 1962, http://archives.radio-canada.ca/politique/provincial_territorial/clips/1080/.

16　Paul-André Linteau, *Quebec Since 1930*, translated by Robert Chodos and Ellen Garmaise (Toronto: Lorimer, 1991), 175–76, 339.

17　Ibid., 30.

18　MRNF, "Close-Up: One of the Best Places for Mining Investment," web page posted 2010, http://www.mrnfp.gouv.qc.ca/english/mines/index.jsp.

19　Fraser Institute, *Survey of Mining Companies 2011–2012* (Calgary: 2012).

20　Ibid., 9.

21　*Globe and Mail* (Toronto), "Top 1000: Ranking Canada's Top 1000 Public Companies by Profit," posted June 28, 2012, http://www.theglobeandmail.com/report-on-business/rob-magazine/top-1000/2012-rankings-of-canadas-top-1000-public-companies-by-profit/article4371923/.

　　　　　　　　　　　　　　　　　　　A Case Study Endnotes

22 Françoise Bertrand, president and director general of the Fédération des chambres de commerce du Québec, « Développer les régions minières du Québec », *Le Devoir* (Montréal), July 8, 2009, our translation, http://www.ledevoir.com/non-classe/258221/developper-les-regions-minieres-du-quebec.

23 Auditor General of Quebec (AGQ), « Interventions gouvernementales dans le secteur minier », report of the Auditor General of Quebec to the National Assembly for 2008–2009, vol. II, Highlights, 2009, http://www.vgq.gouv.qc.ca/en/en_publications/en_rapport-annuel/en_fichiers/en_Highlights2008-2009-V2.pdf.

24 MRNF, "Close-Up on the Department," web page, http://www.mrnf.gouv.qc.ca/english/department/index.jsp, consulted June 20, 2012.

25 AGQ 2009, « Interventions », para. 2.39, our translation.

26 Ibid., para. 2.5, our translation.

27 Finances Québec, "Budget 2010–2011: Choices for the Future: Economic and Budgetary Action Plan," March 2010, 95, http://www.budget.finances.gouv.qc.ca/Budget/2010-2011/en/documents/EconomicActionPlan.pdf.

28 Handal 2010.

29 James Otto, Craig Andrews, Fred Cawood et al. *Mining Royalties: A Global Study of their Impact on Investors, Government, and Civil Society* (Washington, DC: World Bank, 2006), 100, cited in Handal 2010, 43–44.

30 Finances Québec 2010, 96.

31 The increase to 16% took effect January 1, 2012. See Finances Québec, "Profit."

32 Fred McMahon and Jean-François Minardi (Fraser Institute), « Libre opinion : Sombre avenir pour l'industrie minière au Québec », *Le Devoir* (Montréal), April 23, 2010, http://www.ledevoir.com/economie/actualites-economiques/287500/libre-opinion-sombre-avenir-pour-l-industrie-miniere-au-quebec.

33 Finances Québec, "Budget at a Glance," Budget 2012–2013, http://www.budget.finances.gouv.qc.ca/budget/2012-2013/index_en.asp; and KPMG, "Highlights of the 2012 Quebec Budget," March 20, 2012, http://www.kpmg.com/ca/en/issuesandinsights/articlespublications/tnf/pages/tnfc1211.htm.

34 AGQ 2009, « Interventions », para. 2.5; AGQ 2009, Report, 9–10.

35 AGQ 2009, « Interventions », para. 2.38, our translation.

36 MRNF, "Preparing for the Future of Quebec's Mineral Sector: Quebec Mineral Strategy," web page, 2009, http://www.mrnf.gouv.qc.ca/english/publications/mines/strategy/mineral_strategy.pdf.

37 AGQ 2009, « Interventions », para. 2.111, our translation.

38 Deneault, Abadie, and Sacher 2008.

39 MRNF, *Preparing for the Future of Quebec's Mineral Sector*, consultation paper, 2007, 24, http://www.mrnf.gouv.qc.ca/english/publications/mines/strategy/consultation-document.pdf.

40 Northwatch and MiningWatch Canada, *The Boreal Below: Mining Issues and Activities in Canada's Boreal Forest*, May 2008, http://www.miningwatch.ca/sites/ www.miningwatch.ca/files/Boreal_Below_2008_web.pdf.

41 MRNF, *Preparing for the Future of Quebec's Mineral Sector*, 2009.

42 Ibid., 20.

43 Katherine Marshall, "A Job to Die For," *Perspectives*, Statistics Canada Catalogue no. 75-001-XPE Summer 1996, http://www.statcan.gc.ca/studies-etudes/75-001/ archive/e-pdf/2889-eng.pdf; Halifax *Chronicle Herald*, "Mining Still This Country's Most Dangerous Job," May 5, 1997, A2.

44 Martin Frigon and Christian M. Fournier, *Make Money. Salut, Bonsoir!* documentary film (Montréal : Les Productions Virage Inc., 2004), http://diffusionmultimonde.com/en/2004/09/make-money-salut-bonsoir/.

45 AGQ 2009, « Interventions », para. 2.40.

46 MRNF, "Flow-Through Shares," http://www.mrnf.gouv.qc.ca/english/mines/fiscal/ fiscal-incentives-shares.jsp, consulted August 17, 2012.

47 Mark Winfield, Catherine Coumans, Joan Newman Kuyek, François Meloche, and Amy Taylor, *Looking Beneath the Surface: An Assessment of the Value of Public Support for the Metal Mining Industry in Canada*, report on real costs of mining (Ottawa: Pembina Institute for Appropriate Development and Mining-Watch Canada, October 2, 2002), 69, http://www.miningwatch.ca/sites/www. miningwatch.ca/files/belowthesurface-eng_0.pdf.

48 Handal 2010, 23.

49 Detailed corporate information about Canadian numbered companies is available to subscribers at Mintportal.bvdep.com; general information is available free at Canadiancompanies.landoffree.com, consulted August 17, 2012.

50 Finances Québec, "Le Québec, et ses ressources naturelles: Pour en tirer le plein potential," *Budget 2012–2013*, http://www.budget.finances.gouv.qc.ca/ Budget/2012-2013/fr/documents/Ressources.pdf, 25.

51 Finances Québec, "2004–2005 Budget Speech," March 30, 2004, 16, http://www. budget.finances.gouv.qc.ca/budget/2004-2005/en/pdf/BudgetSpeech.pdf.

52 Finances Québec, "L'évasion fiscale au Québec, source et ampleur," *Études économiques, fiscales, et budgétaires*, April 22, 2005, http://www.finances.gouv. qc.ca/documents/EEFB/fr/eefb_vol1_no1.pdf.

53 Confédération des syndicats nationaux (CSN), « La Fédération de la métallurgie-CSN entreprend sa tournée pré-congrès : Rouyn-Noranda accueillera le 46ᵉ congrès de la FM-CSN », news release, October 27, 2008, our translation, http:// cnw.ca/HAN3q.

54 Investissement Québec, "Creation of Ressources Québec – Quebecers Invest $1.2 Billion to Maximize Spinoffs from Natural Resource Development," news release, April 18, 2012, http://www.investquebec.com/en/index.aspx?page=3089.

55 Sidex, "Our Sponsors," http://www.sidex.ca/DefaultSidex.asp?Lang=En, consulted June 20, 2012.

56 Winfield et al. 2002, 66.

57 MRNF, "Sodemex and Sodemex II," May 2002, http://www.mrnf.gouv.qc.ca/
    english/mines/quebec-mines/2002-05/funding.jsp.

58 Winfield et al. 2002, 66.

59 Intergovernmental Working Group on the Mineral Industry (IGWG), *Taxation
    Issues Relating to Exploration and the Restructuring of Resource Taxation* (Halifax:
    September 2003), 23, http://www.nrcan.gc.ca/sites/www.nrcan.gc.ca.minerals-
    metals/files/pdf/mms-smm/busi-indu/met-qfi/2003/igwg-2003-eng.pdf.

60 Louise Laverdure and Jean-Marie Fecteau, *Definition of an Action Plan in Research
    and Development, Trial, and Experimentation to Promote Safety for Under-
    ground Mining Operations*, final report, edited by John E. Udd, CANMET-MMSL
    report 04-037(CR) (Ottawa: Natural Resources Canada, September 28, 2004),
    77, http://www.camiro.org/images/Mining%20Reports/CANMET-MMSL%20
    04-037(CR)%20English%20Report.pdf.

61 Société de développement de la Baie-James (SDBJ), "Mining Sector Investment
    Fund: The SDBJ mining investment fund: financing mining projects," 2012, http://
    www.sdbj.gouv.qc.ca/en/financement/fonds_secteur_minier/.

62 Investissement Québec, "Corporate Profile."

63 Investissement Québec, "Home."

64 Investissement Québec, "Corporate Profile."

65 Investissement Québec, "Raymond Bachand Announces That the Government
    Is Authorizing Investissement Québec to Lend Alcoa a Maximum of $50 mil-
    lion," news release, April 24, 2009, http://www.investquebec.com/en/index.
    aspx?accueil=1&page=2377.

66 Presse Canadienne, « Québec prête 175 millions à Rio Tinto Alcan », *Le Devoir*
    (Montréal), May 8, 2009, http://www.ledevoir.com/2009/05/08/249386.html.

67 Fodé-Moussa Keïta, *Les sociétés minières canadiennes et le développement du
    secteur de l'or : les impacts de leurs activités en Afrique de l'ouest*, M.A. thesis,
    UQAM, September 2007.

68 Winfield et al. 2002, 66.

69 Ibid., 73.

70 MRNF, "Geology," http://www.mrnf.gouv.qc.ca/english/mines/geology/index.
    jsp, consulted June 20, 2012.

71 MRNF, *Preparing for the Future of Quebec's Mineral Sector*, 2009, 14.

72 Handal 2010, 23.

73 Winfield et al. 2002, 64.

74 Environment Canada, Threats to Water Availability in Canada, NWRI scientific
    assessment report series no. 3 and ACSD science assessment series no. 1 (Bur-
    lington, ON: National Water Research Institute, 2004), http://www.ec.gc.ca/
    inre-nwri/0CD66675-AD25-4B23-892C-5396F7876F65/ThreatsEN_03web.pdf;

Gavin Mudd, "Sustainability Reporting and Water Resources: A Preliminary Assessment of Embodied Water and Sustainable Mining," *Mine Water Environment* 27 (2008): 136–144.

75 COREM, "Members," http://www.corem.qc.ca/entreprise/members, consulted August 6, 2012.

76 COREM, "Pre-Competitive Research," http://www.corem.qc.ca/precompetitive-research, consulted August 6, 2012.

77 COREM, "Board of Directors," http://www.corem.qc.ca/entreprise/governance/board-of-directors, consulted August 5, 2012.

78 From 2008–2009 to 2010–2011, $20 million was earmarked for the fund each year, followed by $10 million in subsequent years. See MRNF, "Creation of the Mining Heritage Fund," 2008, http://www.mrnf.gouv.qc.ca/english/mines/quebec-mines/2008-11/heritage.asp.

79 The *Quebec Mining Act*, R.S.Q., c. M-13.1, http://canlii.ca/t/51v5g, has been in force since May 16, 2012. In 2011, the government tabled Bill 14, *An Act Respecting the Development of Mineral Resources in Keeping with the Principles of Sustainable Development*, which increases mineral royalties, prohibits mining development near urban centres, and requires mining companies to post a bond for 100 percent of mining site reclamation costs. "The Bill was the subject of public hearings during 2011 and a number of amendments were subsequently brought to the Bill and approved by a Committee of the National Assembly of Quebec. However, the clause-by-clause adoption of Bill 14 has not been completed despite 43 days of session by the Committee, which adjourned its proceedings a few weeks ago for the summer recess. The issue of royalties on mining resources continues to divide the Committee. The Official Opposition is pushing for an increase of the level of these royalties, which already have been increased by the government." J. M. Madeleine Donahue and Jean Piette, "Canada: Ontario and Quebec Propose Changes to the Respective Mining Legislation and Regulations," July 20, 2012, http://www.mondaq.com/canada/x/188202/Mining/Ontario+And+Quebec+Propose+Changes+To+The+Respective+Mining+Legislation+And+Regulations.

80 Ecojustice, *Setting a Gold Standard: Quebec's Mining Act Reform*, edited by William Amos, Anne Audoin, and Ugo Lapointe, with André Morin, Sylvain Archambault, Mélanie Pouliot, Noah Arshinoff, et al., October 2009, 6, 8, http://www.ecojustice.ca/publications/reports/setting-a-gold-standard/attachment.

81 Handal 2010, 38.

82 Ecojustice 2009, 1, 2.

83 See, for example, Ecojustice, "Commentaire sur la stratégie minérale et modifications suggérées à la *Loi sur les mines*," October 18, 2007, 2, http://www.bibliotheque.assnat.qc.ca/01/mono/2007/12/956566.pdf.

84 Ecojustice 2009, 7.

85 MRNF, "GESTIM Plus: A Mining Title Management System," http://www.mrnf.gouv.qc.ca/english/mines/rights/rights-gestim.jsp.

86 Canadian Boreal Initiative–International Boreal Conservation Campaign, *Mineral Exploration Conflicts in Canada's Boreal Forest*, May 2008, 8, http://www.borealcanada.ca/documents/MiningExplorationConflicts-Report-May2008.pdf.

87 Ecojustice 2009, 7.

88 *Mining Act*, sec. 235.

89 Ecojustice 2009, 4.

90 Alexandre Shields, « Acheter des claims miniers pour protéger sa propriété », *Le Devoir* (Montréal), August 8, 2012, http://www.ledevoir.com/societe/actualites-en-societe/356331/acheter-des-claims-miniers-pour-proteger-sa-propriete.

91 Jean-Pierre Thomassin, « La vérité sur l'industrie minière québécoise », *Le Devoir* (Montréal), May 8, 2008, our translation, http://www.ledevoir.com/2008/05/08/188735.html.

92 Confédération des syndicats nationaux (CSN), « Fermeture 'temporaire' de la mine Meston à Chibougamau : le régime minier québécois doit être revu de fond en comble !», news release, January 29, 2008, our translation, http://www.csn.qc.ca/web/csn/communique/-/ap/Comm29-01-08a.xml.

93 Office of the Auditor General of Canada (AGC), "Abandoned Mines in the North," report of the commissioner of the environment and sustainable development to the House of Commons, chap. 3, October 2002, 3, http://www.oag-bvg.gc.ca/internet/docs/c20021003ce.pdf.

94 Auditor General of Quebec (AGQ), « Interventions gouvernementales dans le secteur minier », *Rapport du VGQ pour l'année 2008–2009*, vol. II, chap. 2, April 1, 2009, para. 2.86, http://www.vgq.gouv.qc.ca/fr/fr_publications/fr_rapport-annuel/fr_2008-2009-T2/fr_Rapport2008-2009-TII-Chap02.pdf; AGQ 2009, "Report," 11.

95 Ecojustice 2009, 5.

96 Gérard Duhaime, Nick Bernard, and Robert Comtois, "An Inventory of Abandoned Mining Exploration Sites in Nunavik, Canada," *Canadian Geographer* 49, no. 3 (2005): 260–71.

97 Yves Chartrand, « Richard Desjardins réclame une enquête publique sur le MRN », *Rue Frontenac*, April 6, 2009, our translation, http://exruefrontenac.com/nouvelles-generales/politiqueprovinciale/3356-richard-desjardins-mines-foret-industrie-forestiere-miniere.

98 Deneault, Abadie, and Sacher 2008.

99 Mathieu Boivin, « Québec invite les minières à s'enrichir chez nous », *Rue Frontenac*, May 1, 2009, our translation, http://exruefrontenac.com/affaires/economie/4675-mathieu-boivin-mines-quebec.

100 SNC-Lavalin, *Étude sur la restauration des mines de cuivre et de cobalt en République Démocratique du Congo*, April 2003, 33, our translation, http://www-wds.worldbank.org/servlet/WDSContentServer/WDSP/IB/2004/12/07/000012009_20041207142559/Original/E7390v120EnvoAuditoGecamines.doc.

101 Yves Chartrand, "Une nouvelle pelure de banane pour le gouvernement Charest," *Rue Frontenac*, April 3, 2009, http://exruefrontenac.com/nouvelles-generales/117-vu-de-la-colline/3212-ychartrand-pelure-charest.

102 Yves Chartrand, "Richard Desjardins réclame une enquête publique sur le MRN," *Rue Frontenac*, April 6, 2009, http://exruefrontenac.com/nouvelles-generales/politiqueprovinciale/3356-richard-desjardins-mines-foret-industrie-forestiere-miniere.

103 Quebec Minister of Sustainable Development, Environment, and Parks, "Gaz de schiste – Les activités de l'industrie seront assujetties au développement de connaissances scientifiques," news release, March 8, 2011, http://www.mddep.gouv.qc.ca/Infuseur/communique.asp?no=1831.

104 Gordon Laxer, "The U.S. Must Go Green to Gain Energy Independence. Canada Must Gain Independence to Go Green," paper presented at the Rethinking Extractive Industries: Regulation, Dispossession, and Emerging Claims conference, York University, Toronto, March 2009, 4, http://www.yorku.ca/cerlac/EI/papers/Laxer.pdf.

105 Gilles Bibeau, *Le Québec transgénique : science, marché, humanité* (Montréal : Boréal, 2004), 155–59.

106 Roméo Bouchard, Jean-Louis Chaumel, Pierre Dubud, Paul Gipe, Gaétan Ruest, and Gabriel Sainte-Marie, *L'éolien, pour qui souffle le vent?* (Montréal : Éditions Écosociété, 2007), 7.

107 MRNF, Plan Nord, 2012.

108 Conseil régional de l'environnement de l'Abitibi-Témiscamingue (CREAT), *Bulletin du CREAT* (Autumn 2008): 2, www.creat08.ca/pdf/bulletins/automne2008.pdf.

109 Environment Canada 1996; Environment Canada, "Mercury in the Food Chain."

110 Observatoire de l'Abitibi-Témiscamingue, « Portrait de l'environnement », February 2007, 64, our translation, http://www.observat.qc.ca/documents/publications/integral_environnement_2007.pdf; Philippe-André Lafrance, Johanne Cyr, Valérie Carange, Alexandre Couturier-Dubé, Jean Dionne, Robert Lacroix, Sophie Proulx, and Malek Zetchi, "Chapter 7: Mine Rehabilitation," in *Report on Mineral Activities in Québec 2011*, DV 2012-02 (Quebec : MRNF, 2011), 113–17, http://www.mrnf.gouv.qc.ca/english/publications/mines/publications/publication-2011-chapitre7.pdf.

111 N. Miramond, D. Miau, and F. Brochard, "Diagnostic du phénomène Drainage Minier Acide sur des mines d'or primaire en Guyane française : Évaluation des risques associés" (Montjoly, Guyane Française: GEM Impact – DIREN, 2006), 5.

112 Ibid.

113 Observatoire de l'Abitibi-Témiscamingue, 64, our translation.

114 Gavin Mudd, "Global Trends in Gold Mining: Towards Quantifying Environmental and Resource Sustainability?" *Resources Policy* 32 (2007): 42–56.

115 Earle A. Ripley, Robert E. Redmann, and Adèle A. Crowder, *Environmental Effects of Mining* (Delray Beach, FA: St. Lucie Press, 1996).

116 Winfield et al. 2002, 3.

117 MRNF, "Chapter 7: Mine Rehabilitation," 2011, 113.

118 Carol Ptacek and David Blowes, Transport of Metals from Mine Tailings Impoundments and Release to Surface Waters: Final Report, May 31, 2002, TSRI Project 192, NWRI Contribution 03-173 (Burlington, ON / Saskatoon, SK: Environment Canada, National Water Research Institute, 2003), 2.

119 Ibid.

120 AGC 2002, para. 3.11.

121 AGC 2002, para. 3.1.

122 Grand Council of the Crees (Eeou Istchee), Cree Regional Authority, annual report 2008–2009, www.gcc.ca/pdf/GCC-CRA-Annual-Report-2008-2009. pdf; Radio-Canada – Abitibi-Témiscamingue, "Importantes conséquences environnementales," report broadcast July 2, 2008, http://www.radio-canada.ca/regions/abitibi/2008/07/02/005-digue_chapais_n.shtml.

123 AGQ 2009, « Interventions », paras. 2.72–2.84.

124 Quebec Mining Association (QMA), « Il n'y a pas de bombe à retardement environnementale et l'industrie minière du Québec s'occupe de façon responsable de la restauration de ses sites miniers », news release, July 11, 2008, our translation, http://cnw.ca/IoLeh.

125 MRNF 2009, 33.

126 AGQ 2009, « Interventions », para. 2.22.

127 Katie Daubs, "Asbestos Report 'Misused', Scientists Said," Ottawa Citizen, May 28, 2008, http://www2.canada.com/ottawacitizen/news/story.html?id=4c342ebe-2633-4ea4-bc06-34797b8ed932.

128 Deneault, Abadie, and Sacher 2008.

129 M. T. Brondeau, T. Calvel, M. Falcy, T. Jargot, M. Reynier, and O. Schneider, « Amiante », Fiche toxicologique numéro 145, Services techniques et médicaux de l'INRS, 1997, www.afim.asso.fr/SST/maladies/ft145.pdf.

130 World Health Organization (WHO), "Elimination of Asbestos-Related Diseases," September 2006, 1, http://www.who.int/occupational_health/publications/asbestosrelateddiseases.pdf.

131 CBC News, "Asbestos: The Magic Mineral That Was Once Canada's Gold," June 10, 2009, http://www.cbc.ca/news/canada/story/2009/06/10/f-asbestos-safety.html.

132 United States Department of the Interior – United States Geological Survey (USGS), 2010 Minerals Yearbook: Asbestos, advance release, August 2011, 8.1, http://minerals.usgs.gov/minerals/pubs/commodity/asbestos/myb1-2010-asbes.pdf.

133 Presse Canadienne, « Amiante : la Société canadienne du cancer interpelle Jean Charest », June 29, 2010, our translation, http://www.lesaffaires.com/secteurs-d-activite/mines-et-metaux/amiante—la-societe-canadienne-du-cancer-interpelle-jean-charest/516156.

134 USGS 2011.

135 Amir Attaran, David R. Boyd, and Matthew B. Stanbrook, "Asbestos Mortality: A Canadian Export," *Canadian Medical Association Journal* (*CMAJ*), October 21, 2008, 871, http://www.cmaj.ca/content/179/9/871.full.pdf+html, citing AGC 2006; Roger Collier, "Health Advocates Assail Canada's Asbestos Stance," *CMAJ*, December 2, 2008, http://www.cmaj.ca/cgi/content/full/179/12/1257.

136 Presse Canadienne, « L'arrêt du financement fédéral de l'Institut du chrysotile réclamé », January 23, 2009, http://www.lesaffaires.com/article/0/mines-et-metaux/2009-01-23/488331/larretecirct-du-financement-feteacutede-teacuteral-de-linstitut-du-chrysotile-reteacuteclameteacute.fr.html.

137 Ibid.

138 Association nationale de défense des victimes de l'amiante (ANDEVA), « Une dégonflade en forme d'aveu : L'Institut du chrysotile canadien renonce à poursuivre l'ANDEVA en justice », March 4, 2009, our translation, http://andeva.fr/?Une-degonflade-en-forme-d-aveu-1.

139 Marc Hindry, « Une industrie meurtrière et moribonde », *Bulletin de l'ANDEVA*, no. 24, (September 2007), our translation, http://andeva.fr/?DOSSIER-L-AMIANTE-AU-CANADA.

140 The Rotterdam Convention on the Prior Informed Consent Procedure for Certain Hazardous Chemicals and Pesticides in International Trade, more commonly known simply as the Rotterdam Convention, is a United Nations treaty to promote shared responsibilities in relation to importation of hazardous chemicals. The convention was adopted in Rotterdam on September 10, 1998, and entered into force on February 24, 2004. See United Nations Environment Programme (UNEP), Secretariat of the Rotterdam Convention, 2004, http://www.pic.int/.

141 Canadian Press, "Chrysotile Asbestos: Harper Government Defends Carcinogen Despite Rotterdam Pressure," June 15, 2011, http://www.huffingtonpost.ca/2011/06/15/chrysotile-asbestos-harpe_n_877251.html; Julia Belluz, "Can Asbestos Be Used 'Safely'?", *Maclean's*, June 21, 2011, http://www2.macleans.ca/2011/06/21/can-asbestos-be-used-safely/.

142 Collier 2008.

143 Ibid.

144 Canadian Association of Physicians for the Environment (CAPE), "Letter to Prime Minister Stephen Harper," June 14, 2011, http://www.asbestosdiseaseawareness.org/wp-content/uploads/Letter-to-Prime-Minister-Harper-Rotterdam-June-14-2011.pdf.

145 Hervé Kempf, "Asbestos, la ville maudite de l'amiante," *Le Monde*, December 28, 2005.

146 *The Economist*, "Hazardous Hypocrisy: A Curious Liking for Asbestos," October 23, 2008, http://www.economist.com/world/americas/displaystory.cfm?story_id=12480452.

147 Micheline Marier, William Charney, Richard Rousseau, Roch Lanthier, and John Van Raalte, "Exploratory Sampling of Asbestos in Residences near Thetford Mines: The Public Health Threat in Quebec," *International Journal of Occupational*

and *Environmental Health* 13, no. 4 (2007): 386–97, http://www.galenicom.com/it/article/18085052/Exploratory+sampling+of+asbestos+in+residences+near+Thetford+Mines:+the+public+health+threat+in+Quebe; and Canadian Broadcasting Corporation (CBC), "Quebec Asbestos Mining Town 'Severely Contaminated': Report," November 7, 2007, http://www.cbc.ca/news/health/story/2007/11/06/asbestos-thetford.html.

148 Ricardo Codina, « De l'amiante dans l'air de Thetford Mines », *La vie rurale*, November 7, 2007, our translation, www.la-vie-rurale.ca/contenu/15738.

149 USGS 2011.

150 MRNF 2009, 17.

151 George Novack, *Genocide against the Indians: Its Role in the Rise of US Capitalism* (New York, Pathfinder Press, 1972).

152 Oujé-Bougoumou Community Internet Gateway, "Our History," http://www.ouje.ca/content/our-story/history.php, consulted June 20, 2012.

153 Radio-Canada – Abitibi-Témiscamingue 2008.

154 C. L. Covel and D. Master, *Sediment, Surface Water, and Fish Quality Investigation: Oujé-Bougoumou Cree Nation Territory Quebec, Canada* (Lyndeborough, NH: Covel and Associates, 2001); Neil Diamond and Jean-Pierre Maher, *Heavy Metal: A Mining Disaster in Northern Quebec*, documentary film (Montréal : ReZolution Pictures International, 2005), http://www.rezolutionpictures.com/productions/documentaries/heavy-metal/.

155 Diamond and Maher 2005.

156 Environment Australia, Department of the Environment, "Cyanide Management, Best Practice," *Environmental Management in Mining* 40 (1998), http://www.ret.gov.au/resources/Documents/LPSDP/BPEMCyanide.pdf; Robert Moran, "Cyanide Uncertainties: Observations on the Chemistry, Toxicity, and Analysis of Cyanide in Mining-Related Waters," edited by Susan Brackett (Washington, DC: Mineral Policy Center [now Earthworks], 1998), http://earthworksaction.org/pubs/cyanideuncertainties.pdf; Bernd G. Lottermoser, *Mine Wastes: Characterization, Treatment, and Environmental Impacts*, 2nd ed. (Berlin and Heidelberg: Springer-Verlag, 2007), 193; UNEP; David A. Dzombak, Rajat S. Ghosh, and George M. Wong-Chong, *Cyanide in Water and Soil: Chemistry, Risk, and Management* (Boca Raton, FA: CRC Press/Taylor and Francis, 2006), 8.

157 GENIVAR, *Canadian Malartic Gold Mine Project Environmental Impact Study Preliminary Version Summary,* GENIVAR Limited Partnership's report to Osisko Mining Corporation, GENIVAR AA106790, October 2008, 13, http://www.osisko.com/pdfs/OSK%20EIA%20Summary%20English%20Nov%2014%202008.pdf.

158 Osisko Exploration Ltd., "Osisko Reports First Quarter 2012 Results: Mine Operating Profits of $70.5 Million, Net Profit of $29.4 Million," news release, August 9, 2012, http://www.osisko.com/en/press/2012/08/09/708/osisko-reports-second-quarter-2012-results.html; Nature Quebec, *Le Projet Canadian Malartic d'Osisko : Neuf ans de prospérité éphémère, des décennies d'impacts negatives*, Mémoire

Présenté dans le Cadre des Consultations du Bureau d'Audiences Publiques sur l'Environnement (BAPE), Avril 2009, 10, http://www.bape.gouv.qc.ca/sections/mandats/Mines_Malartic/documents/DM80.pdf.

159 Plan Nord promises to create twenty thousand jobs a year for twenty-five years. See Plan Nord, "Building Northern Quebec Together: The Project of a Generation," http://plannord.gouv.qc.ca/english/index.asp, consulted August 6, 2012.

160 Daniel Leblanc, "Charest Unveils Plan to Create 250,000 Jobs in Quebec," *Globe and Mail* (Toronto), August 2, 2012. http://www.theglobeandmail.com/news/politics/elections/charest-unveils-plan-to-create-250000-jobs-in-quebec/article4457383/, consulted August 6, 2012.

161 Albert Memmi, *The Colonizer and the Colonized* (Boston: Beacon, 1991).

162 Abitibi-Témiscamingue Nord-du-Québec (FTQ), « Le 'boom minier' doit aussi profiter aux travailleurs de la région », August 23, 2007, our translation, http://www.abitibi-nordqc.ftq.qc.ca/modules/nouvelles/nouvelle.php?id=10&langue=fr.

163 The Canadian Malartic deposit was discovered in 1926 and underground development began in 1928. See Osisko Exploration Ltd., *Canadian Malartic Gold Deposit, Quebec, Three to Four Million Ounce Gold Potential*, n.d., 3, http://www.osisko.com/pdfs/media_art_osisko_malartic_summary.pdf; and "Osisko on a Roll in Quebec," *Planning for Profits*, report on mining special issue (Winter 2006): 34, http://www.osisko.com/pdfs/media_art_pfp_osisko_quebec.pdf.

164 Deneault, Abadie, and Sacher 2008.

165 Ibid.

166 GENIVAR, "What We Do: Canadian Malartic Gold Mine Project, Malartic, QC, Canada, Osisko Mining Corporation, http://www.genivar.com/en/what-we-do/environment/approval-and-permit/Pages/canadian-malartic.aspx.

167 Osisko Exploration Ltd., "Osisko Officially Inaugurates the Canadian Malartic Mine," news release. May 31, 2011, http://www.osisko.com/en/press/2011/05/31/609/osisko-officially-inaugurates-the-canadian-malartic-mine.html.

168 Deneault, Abadie, and Sacher 2008.

169 Pierre André, "Les acteurs locaux et les projets développement. Situation et défi de la participation citoyenne," paper presented at a conference on Les savoirs locaux, Défis pour la conservation des ressources naturelles, organized by the Chaire d'études du Mexique contemporain and the Centre de développement de la recherche internationale en environnement (CEDRIE), Université de Montréal, April 27–28, 2009.

170 Véronique Hivon, « Un système de justice simplifié et accessible, une priorité pour Véronique Hivon », *Journal L'Action* (Joliette, Quebec), May 6, 2009, our translation, http://www.facebook.com/note.php?note_id=107891161530.

171 André 2009.

172 Collectif de spécialistes en consultation du public, « Gaz de schiste – Un test pour l'indépendance du BAPE », *Le Devoir* (Montréal), September 17, 2010, our translation, http://www.ledevoir.com/politique/quebec/296356/gaz-de-schiste-un-test-pour-l-independance-du-bape.

173 GENIVAR, *Canadian Malartic Gold Mine Project Environmental Impact Study Preliminary Version Summary,* GENIVAR Limited Partnership's report to Osisko Mining Corporation, GENIVAR AA106790, October 2008, 6, http://www.osisko.com/pdfs/OSK%20EIA%20Summary%20English%20Nov%2014%202008.pdf.

174 *La Frontière* (Rouyn-Noranda), *Cahier spécial mines*, 2008, our translation.

175 Marc-Urbain Proulx, « La dette de Rio Tinto Alcan et le Québec », *Le Devoir* (Montréal), January 3 and 4, 2009, our translation, http://www.ledevoir.com/2009/01/03/225527.html.

176 Liberal Party of Quebec, speech by Jean Charest in Lévis, September 2008, http://www.plq.org/fr/PlanNord_energies.php.

177 Transport Québec, "Québec investit 106 millions $ dans les aéroports du Nunavik et de la Côte-Nord," March 31, 2009, http://www.infrastructures.gouv.qc.ca/nouvelles/details-nouvelle.asp?contenu=8.

178 Plan Nord, « Le cadre financier du Plan Nord: Création du Fonds du Plan Nord », 2011, http://plannord.gouv.qc.ca/financier/fonds.asp.

179 Duhaime, Bernard, and Comtois 2005; Transport Québec 2009; MRNF, "Les secteurs chauds de l'exploration de l'uranium," map, January 2009, http://www.mrnf.gouv.qc.ca/mines/quebec-mines/2009-02/uranium3-g.jpg.

180 MRNF 2009.

181 Plan Nord, « Les transports et les communications: Développer un réseau intégré de transport », 2011, http://www.plannord.gouv.qc.ca/transports/reseau.asp; MRNF Plan Nord, *Faire le Nord ensemble: Le chanter d'une generation*, 2011-1001, 2011, http://www.plannord.gouv.qc.ca/documents/plan-action.pdf.

182 Assembly of First Nations of Quebec and Labrador (AFNQL), "The Plan Nord (North Plan) and the First Nations: What Is Jean Charest's Plan?", news release, March 11, 2009, http://www.apnql-afnql.com/en/actualites/pdf/comm-2009-03-11.pdf.

183 Ibid.

184 Assembly of First Nations of Quebec and Labrador (AFNQL), "Plan Nord: An Opportunity for Jean Charest to Establish a New and Respectful Relationship with First Nations," news release, September 29, 2008, http://www.apnql-afnql.com/en/actualites/pdf/Comm-2008-09-29.pdf.

185 Ibid.

186 Turtle Island Native Network, "Cree Nation and Quebec Sign Governance Agreement," July 24, 2012, http://www.turtleisland.org/discussion/viewtopic.php?f=11&t=10179&start=0.

187 Hydro-Québec, "Project News: Eastmain 1-A/Sarcelle/Rupert," Bulletin No. 1, May 2011, http://www.hydroquebec.com/rupert/en/pdf/bulletin_2011_05.pdf.

188 Kristin Craik, "Eastmain-1-A-Sarcelle-Rupert Hydropower Project: The Beneficial Renewable Energy Solution," *Business Review Canada* (May 2012): 198–215 at 215, http://www.businessreviewcanada.ca/magazines/10936.

189 Hydro-Québec, "Project News: Eastmain 1-A/Sarcelle/Rupert," Bulletin No. 1, May 2011, http://www.hydroquebec.com/rupert/en/pdf/bulletin_2011_05.pdf.

190 Government of Quebec, "Projets hydroélectriques – Québec développe à plein régime son potentiel hydroélectrique," October 3, 2007, http://www.lelezard. com/communique-73128.html; and Kristin Craik, "Eastmain-1-A-Sarcelle-Rupert Hydropower Project: The Beneficial Renewable Energy Solution," *Business Review Canada* (May 2012): 198–215 at 212, 215, http://www.businessreviewcanada.ca/ magazines/10936.

191 Environment Canada, *The State of Canada's Environment* (Ottawa: Government of Canada, 1996).

192 Environment Canada, "Mercury in the Food Chain," 2010, http://www.ec.gc.ca/ mercure-mercury/default.asp?lang=en&n=d721ac1f-1.

193 Duhaime, Bernard, and Comtois 2005, 262.

194 MRNF 2009, 14.

195 Anna Bednik, « Bataille pour l'uranium au Niger », *Le Monde Diplomatique*, June 2008, our translation, http://www.monde-diplomatique.fr/2008/06/ BEDNIK/15976.

196 Marc Trezzini, « Après Tchernobyl, un 'nouveau souffle' pour l'uranium », DATAS, our translation, http://www.datas.ch/article.php?id=445.

197 IndexMundi, "UxC Uranium U3O8 Swap Futures End of Day Settlement Price," 2012, http://www.indexmundi.com/commodities/?commodity=uranium&mo nths=120.

198 Dave Brown, "China Aggressively Moving Forward Nuclear Power Projects," *Uranium Investing News*, June 13, 2012, http://uraniuminvestingnews.com/11689/ china-aggressively-moving-forward-nuclear-power-projects-uranium-shanghai- stock-exchange.html; Daily News and Analysis, "India to Launch 16 New Nuclear Reactors," June 1, 2012, http://www.dnaindia.com/scitech/report_india-to-launch- 16-new-nuclear-reactors_1696773.

199 Katherine Yih, Albert Donnay, Annalee Yassi, A. James Ruttenber, and Scott Saleska, "Uranium Mining and Milling for Military Purposes," in *Nuclear Wastelands: A Global Guide to Nuclear Weapons Production and Its Health and Environmental Effects*, edited by Arjun Makhijani, Howard Hu, and Katherine Yih, 105–69 (Cambridge: MIT Press, 2000), 126.

200 Ibid., 108, 126.

201 World Nuclear Association, "Uranium in Canada," May 2012, http://www.world- nuclear.org/info/inf49.html.

202 Plan Nord, *Building Northern Québec Together: The Project of a Generation*, 2011, 59, http://plannord.gouv.qc.ca/english/documents/action-plan.pdf.

203 West Quebec Coalition against Mining Uranium, "West Quebec Mining Claims," March 14, 2012, http://no-uranium.blogspot.ca/.

204 Isabelle Gingras and Bruno Imbeault, « Pour un moratoire sur les mines d'uranium au Québec », *Le Devoir* (Montréal), December 8, 2009, http://www.ledevoir.com/economie/actualites-economiques/278773/pour-un-moratoire-sur-les-mines-d-uranium-au-quebec.

205 Community Coalition against Mining Uranium, "A Matter of Conscience," March 2008, http://www.ccamu.ca/pdfs/conscience-final-mar-08.pdf.

206 Aaron Mercredi, "Mining in Ontario: Colonial Conquest of Indigenous People," *Fire This Time* 5, no. 2, http://www.firethistime.net/fttV5N2_mining.html.

207 *Frontenac Ventures Corporation v. Ardoch Algonquin First Nation*, 2008 CanLII 8247 (ON SC), http://canlii.ca/t/1vxh4.

208 Yih et al. 2000, 105.

209 Robert Brooks and Anita Seth, "The Uranium Burden," Institute for Energy and Environmental Research, *Science for Democratic Action* 8, no. 4 (2000): 1–5, http://ieer.org/wp/wp-content/uploads/2012/02/8-4.pdf.

210 Ibid.

211 Ibid.

212 Yih et al. 2000, 129, 133.

213 Magnus Isacsson, *Uranium*, documentary film, produced by Dale Phillips (Montreal: National Film Board of Canada, 1990), http://www3.onf.ca/enclasse/doclens/visau/index.php?mode=view&filmId=5080&language=french&sort=title&PHPSESSID=964090d8c9aa05c18cc6b8ee3187435d.

214 Yih et al. 2000, 131.

215 Auditor General of Canada (AGC), "Radioactive Waste Cleanup in Port Hope, Ontario," *Environment and Sustainable Development Environmental Petitions: Petitions Catalogue*, January 4, 2008, http://www.oag-bvg.gc.ca/internet/English/pet_232_e_30304.html.

216 Ibid.

217 Yih et al. 2000, 136.

218 Wladimir Tchertkoff and Emanuela Andreoli, *Le Sacrifice*, documentary film (Origlio, Switzerland : Feldat-Film, 2003).

219 Yih et al. 2000, 106.

220 MRNF, "Québec, the Best Place in the World for Mineral Exploration," http://www.mrnf.gouv.qc.ca/english/international/mines.jsp, consulted August 7, 2012.

221 Diane Francis, "Quebec: World's Smartest Mining Jurisdiction," *Financial Post*, June 18, 2008, http://www.stockhouse.com/Blogs/ViewDetailedPost.aspx?p=76668.

222 Fraser Institute, *Survey of Mining Companies 2008–2009* (Calgary: 2009), http://www.fraserinstitute.org/research-news/display.aspx?id=13454.

223 SNC-Lavalin 2003, 29, our translation.

224 Fawzia Sheikh, "Native Canadians Fear Mining Boom in 'Ring of Fire'," *First Nations Environmental Health Innovation Network*, July 30, 2012, http://www.fnehin.ca/site.php/news/native_canadians_fear_mining_boom_in_ring_of_fire/; William Hipwell, Katy Mamen, Viviane Weitzner and Gail Whiteman, *Aboriginal Peoples and Mining in Canada: Consultation, Participation, and Prospects for Change*, working discussion paper, North-South Institute (Ottawa), January 2002, http://metisportals.ca/MetisRights/wp/wp-admin/images/Aboriginal%20 Peoples%20and%20Mining%20in%20Canada.pdf.

225 Erin Weir, "Foreign Control of Canadian Mining," *Progressive Economics Forum*, March 8, 2010, http://www.progressive-economics.ca/2010/03/08/foreign-control-canadian-mining/.

226 Katia Opalka, "Oil and Gas: The View from Canada," *Natural Resources & Environment* 26, no. 2 (Fall 2011): 1–4 at 1, http://www.cba.org/cba/newsletters-sections/pdf/2012-02-neerls2.pdf.

Conclusion
Some Issues We Need to Address

1 TMX Group, "A Capital Opportunity: Mining," slide presentation, slide 22.

2 Alain Deneault, *Offshore: Tax Havens and the Rule of Global Crime*, translated by George Holoch (New York: New Press, 2012).

3 Robin Fisher, *Contact and Conflict: Indian-European Relations in British Columbia, 1774–1890*, 2nd ed. (Vancouver: University of British Columbia Press, 1992), 96.

4 Michèle DuCharme, "The Canadian Origins of South African Apartheid?", *Currents: Readings in Race Relations* 3, no. 4 (1986): 1–32.

5 Alain Deneault and Aline Tremblay, *Mapping Financial Secrecy*, report on Canada (London: Tax Justice Network, October 2011), http://www.secrecyjurisdictions.com/PDF/Canada.pdf.

6 Department of Foreign Affairs and International Trade (DFAIT), "Building the Canadian Advantage: A Corporate Social Responsibility (CSR) Strategy for the Canadian International Extractive Sector," March 2009, http://www.international.gc.ca/trade-agreements-accords-commerciaux/ds/csr-strategy-rse-stategie.aspx?lang=eng&view=d.

7 Chen-I Lin and Allison Schuster, "Hydroelectricity Investment in Democratic Republic of the Congo: The Grand Inga," paper prepared for civil and environmental engineering (Lin) and political science (Schuster) departments, Tufts University, March 2009, http://wikis.uit.tufts.edu/confluence/display/aquapedia/Hydroelectricty+Investment+in+the+Democratic+Republic+of+the+Congo+-+The+Grand+Inga; and « Avant-projet international Moanda, site promotionnel », http://s4.e-monsite.com/2011/05/27/72955536plagiat-1-pdf.pdf.

8   United Nations Committee on the Elimination of Racial Discrimination (CERD), "Concluding Observations for Canada," UN Doc CERD/C/CAN/CO/18, May 25, 2007, http://www2.ohchr.org/english/bodies/cerd/docs/CERD.C.CAN.CO.18.doc.

9   Aboriginal Affairs and Northern Development Canada, "Canada's Statement of Support on the United Nations Declaration on the Rights of Indigenous Peoples," November 12, 2010, http://www.aadnc-aandc.gc.ca/eng/1309374239861/1309374546142.

10 Georges Perec, *Things: A Story of the Sixties; A Man Asleep,* translated by David Bellos (London: Collins Harvill, 1990), 119.

Index

Trudel, Pierre 62
TSX Venture Exchange (TSXV) 15, 16, 37, 87–88
Tunisia 43, 163

U.S. Institute for Energy and Environmental Research 174
Uganda 45–46
UN Committee on the Elimination of Racial Discrimination (CERD) 45, 50
UN Declaration on the Rights of Indigenous Peoples 40, 50, 176, 185
UN High Commissioner for Human Rights 45, 46
UN Panel of Experts on the Illegal Exploitation of Natural Resources and Other Forms of Wealth of the Democratic Republic of Congo 46
UN Sub-Commission on the Promotion and Protection of Human Rights 54
Ungava Trough 168
United Canadas 101–102
United States Environmental Protection Agency 161
Université de Montréal 25, 62, 165
Université du Québec à Montréal 30
University of Alberta Parkland Institute 151
University of Toronto Lassonde Institute of Mining 68, 69
University of Toronto Munk Centre for International Relations 68, 79

University of Waterloo 154
University of Western Ontario and University of Dar es Salaam Institute of Development Studies 69
uranium 1, 58, 107, 114, 129, 167 170–77
Uranium (documentary film) 172

Vancouver Stock Exchange 19, 121
Vickers Porcupine 109

War Eagle mine 97
Weber, Max 80, 87–89, 94, 123, 124
Wesdome Gold Mines 131
West Africa 4
West, James 87
Whitehorse Mining Initiative 37
Wilfrid Laurier University 24
Windfall Oils and Mines 118
Winnipeg Stock Exchange 108
World Bank 6, 11, 22, 39, 43, 45, 59, 71, 74, 129, 135, 150, 166, 175, 176, 182
World Bank International Finance Corp. 166
World Health Organization 5, 56
World University Service of Canada 44
World Vision 44
WorldCom 25
Wright, Scott 20

Xstrata 64, 130, 131, 132, 144, 148

Zaire 38
Zambia 39
Zimbabwe 39

ABOUT THE AUTHORS

Alain Deneault teaches critical thought in the political science department at the Université de Montréal and conducts research for the Quebec section of the Tax Justice Network. He is co-author of the book *Noir Canada: Pillage, corruption, et criminalité en Afrique* (Écosociété, 2008). His books most recently translated into English include *Offshore: Tax Havens and the Rule of Global Crime* (New Press, 2012) and *Paul Martin and Companies: Sixty Theses on the Alegal Nature of Tax Havens* (Talonbooks, 2005).

William Sacher holds a PhD in atmospheric sciences from McGill University and is currently a doctoral candidate in development economy at the Latin American School of Social Sciences (FLACSO). He has published numerous articles and reports about mining and the exploitation of natural resources and is co-author of the book *Noir Canada: Pillage, corruption, et criminalité en Afrique* (Écosociété, 2008), which received the 2009 Richard Arès Award in Montreal, Quebec.

For more information, including tables based on reports of the Canada Pension Plan Investment Board and the Caisse de dépôt et placement du Québec that show Canadian public fund investments in mining corporations, visit www.imperialcanada.ca.